MY YEAR IN THE ONLINE LEFT

SOCIAL MEDIA, SOLIDARITY AND ARMCHAIR ACTIVISM

ERIC W. SAEGER

Fells Carson Publishing
www.fellscarson.com

Copyright © 2024 by Eric Saeger
All rights reserved.

Library of Congress Cataloging Data
Saeger, Eric.
My Year in the Online Left: Social Media, Solidarity and Armchair Activism
    Registration Number TXu 2-088-829
    Year of completion: 2024
    ISBN-13: 978-1-7325835-5-9
    ISBN-10: 1-7325835-5-9

First Edition

10 9 8 7 6 5 4 3 2 1

For Jen, and the friends I made along the way.

"This is always an unpopular undertaking, and usually everyone is offended."
– Saul Alinsky, *John L. Lewis: An Unauthorized Biography*

Contents

INTRODUCTION	i
1: MEET THE ONLINE LEFT	1
2: THE DECLINE OF CORPORATE SOCIAL MEDIA	37
3: TWITTER IS DEAD, LONG LIVE THE FEDIVERSE	79
4: DIGITAL DIVIDES	101
5: IT'S REALLY, TRULY, MADLY THE CLASS WAR, FOLKS	151
6: PUTTING IT ALL TOGETHER: RULES FOR ONLINE RADICALS	220
ACKNOWLEDGMENTS	237
NOTES	239
INDEX	259

Introduction

Many—hopefully most—readers will be happy to note that this book is not an academic exercise. That said, we'll get into some mildly complicated material as we progress, all of which I'll try to translate as legibly as possible. It's stuff I learned during the time I spent collaborating, canoodling, and arguing with various types of leftists on Twitter (renamed "X" after Elon Musk bought it, but longtime Twitter users still refer to it as Twitter and probably always will) and elsewhere (technically it's been four years and counting at this writing, not just a single "year"; the title refers to a foolish experiment I forced myself to undertake, which we'll chat about later).

But it's not an academic exercise, I swear. It's intended as something of an "online travel guide" for beginner activists of all left-leaning persuasions, from Democratic supporters to anarchists, who want to understand the current social media zeitgeist, but we won't get too serious about even that. At the same time, it's offered to the general public as "infotainment," a collection of things you might want to know if you spend any of your spare time discussing leftist politics and such on the big corporate social media platforms. Let me clarify that when I refer to the "left," I mean the "non-right," i.e., the political left in the broadest possible sense. Conservatives and other curious parties are welcome aboard, of course.

I view this book not as a guide for "being correctly leftist on Twitter" and elsewhere but instead as a compendium of historical and technical facts, general observations, and gently offered suggestions that will hopefully inspire politically active social media users to look past their differences, discover their common dreams and complaints, and engage with others in a more informed, mature, and constructive manner, ultimately toward the effort of helping activists and organizers spread their messaging and build solidarity behind common causes.

You may detect a Marxist slant to these doings, but this book isn't necessarily a socialist recruitment tool, nor is it an establishment propaganda piece bent on legitimizing the Democrats. Although I believe that basically everything that's causing the vast majority of citizens to feel suffocated by America's socioeconomic atmosphere can be attributed, in one way or another, to the ongoing and ridiculously lopsided "class war" between America's oligarchs and everyone else, I'm not trying to persuade anyone to run out and buy a hammer-and-sickle logo gym bag to prove that they're "down with the struggle." I'm simply saying that we need to ease up on each other, that the endless internecine warfare that's divided the left for decades is in need of a ceasefire.

At the moment, the left appears to be hopelessly split. Liberals and socialists, the two major camps of the left, are embroiled in a holy war, each side celebrating its patron saints (Barack Obama and Karl Marx, respectively) and cursing its perceived devils (Donald Trump, Hillary Clinton). Their cold, robotic estrangement is remindful of the two halves of the RMS *Titanic* resting and rusticling on the floor of the Atlantic Ocean, around 600 yards apart, where they lie in wait, triple-dog-daring the bored and wealthy to test its potentially crushing depth. Both sides are dedicated to human equality, but neither one has a crystal clear picture of the beliefs they have in common or the skills and attributes each side brings to the table. I hope to clear that up a bit.

Since much of the friction happens online, we'll look at the emergence of social media spaces that, unlike divisive corporate platforms like Twitter and Facebook, offer calmer, less alienating environments where cohesion and understanding between all "online leftists" might flourish and where real solidarity between regular citizens could develop without interference from Big Tech. With any luck, mutual understanding will lead to spectacular, nonviolent acts of civil disobedience that will put our oligarchs on notice.

Toward the effort of building that all-important activism-minded consensus, we'll look at such things as the rapid growth of independent news media, or "citizens' journalism," and how that growing sphere might improve itself.

We'll talk about your money, too, and why you have less of it than you should. Recently, owing to America's hyper-accelerated jump in wealth inequality, a lot of online leftists have become morbidly fascinated with the dreary subject of macro-level economics, specifically its mechanics and history. Since that's what many of you want to know more about, we'll get to know a group of experts I think of as "punk economists," a term that refers to the growing army of "heterodox" economists and niche historians who speak nothing but uncensored truth about the history and current realities of America's economic system. Those people have brilliant suggestions on how to fix it and thereby "save America." Some of their findings are guaranteed to enrage you. We'll spend a lot of time on that, I assure you, but not now. Like little Regan said in the 1973 film *The Exorcist*: In time. It'll have to wait until Chapter 5.

It's time to stop all the online nonsense, get properly informed, and grow some solidarity, is the idea. Hopefully, this book will help with that.

1

Meet the Online Left

I. Actually, First, Meet the Fifth Estate

Today, there are many reasons for the left—scratch that: "the 99 percent," meaning everyone who has to work for a living, including conservatives—to organize, protest, boycott, and engage in sustained nonviolent civil disobedience. Two big reasons are the climate crisis, which has essentially been unaddressed by our oligarchs, and the growing misery factor of everyday life in the United States, which poses a different kind of threat: A population composed of chronically unhappy citizens usually leads to increased levels of nationalism, as embodied nowadays by the growing number of small but determined white supremacist groups scattered all over America.

The mainstream corporate media constantly chatters about those guys, despite their actual numbers' remaining at a less-than-insignificant level. What we should really be worried about is not feisty little platoons of lonely, Pop Tart-hoarding survivalists in hockey pads and toy badges marching for "the right to be white" but the fact that the cultural glue that binds all Americans to each other is running out of any tensile strength, thereby "posing a threat to democracy," as the liberal media tells us (because "threatening democracy" sounds a lot less urgent than "diligently working to reduce America to a smoking crater").

But let's back up a second because there it is, up there, the word "democracy." According to the mainstream liberal media, "democracy," the classic liberal socioeconomic philosophy that guides our country's sociopolitical landscape, is what "we're fighting to preserve."

But what is "democracy," hallowed be its name? According to the Oxford English Dictionary, it's this:

> Government by the people; that form of government in which the sovereign power resides in the people as a whole, and is exercised either directly by them (as in the small republics of antiquity) or by officers elected by them.

And there it is, that pesky conjunction: "or." The Cambridge English Dictionary (which, unlike Oxford, is kind enough not to demand a $100 yearly subscription fee to look through it for ten seconds) defines "or" as a word "used to connect different possibilities."

I'll drop the pedantry because people hate it. Here it is: America doesn't have a real democracy anymore, if it ever did, at least going by the dictionary definition of the word.

Suppose we define democracy in its truest sense, as congruency between the will of the people and the public policies their "duly elected" representatives deliver. In that case, it doesn't hold up under any real scrutiny (although to be fair, Aristotle used to say that all democracies eventually become oligarchies, which is the only sure sign that we *used* to have one, at least). Policies favored by the public are chosen by American lawmakers only 59 percent of the time, just slightly better than if the representatives had flipped a coin (most revealing is the disconnect between the public's genuine desire to have term limits imposed on representatives, who vote against the idea 68 percent of the time[1]).

That alone—the fact that our political class has become as dynastic as the Medicis—is proof that America's system isn't possessed of the key feature Renaissance philosopher Niccolò Machiavelli considered a must-have for maintaining a healthy republic, which is what many citizens think we have (sans the "healthy" part). Republics are governed by charters, like our own Constitution, not tiny, powerful groups.

So, which thingamajig do we have, a republic or a democracy? Well, the late author Chalmers Johnson asserted that we haven't had a legitimate republic since Congress voted to give George W. Bush free rein to destroy Iraq after the 9/11 terrorist attacks, events Iraq had nothing whatsoever to do with. On paper, Bush had permission to use "any means necessary" to wage war on the Iraqis. Thus Bush, Johnson pronounced, was allowed to ignore the Constitution, and ergo, America was officially no longer a republic.

What about a democracy. Is that what we have?

Good question. The optics tell voters that our duly elected representatives couldn't care less what they think they have. In fact, they'd prefer it if the citizenry would just shut up. Generally, political protests are discouraged by both parties of the Democratic/Republican duopoly and roundly ignored by the mainstream media. That's to be expected, of course, given that the duopoly and the establishment media are controlled by a coalition of (mostly) anti-populist billionaires who hold more wealth than the government, a situation that's led to rule by an increasingly overconfident oligarchy. As for the tattered and torn charter of our republic, Charles Koch, the extreme right-wing fossil fuel baron, is the person currently working the hardest to rewrite the Constitution[2] and make it less egalitarian than it is (as we'll discuss, it was originally written by a gaggle of wealthy aristocrats who were more concerned about protecting their property from domestic threats than ensuring that our laws benefitted average citizens. Ipso facto, we don't have a functioning democracy).

At the purely political level, our system is distressingly close to descending into "anocracy," a mortally sickened form of government that's part democracy and part dictatorship. Anocracy, as political scientist Barbara F. Walter discussed in her 2022 book *How Civil Wars Start,* is a super-fertilizer for growing bad outcomes like, you guessed it, civil wars. That isn't to say that we're likely to see extended bombing runs by B-21 Raider jets on Biloxi or Boston; America is too big and spread out for that. If a "second American civil war" ever does come to pass, it'll most likely resemble the Syrian civil war, punctuated by flare-ups of widely scattered violence, especially in areas where large groups bond over race, which is another telltale symptom of anocracy. Of course, if the worst did happen, our oligarchs would want any rambunctious hostilities to cease immediately so they could go back to the business of screwing everyone, which means they'd trot out the military to cool things down in the more chaotic zones. But which military would they hire to do the messy work, the U.S. military or the privatized armies operated by right-wing zealots like Eric Prince? There are a lot of ways things could go south.

But is America really *that* screwed up? It depends on whom you ask. As early as 2014, researchers at Princeton University concluded that America is no longer a democracy but an oligarchy.³ For her part, Walter maintains that the United States is a "factionalized anocracy," wavering between autocracy and democracy. I think she's being overly polite in that assessment, and so do a lot of other people.

"Like who?" you ask, the answer to which allows us to segue into a proper introduction to the "online left," since the fastest way to get to know someone is to know what kind of media they consume. In this case, the "who" is "Fifth Estate" journalists, experts, academics, and historians, nearly all of whom believe we no longer have a real democracy. Neither do many of their peers and colleagues, but they're either too intimidated by (or financially dependent on) the establishment to admit it.

I should probably explain what the "Fifth Estate" is. The phrase's definition isn't etched in stone yet, but it's emerging as an expression that identifies independent (i.e., not corporate-sponsored) journalism and punditry that's usually presented through internet platforms as opposed to being offered through more traditional outlets like cable television, corporate newspapers and so on. It refers to a new player in the classic "estates of the realm" socioeconomic hierarchy, joining the First Estate (the "nobility," i.e., a society's wealthiest elites), the Second (the clergy), the Third (ordinary citizens) and the Fourth (the popular press). For our purposes, this new group, the Fifth Estate, defines the broad cohort of self-supporting, non-establishment-beholden writers, pundits, independent journalists, podcasters, regular citizens with YouTube channels or whatnot; in short, outlets that focus on the unvarnished truths behind matters of sociopolitical ideas and happenings.

Former Oxford Internet Institute director William Dutton atomizes the phrase further, which is his wont, being that he coined it. He argues that the Fifth Estate comprises literally all "networked individuals" who, through independent, internet-based platforms, strive to hold the wealthy accountable and challenge mainstream reporting on virtually any issue, generally toward the aim of building widespread consensus on socioeconomic and political news items, all so that citizens can figure out where to direct their own investigative and/or activist energies.

Dutton's is the most helpful definition if we dumbify it to mean "the great internet hivemind," which he doesn't specifically do. Rather, he defines the Fifth Estate as a "network of networks" comprising social groups that exist without home bases, with each individual person serving as a "portal" or "network node." I've looked at his rather tangled definition upside down and sideways and concluded that his position is that the Fifth Estate is indeed the great internet hivemind, but I wouldn't bet two dollars that I've got it right. A wobbly political centrist like *The New York Times'* Thomas Friedman, Dutton—who in February 2024 expressed support for Republican presidential nominee Nikki Haley in a Twitter post that received no attention whatsoever—appears to be more of a pie-in-the-sky pseudo-futurist than someone who has any working knowledge of current computer technology or understanding of social media subcultures. But either way, his term fits the bill. The Fifth Estate focuses on subjects that the Fourth Estate isn't allowed to cover because those subjects pose threats to the reputations of the entities that run America: oligarchs, corporate entities, the military-industrial complex folks, etc. Those elites also own and operate the Fourth Estate companies that distribute mainstream news.

The Fifth Estate challenges the status quo through its very existence. It's the free press arm of the Third Estate; in other words, it truly is the people's media and is hastening the Fourth Estate's extinction. The Fifth Estate is the antithesis of the Fourth, whose blurring of the line between reporting and opinion, journalist Zaid Jilani wrote, "has been a disaster for the country. It's led to more polarization and less trust in the mass media. I think reporters should generally stick to reporting the facts."

That points to the defining distinction between the Fourth and Fifth Estates. While both bodies constantly editorialize when they're delivering news stories, the mainstream media's critiques aim to defend the enormously wealthy interests that pay its bills, whereas independent media figures can look at a story from every angle with an eye toward informing the public what's in their best collective interests.

If the Fourth Estate were doing its job—consistently and objectively reporting facts about (while offering honest analysis on) "complicated" issues without any interference from moneyed interests—it would eventually lead to citizens' challenging the "capital order" (a term concocted by Italian economist Clara Mattei, pointing to the implicit caste system that characterizes Western socioeconomics today, wherein the minuscule wealthy minority holds dominance over the economic super-majority). Given that they're well aware of that, our oligarchs and corporate elites are wise to fear the truth. Surely there'd be trouble if the citizenry, suddenly finding itself in possession of every detail of every dirty trick the First Estate has ever pulled, became radicalized. The Fifth Estate's imperative is to push that envelope, to work tirelessly to inform citizens about matters that reveal extreme misconduct or incompetence on the part of the world's most influential people and organizations. Members of the Fifth Estate offer that information freely and fearlessly, aware that their voices could be silenced by corporate or political censors at any moment.

All in all, I'd say Dutton has the *potential* to be a card-carrying member of the Fifth Estate, but he's either obfuscating his own findings out of fear that his scholarly colleagues will shun him for his ideas or he's incapable of using plain language in his writing. It's probably the latter: As is the case with too many scholars who try to communicate their ideas for public consumption, Dutton's sesquipedalian ramblings bring to mind a 2021 exchange between two Reddit users in reaction to a podcast focused on Modern Monetary Theory. One "Redditor" (Reddit user) asks, "Am I too dumb to understand any of what they're talking about?" to which another replies, "You're not. They were too dumb to put it into plain language."

Putting that analysis aside for the time being, the takeaway is that the Fifth Estate is quickly replacing the Fourth as the cultural pillar citizens look to for truth. As Dutton would put it, the Fourth Estate is no longer interested in checking the power of governments, industry, and business. The mainstream press has become nothing more than the propaganda ministry of oligarchic capitalism and its slobbering pit bull sidekick, imperial-mercantilist aggression enforced by our military. It no longer stands as the inquisitor of the empire, if, in fact, it ever really did, aside from rare frenzies of coverage regarding things like the Watergate and Iran-Contra kerfuffles. Indeed, nowadays, the Fourth Estate fixates more on the *sources* of journalistic leaks, such as Julian Assange, than it does on the villains and systemic flaws its stories expose.

If you'll indulge me, it's an excellent time to set the record straight with an etymological tangent. Currently, the phrase

"Fifth Estate" does mean different things to different people. In his 2016 book *The Fifth Estate: Think Tanks, Public Policy, and Governance*, James McGann uses the phrase to identify the political think tanks that help shape and coordinate our legislation. Obviously, McGann is referring not to independent journalists but to what most would consider an elite propaganda arm of the First Estate. McGann's been accused of being an apologist for think tanks, but by no means are the organizations he covers driven by the same directives as Charles Koch's rat's nest of libertarian pro-business, anti-worker think tanks, you know, the ones that make up ridiculous phrases like "clean coal" and whatnot.

I could go on, so let's; I want to help Dutton make his definition stick, so let's face the ambiguity head-on. *Fifth Estate* is the title of a 2018 murder mystery novel by Jason Blacker, a 1987 autobiographical book by Italian writer Ferdinando Camon, and two books that were released in 1978; a nonfiction book that examined Britain's trade unions and a novel about deep governmental corruption from *The French Connection* author Robin Moore. The 2018 novel *Breaking News: A Story of the 5th Estate*, written by Jim Boston, is actually focused on the *Fourth* Estate (specifically, mainstream television news), not the Fifth. And finally, in 1926, a same-titled book written by Jerome Travers and James Crowell was a whimsical treatise on the game of golf.

Published in 2023, Dutton's own *Fifth Estate* lays out the internet's potential for putting the First and Fourth Estates on notice. The book was published by Oxford Press, which immediately alerts us to its nature, that of an academic endeavor that one reviewer recommended for "researchers, business leaders," and such. Like most books written by upper academics who worry too much about how their colleagues will judge their painstakingly sculpted prose, a brief scan of the text finds it all but inaccessible, full of stuff that demands the reader add links to Wikipedia and thesaurus.com to their smartphone's home screens before trying to wrestle with it. Personally, I'd rather read Target's 50-mile-long wi-fi user agreement toward finding the part where they admit that they'll be sending Nabisco spam to my email box for months on end if one of their store's surveillance cameras catches me picking up a box of Oreos in one of their stores, but they're your eyeballs.

(Please note that all the business above is not intended to bash Dutton, who's earned no small measure of respect for identifying online punditry as a force to be reckoned with. I've been an arts critic for more years than I care to admit, and like they say, critics gotta critic.)

The most well-known Fifth Estate reporters, pundits and personalities belong to an exclusive, informal club, a group of workaholic "netizens" (frequent users of social media and other internet discussion spaces) who've attained cognoscenti status in certain circles. They're "internet popular" people with well-informed, snarky, urban, and blaringly hip mindsets commonly found in Twitter culture. They're ideological influencers, or "thoughtfluencers" whose high visibility and mutual collegial respect tell us they're in a different class than the casual internet user who posts the occasional "I hate Trump" on Facebook. Suffice to say that well-established Fifth Estate figures sit far closer to the center of the hivemind than infrequent internet users.

By now I assume we've reached the point when some readers are wondering which Fifth Estate newspeople and pundits I'd recommend they investigate based on their long records of hard work, trustworthiness, courage, and smarts.

People occasionally ask me that on Twitter, so here goes. Briahna Joy Gray (of the *Bad Faith* podcast) is at the top of my list these days, followed by, in no particular order, Katie Halper (of *Useful Idiots*), Paul Jay (*Real News Network*), Amy Goodman (*Democracy Now!*), Sam Seder (*The Majority Report*) and the criminally underserved Abby Martin of *The Empire Files*. Those and other Fifth Estate figures had their watershed moment in 2023 when media coverage of the U.S.-assisted genocide of Palestinians in the Gaza Strip by Israeli Prime Minister Benjamin Netanyahu's Israel Defense Force (IDF) exposed the divide between the pro-imperialist Fourth Estate and the populist Fifth Estate in stark relief. In America, cable news viewers comprised the only demographic of news consumers that didn't believe Netanyahu was committing genocide.[4]

The polarization between corporate and independent media has been evident for years now. Unlike the Fourth Estate, the Fifth has consistently tried to warn Americans that our country has serious problems that almost no member of the blue-red duopoly admits seeing. Those problems have been allowed to fester and are now approaching critical mass. With regard to who's to blame for it all, fingers point in all directions by a population that for decades has been systematically and criminally under-informed, disinformed and misinformed about socioeconomic realities by mainstream economics "experts" and the Fourth Estate. Distressingly, the mainstream media, that all-powerful hegemon of American culture, receives auxiliary support from certain self-serving online thoughtfluencers, fringe Fifth Estate figures who, as a friend put it, aren't trying to fix the problems we have but are instead working to grow financially secure enough that the problems don't apply to them.

That's a harsh way of putting it, but yes, at times, Fifth Estate success can, ironically, work to obstruct the path to cultural, socioeconomic, and political betterment. Too often—and I'll put this as delicately as possible—Fifth Estate "stardom" exposes a built-in defect of anti-establishment struggle within our capitalist context. Before his passing, British writer Mark Fisher noted that capitalist philosophy is so deeply ingrained in our collective mindset that we can't imagine a world where everything isn't perceived as being some sort of commodity. As such, when even the most earnest "social media celebrity" successfully builds a profitable anti-neoliberal (or pro-socialist or "pro-benevolent capitalist") platform on a corporate social media site, it can be hard to reject American capitalism entirely. It's a given that cognitive dissonance can surface when one is reaping riches from the same system under which one has built a successful social media platform by speaking ill of it.

A lot of riches can be reaped by knocking the system. Documentary filmmaker Michael Moore, whose anti-establishment movie credits include *Bowling For Columbine* and *Fahrenheit 9/11*, has achieved no small amount of fame for parlaying his existential disdain for things like inadequate gun control laws and "cheap labor conservatism" into deals with major entertainment companies owned by the same corporate behemoths he derides. Why does the corporatocracy let him get away with it? "They don't believe in anything," Moore offers during the last few minutes of the 2004 documentary *The Corporation*. "They put me on [the mainstream media] because they know that there's millions of people that want to see my film or watch the TV show, and so they're going to make money." Moore sees himself as exploiting a "flaw in capitalism" and seems content with knowing that the corporatocracy views rebellious dissension as a marketable commodity, albeit with limits, as many Fifth Estate figures have found out (I should add here that not every independent journalist is a brilliant humorist who started their career with $58,000 in seed money won in a lawsuit against the nonprofit American progressive magazine *Mother Jones*. That's certainly not to begrudge Moore; at least his windfall didn't go to someone criminally annoying like Ben Shapiro).

Too many independent media figures have their price, is what I'm getting at, whether in the form of money or online "clout," sometimes referred to as "platform capital" (the currency of social media, a form of street credibility one earns by amassing teeming hordes of fans and followers who regale their posts and other efforts with great numbers of likes, retweets, shares, and such). It's natural for any media figure to be tempted to expand and grow their platform's "brand" by any means necessary, which, for some Fifth Estate figures, can become their prime directive, supplanting the intents of their original heart-driven activism while keeping the left splintered.

So, then. As we trudge on, I'll describe what I view as the "online left" and examine the question of whether or not regular people—sometimes identified as "normies," i.e., people who get nearly all their news and opinion from mainstream sources like corporate news service articles and cable television shows—actually do believe that the political and cultural doings and happenings that originate on the internet are in any way "real" or meaningful.

II. Activism and the Fifth Estate

The "online left" is a contentious term. As I said, I'll use it in the broadest possible sense. Even if you're convinced you know what the online left is, I'd encourage you to keep reading, as it covers some basics that may expand your thinking. In time, we'll go over the things that have worked to prevent the "very online" members of the American left from stepping outside their siloed internet subgroups and combining their forces to serve as an adjunct to organized activism.

Repeat: adjunct. Although I'll argue in these pages that the internet has been underused by left-minded organizers and political activists of all stripes, I'm the first to admit that "the revolution will not be tweeted." Acts of internet activism—"slacktivism," if you insist—regardless of their intensity or virality, cannot in some ways match the organic *humanness* of such things as marches, sit-ins and other forms of protest that require the physical presence of people. Indeed, since the dawn of the internet, there's been the sense that, owing to their mysterious, virtual origins, things that develop online are somehow not part of the real world. In the all-too-recent past, every time an online activist effort threatened to accomplish anything, naysayers appeared, glibly rejecting the idea that people yakking on the internet could ever prove helpful to movements. For example, in 2010, author and constant Fourth Estate fixture Malcolm Gladwell argued in a *New Yorker* thinkpiece titled "Small Change: Why the revolution will not be tweeted,"[5] that relationships formed online are too superficial to empower activist causes. He contended that online movements are "built around weak ties" and can't be taken seriously. To bolster his position, Gladwell cited an act of civil disobedience that took place in 1960. Four freshmen from North Carolina's all-Black Agricultural and

Technical State University staged a sit-in at the lunch counter of the Greensboro Woolworth's store. Ignoring the store's adherence to Jim Crow laws, one of the students ordered a cup of coffee. The order was refused, and the student was informed, "We don't serve Negroes here." A battle of wills ensued. The four students sat at the counter for six days as tensions mounted inside and outside the store. In the end, a bomb threat forced the evacuation of the entire building, also serving to scatter the crowd of sign-carrying protesters who were marching in front of its classically quaint-looking façade.

Although that effort came to naught, the tactic caught on. Copycat sit-ins began popping up in Virginia, South Carolina, Tennessee, and, eventually, as far as Texas. The Greensboro Sit-In is now considered a historic event that brought the fight for civil rights to the national stage. Its nonviolent approach inspired the Freedom Riders (a collective of activist groups that toured the American South by bus in 1961 to protest segregated bus terminals) and other groups to advance the cause of integration in the South and, by extension, further the cause of equal rights in the United States.

The Greensboro store became a site of legend. In 2010, on the 50th anniversary of the sit-in, the building was re-introduced to the public as the International Civil Rights Center and Museum.

Now, the internet obviously played no part in those events, but it certainly would have if it had existed on the ubiquitous scale it does today. Gladwell—who, I would hope, looks back with a bare modicum of regret at ever having written that article, all things considered—was all too eager to ignore the fact that the students' act of civil disobedience would have assuredly "blown up" on today's social media sphere, which would have likely led to broader pushback (and many more copycat sit-ins) from outraged citizens of all persuasions, likely within a much shorter time frame.

In the 2010 article, Gladwell played the role of a stubbornly skeptical, ostentatiously metropolitan fuddy-duddy singularly unimpressed with any activist effort that doesn't manifest a physical presence. It wasn't his finest hour, but he's gotten a few things right over the years. In the same article, he chided former national security adviser Mark Pfeifle's call to nominate Twitter for the Nobel Peace Prize (that'd be like nominating the U.S. Post Office for a Pulitzer Prize in honor of all the books that have been sent through the mail). He also accused Western journalists of incompetence because they didn't tweet in Farsi when they tried to help organizers in Iran coordinate and further expand the 2009 protests denouncing the re-election efforts of populist president Mahmoud Ahmadinejad. Such criticism may have had an effect: It's now somewhat common to see Westerners tweeting in Yemeni Arabic, Ukrainian and such when discussing front-page current events in other countries.

But as for Gladwell's rant against slacktivism, that received its comeuppance two days after it was published when NPR reprinted a blog post written by San Francisco-based entrepreneur Dave Pell.[6] In the piece, Pell dismissed Gladwell's unbidden nonsense with venom: "Yes, folks," he deadpanned, "The Civil Rights movement took place at a time before Twitter. For those scoring at home, the same is true for every notable historical event from the Big Bang through the release of Destiny Child's 'Bootylicious' video." Fun stuff, and then Pell pointed out the obvious. "The real-time, social web is clearly not a required element to organize and execute a high-impact revolution. Neither is a megaphone, but it sure makes it easier for the folks in the back to hear you."

Bless his heart, Gladwell still has a fetish for being wrong about Information Age developments. In November 2022, for instance, he participated in a much-publicized Munk Debate focused on traditional mainstream media's usefulness in the age of independent media. In it, he and a rather lost-looking Michelle Goldberg (Gladwell's debate partner and fellow op-ed-bloviating Gothamite) had their hats handed to them by the team of author Matt Taibbi and Douglas Murray of U.K. magazine *The Spectator*, who easily swayed 67 percent of the debate's live audience to vote in favor of the statement "Be it resolved, don't trust the mainstream media."

Really, with sincere apologies to your favorite cable news pundit, I don't believe the mainstream media has very long to live. In a 2022 Gallup poll, only seven percent of respondents confessed to having "a great deal" of trust and confidence in mainstream newspapers, TV and radio, whereas 66% said they have very little to no confidence in them. Given that, as the Fifth Estate matures and becomes more widely accepted, it will eventually lure most citizens away from the corporate media. As things stand, the truth is out there, and it's not terribly difficult for people to find, but its spread has been slow owing to many factors.

Stick with it, is my advice to truth-seekers. When you finally see the Fourth Estate's colossal disinformation dump for what it is, you'll be an honorary intelligentsia, reading *The New York Times* "only for the line," as Chalmers Johnson once put it. Johnson uttered that comment years before author/activist Amber A'Lee Frost told her *Chapo Trap House* podcast listeners about her similar daily reading habits: Every day, she spends five minutes reading the *New York Times* to catch up with the latest trending topics in establishment propaganda, then reads the *Financial Times* cover to cover to ascertain what the oligarchs are actually planning.

In sum, America's news media consumption habits are what keep its citizenry confused. Whether you trust the *Times* or not, it was the most-read news site in America as of September 2023, followed by CNN, MSN, Fox News and Yahoo Finance.[7]

Of course, many "not very online" outsiders don't take Fifth Estate media content seriously because independent show hosts push the "fourth wall" envelope much farther than the tightly produced network and cable news-and-talk shows they're accustomed to consuming. Fifth Estate creators often fill hours with distracted tangents, casual chatting and off-topic observations, actively encouraging audiences to perceive them as "unprofessional" in a manner that jibes with the "microblogging" designation attached to Twitter. "It's just an internet thing," folks think, mainly because they've never indulged in it. Fifth estate media can be kludgy and loose, yes, but let's face it, anything's better than the mainstream media, the *Pravda* of American free- market capitalism.

Ultimately, it falls on the public to be more selective about the *reality* in which it lives. Regardless of how one becomes informed—whether through talking to others, reading, or following Fifth Estate figures—keep in mind that the keys to change are organization and solidarity. There's strength in numbers, but without collective resolve and mutual respect for the beliefs and opinions of others, numbers mean nothing.

III. What is the Online Left?

For our purposes, the "online left" refers to a demographic that includes anyone who holds few if any conservative beliefs, is dissatisfied with the Democratic Party to some wide-ranging degree, and has developed a great deal of political awareness by spending the bulk of their social media time conferring and brainstorming with casual acquaintances and total strangers on sociopolitical and socioeconomic subjects.

Another defining characteristic is its hip, snarky *je ne sais quoi*, a generally nihilistic attitude redolent of Twitter culture. Because of that, the "Twitter Left" might be more descriptive than "online left" since it would probably resonate with casual internet users who consider *all* Fifth Estate media—from its most popular talk shows (e.g., *The Young Turks*, *Breaking Points*, etc.) to the most obscure one-person operation featuring some YouTube guy explaining Trotskyism to his iguana—to be amateurish, unintelligible, unverified, fringe babblings that could be condensed into 280-character tweets.

I chose "Online Left" as part of this book's title rather than "Twitter Left" for two reasons. For one, owing to many factors we'll discuss later, Twitter itself is in dire straits at this 2024 writing, which would doom any book with Twitter in its title. Also, the term "online left" doesn't strictly apply to people who are active on Twitter. In fact, "online left" doesn't have a standard definition, so it's more open to interpretation. Ultimately, it evokes internet activity in which sentiments are decidedly *non-anti-humanitarian*. Suffice to say, then, there are many millions of members of the online left, folks who add their thoughts to the left hemisphere of the hivemind, whether through posting daily 2,000-word essays to socialism-focused Discord groups or rare, sporadic "I agree" replies to Facebook posts that resonate with them enough to lure them out of their shells.

As well, the mainstream hasn't really settled on what the phrase "online left" signifies. Apart from applying the label to all things politically radical, various journalists have used it to describe the type of staunch center-left voter who may or may not support establishment Democrats (Biden et al.) and progressive voters who support politicians like Vermont Senator Bernie Sanders. Some would argue that "real online leftists" hold staunchly anti-establishment, antiauthoritarian, and/or Marxist views and have no faith in the Democratic Party at all.

It certainly varies and has been a point of confusion to a general public that's politically and ideologically lost to begin with, grossly misled by right-wing media figures who brand Democrats and socialists alike as "radical leftists." Indeed, Democratic voters are commonly described as "leftists" by liberal pundits as well (for example, in democratic strategist Max Burns' November 2021 article for NBCNews.com, titled "Anti-Biden Conservative Chant 'Let's Go Brandon' Is Bait The Left Mistakenly Took"). Any web search for the term "online left" reveals that, although most think pieces tend to characterize the online left as an army of anti-establishment types (as found in CNN.com's December 2019 article "#NeverPete: How Buttigieg Has Drawn The Fury Of The Online Left"), it's not uncommon to see the online left identified as a Democratic-voting segment deeply rooted in "woke culture."

V. The Democratic Left?

Anyhow, yes, although a lot of progressives and socialists wouldn't approve, I'm including in the list of groups that comprise the aggregate "online left" the Democrats, that gigantic army of centrist-leaning liberals who view politics through a red vs. blue team-sports-type lens; for the most part their primary directive is keeping Republican politicians away from power. Those voters spend a lot of their social media time rehashing and condemning right-wing outrages (including the January 6, 2021, assault on the US Capitol building) and miscellaneous ideas the MAGA [Make America Great Again] Republicans have floated since the rise of their leader, Donald Trump.

In the opinion of many farther-leftists—people who stay on top of anti-establishment thought and/or read a lot of progressive and/or socialist literature—bashing Donald Trump and his minions is entry-level stuff, and they recoil from it. Anyone with eyes, they assume, can see that Republican politicians are unspeakable fiends who can't and don't try to hide their pro-business, anti-labor, performatively xenophobic ideology, so what's the use in discussing them? In fact, in the eyes of traditional leftists and progressives, the Democratic Party isn't much better than the Republican Party, if at all, given that its mindset is, like the Republicans', steeped in free market economic philosophy and trigger-happy imperialism. I'll submit my entry for Understatement of the Millennium by stating that this divide has caused a lot of friction within the online left. If there's anything that isn't difficult to find on Twitter, it's a farther-leftist who seems to hate Democrats as much as, if not more than, they do Republicans. "Both parties serve the same corporate interests," they yell.

Sadly, that's a case of history repeating itself. Minor quibbles between left-leaning groups have reduced America's left to a brawling mass of humanity that can't even agree on what *leftism itself* is. In that, we've become as confused about ourselves—and the things we want to achieve—as Germany's warring radical left and center-left factions were during the last years of the Weimar Republic, before Hitler's Nazis made up their minds for them. Back then, Ernst Thälmann, chief of the Stalin-influenced Communist Party of Germany (KDP), worked to depict the center-left—led by the Social Democratic Party of Germany (SPD)—as being as emblematic a symptom of capitalism as the Nazis. Confident that if Hitler won in 1933 he'd bungle everything in sight, Thälmann anticipated that a flood of Nazi supporters would eventually rush to the safe confines of the KPD. That was a disastrously wrong assumption. "Dogmatic, passionate, stubborn and stupid," British journalist David Winner wrote of Thälmann, "the former Hamburg dockworker divided the left and became one of the right's first victims. Within weeks of Hitler's takeover in 1933, he, along with thousands of other communists, was arrested and tortured. Unlike many of them, he survived in prison for 11 years before being murdered on Hitler's orders in 1944."[8]

Don't worry, Marxists; I haven't forgotten that the center-left SDF hired far-right Freikorps paramilitaries to murder Rosa Luxemburg and a bunch of other KPD radicals, nor do I believe Donald Trump poses the same existential threats as Hitler (I doubt Trump could spell "Schicklgruber" correctly if he had 5,000 guesses). But is it really accurate to say that the Democrats serve the same corporate interests as the Republicans?

Okay, they do to some extent, but in fairness, that criticism isn't completely on-target. The Democrats are in thrall to more insidious, superficially honorable corruptions, darkness-dwelling forces like Wall Street and Big Tech, as opposed to the Republicans, who gravitate to in-your-face, garishly harmful things like fossil fuel extraction, Wild West gun laws, and all things misogynist. Meanwhile, it's not like Democratic voters are blissfully oblivious to the fact that they're backing an impotent, often hypocritical party. Once you get to know a few deeply informed Democratic activists well enough to feel safe asking them about it (I should have received the Internet Medal of Honor for trying that on Twitter), they'll readily admit that the party has a lot of profoundly discouraging faults and weaknesses. They're quite aware that the party's politicians are all but incapable of denying the wishes of the oligarchy and too reliant on funding from the proverbial military-industrial complex, the corporatocratic force that habitually plunges the United States into wars of aggression in the name of imperial expansion and corporate profiteering.

In fact, if they've done any investigation at all, and many of them have, Democratic-voting liberals are miserably cognizant that their party has become an unappreciated, alarmingly underfunded political wing whose political representatives can nowadays do little more than offer condolences to the working classes for losing battle after battle in defense of them. When they're not spending nearly all their non-campaign-fundraising time (which, for most elected congresspersons and senators, is a 40-hour-a-week job) they're often working to clean up frivolous anti-labor, anti-consumer-protection or otherwise patently crappy legislative messes that the Republicans left behind after losing majority control of one or more governmental branches.

And so, dismissing all Democratic politicians as mindless, pretentious, less-conservative Republicans who are only feigning any dedication to supporting the rights of minorities and improving the lot of all citizens is more than a little meanspirited, really. Why? Because it wasn't always like this.

In the years after World War II, the middle class was in great shape. One wage-earner could support an entire family on one paycheck alone. In those days, the (more or less) antibusiness Democrats were in charge and seemed unbeatable, with good reason: The Republicans' pro-business/anti-labor agenda made them appear out of touch with regular people. It left Team Red fighting an uphill, unwinnable battle for cultural credibility. That continued happily until the 1970s, when the corporatists mounted an all-in effort to rid themselves of their two most aggravating problems.

On one hand were America's labor unions, and on the other was Ralph Nader's squadron of consumer/voter advocacy groups, all of which still exist today, albeit with nowhere near the influence they had when they were founded. The groups included the Public Interest Research Group (which focuses on grassroots organizing and direct advocacy on issues like consumer protection, public health and transportation), the Center for Auto Safety, and Public Citizen, a group dedicated to pressuring politicians to vote in the public's interests. Egalitarian entities like those thwarted the business elites' dream of an unregulated free market powered by employees who toiled at their jobs for low wages.

Of course, before all that, the Democrats had faced other obstacles. In 1948, the Strom Thurmond-led Dixiecrats, a segment of the Democratic Party that was opposed to racial segregation and supportive of Jim Crow laws, tried to break off from the Democrats but failed, which led to an uneasy peace within the party. In 1968, Republican presidential candidate Richard Nixon took advantage of that tension, directing some of his messaging at conservative Democrats, and won the election. That was the beginning of the end for the Democratic Party as a powerful force for regular citizens. By the 1970s, the Godzillas of industry had grown tired of having their bottom lines slashed by things like organized labor, high wage standards, near-full employment and Nader's sticking his nose in everything.

The corporations struck back in the early '70s, launching the "Corporate Proxy Movement," which still dominates our politics today. The corporatocracy mobilized against labor, leveraging their insurmountable economic power to pressure elected officials to support legislation favorable to business interests. The movement's instigator was conservative fixture Lewis Powell, a grandfatherly, professorial-looking Harvard Law grad whose name, incidentally, is shared by an American Confederate soldier who attempted to murder then-Secretary of State William Henry Seward as part of the Abraham Lincoln assassination plot. In 1971, Powell, at the behest of the US Chamber of Commerce's Education Committee, wrote a letter, accidentally released to the public, which came to be known as "the Powell memo." Titled "Attack on the American Free Enterprise System," the note conveyed paranoid warnings of a "war against capitalism," which prompted many top corporate leaders to move their headquarters from New York City to Washington, D.C., so they could be right in the faces of the politicians whose votes they needed to succeed in their aims.

Nixon had already given the corporations and their lobbyists a big assist in that area, signing off on the Legislative Reorganization Act of 1970. It forced transparency on Congress by recording individual lawmakers' votes on bills, where there had been no public record before. The act allowed lobbyists to know which congresspersons were in their corner and which ones weren't, so they'd know which politicians to fund or defund. Prior to that, the vast majority of legislation was discussed in secret, as Thomas Mann and Norm Ornstein describe in their 2006 book *The Broken Branch*. "Nearly all key committee meetings – at which bills were 'marked up', put together, and amended piece-by-piece, and where conference panels met – were held in secret, behind closed doors. In the absence of the public and press, and with no recorded votes, chairmen could wheel and deal, and cajole or coerce their members, relatively free of outside pressure or influence."

The elites were already on the march in those days. The top U.S. income tax rate had been reduced to 70 percent in 1965 from a high of 92 percent in 1952 and 1953. World War II was long over by the 1960s, so the number of available workers had returned to levels that erased labor's leverage. The corporatocracy was ready to retake control.

Suddenly finding themselves under ferocious attack by dark forces that wanted to wipe them off the political map, the Democratic Party froze, electing not to fight back against the corporatocracy with any intensity. 1995 rolled around, and with Bill Clinton facing hostile Republican majorities in the House and Senate, the party surrendered to the forces of neoliberalism, a Reagan-hatched variant of capitalist philosophy that writer Naomi Klein described as being desirous of "privatization of the public sphere, deregulation of the corporate sector, and the lowering of income and corporate taxes, paid for with cuts to public spending."

Nowadays, the Democrats are essentially a zombie party, flailing around in political quicksand, begging for campaign funding from the same anti-humanitarian enemies they'd sworn to reign in just decades ago. But that's the fault of fearful, unimaginative Democratic politicians, though, and doesn't necessarily dissuade me from considering center-left Democrats to be a bona fide wing of the aggregate online left. In private, they admit to being as frustrated with the party's political sclerosis as anyone else is.

In the meantime, the anti-authoritarian left needs all the

friends it can get. Unlike liberals, who are content to work within the complex political realities they're faced with, farther-leftists cannot obtain (and often claim not to even want) support from any arm of the mainstream. They receive little to no support from public figures, particularly celebrities (beholden to and enriched by the system, famous people stay out of the proverbial class war, rarely risking some tiny fraction of their platform capital by firing off a few hashtagged tweets that might entice or inspire some of their zillions of followers to participate in boycotts, strikes, and other grassroots actions that challenge systemic economic unfairness). As well, unlike Democratic activists, anti-establishment leftists have very few highly skilled, well-paid organizers working to spread their messages.

Relatedly, third-party-supporting leftists would do well to consider that many Democratic activists know a lot about organizing and managing political campaigns. Because of that, farther-left political activists could try viewing them less as mortal enemies than as potential mentors in one capacity or another. In the interest of expanding their movements, the farther-left has no choice but to engage with the center-left on a selective basis at least, maybe approaching liberals whose faith in the Democrats seems to be withering. Twitter searches for word combinations like "disappointed" and "Biden" would help locate them.

By the same token, liberals would do well to show a little more respect for enthusiastic grassroots activists of all ages, even if they aren't well-versed in "the realities of politics." The aggregate left needs true believers possessed of boundless energy if it's going to accomplish anything greater than keeping monsters like Trump out of the Oval Office, especially given that someone much worse—more mission-driven and less self-obsessed—will eventually take Trump's place. If we take to heart the sentiment of late-1800s-era U.K. Prime Minister William E. Gladstone, "Good ends can rarely be attained in politics without passion," where does that leave the 50something liberal from Baltimore who's feeling depressed and deflated after posting dozens of roundly ignored tweets lamenting the lack of voting rights for Blacks in Alabama?

Despite the apparent disgust farther-leftists exhibit when they catch someone expressing support for establishment figures like U.S. Representative Nancy Pelosi (a senior Democrat who's faced an alarming number of insider trading accusations), it wouldn't hurt leftists to get into the habit of using measured tones when interacting with them rather than immediately dismissing everything they say out of hand. Serious Democratic activists feel deeply insulted when farther-leftists write them off as clueless "Blue MAGAs" and "BlueAnons" whose work is pointless. They don't like it when farther-leftists fire off incendiary tweets and Facebook posts accusing them of being bots (semi-intelligent little automated programs), trolls, or useful idiots for the party who only cyber-holler catchphrases like "vote blue no matter who" because they're too ignorant to accept that the system is hopelessly broken and can only be saved by radical change. They do know that; they're just not sold on the idea of widespread upheaval. In the end, both sides would benefit from engaging in rational discussion steeped in critical thinking rather than indulging their egos in the kabuki of heated rhetoric.

Democratic supporters aren't the only ones feeling battered. Unlike the conservative sphere, every non-right-wing platform receives the harshest criticism from within, from leftist groups that think they know better. The Green Party can't get its candidates on ballot forms. Bernie Sanders supporters have politically unrealistic expectations.

And then there are the Marxists, who've been hamstrung by decades of pushback, not only from paranoid numskulls like Joseph McCarthy but from the U.S. government itself. Ardent socialists have (allegedly, I must note, for the lawyers) been hampered by propaganda programs like Operation Mockingbird, widely believed to have been a Central Intelligence Agency-led effort to manipulate the mainstream media to grow anti-communist public opinion. (While we're at it, it's important to note that although no smoking gun has ever been produced proving the existence of Operation Mockingbird to the satisfaction of all interested parties, it's a subject any history teacher can present as established fact to schoolchildren aged 11 to 16 in the United Kingdom and elsewhere.[9])

Owing to its generally more humanitarian, egalitarian mindset and an apparent inability to ignore trolls and bots, the aggregate left is much more prone to descend into internecine skirmishes than the right. Not to be too flip about it, but the only litmus test the right goes by when evaluating a politician would appear to be the following: If the candidate supports something that's bad for women, minorities, the environment, immigrants, people who don't want mentally ill people to get their hands on guns, animals, people in foreign countries, people who believe education is important, etc., that person has their unanimous approval. That's of course an oversimplification that should be rejected out of hand; obviously people are complex. Very few right-leaning voters share every single belief that the political right—referring to the Trump-venerating right that the Republican Party has become—tries to instill in them. For example, one of my conservative friends on Twitter is opposed to the practice of grade schools holding schoolroom talks by members of the LGBTQIA+ community so that kids might learn more about them and themselves. Yet he hates that college has become unaffordable for too many people, and he thinks the current level of wealth inequality is shameful. What I'm getting at is that with enough effort, some center-right conservatives could be converted to leftists.

In line with that, all leftist activists could learn something from conservative movements. Even with all their differences (and we'll discuss more of them later), the collective right spends little to no time on internal bickering, not anywhere near as much as the left does. One explanation for that is that the right organizes better. They develop long-term strategies, not just short-term ones, a left-plaguing problem described by Deepak Bhargava and Stephanie Luce in their 2024 book *Practical Radicals*. "[Leftist] organizers rarely get the opportunity to step back and reflect on their work and the broader movement because they're in a grind of crises and campaigns," they write. "This contrasts with what we have learned about how right-wingers train leaders at business schools and in the military, which emphasize strategy and vision rather than technical know-how."

Although the authors admit that building unity between left-leaning activists and movements may not come quickly, they maintain that it's crucial to achieve, one person or group at a time. Currently, the left is on the ropes, while the right is in position to punch down. It took years of right-wing strategizing for things to get to this point. They covered every base, including early internet forums in the 1980s. As I wrote in *Russian Nazi Troll Bots*, right-wingers of that era plainly saw that most internet users—largely comprising academics and other upper middle class folks—saw their anti-labor messaging for what it was and rejected it completely. Conservative groups responded to that challenge by engaging in organized online trolling. Groups associated with the Young Republicans created hundreds of fake user accounts and coordinated their efforts, posting countless messages on sites like Daily Kos and "Recommending," Liking or responding positively to their own posts en masse, busily "manufacturing consensus" until it seemed as though the internet was inhabited mainly by conservative users.

Today, the right reigns supreme in activist strategy, on the internet and everywhere else. Working in tandem with conservative media outlets like Fox News, the shadowy doings of "dark money"—election campaign funding from nonprofit 501(c)(4) groups that present themselves as benevolent organizations and aren't required to disclose the identities of their donors—keep Republican politicians, and, by extension, their voters, in perpetual lockstep, pigheadedly supporting the interests of fossil fuel companies, the National Rifle Association, etc., and meanwhile ignoring any elephants in the room such as climate catastrophes and schoolrooms full of dead kids. Sitting in cult-like obeisance, the Republican pundit class awaits instructions from the party's malevolent think tanks before reacting en masse to troublesome news stories, like the 2012 Sandy Hook, Connecticut, grade school massacre, when the right countered outraged calls for gun control with tin foil-hatted conspiracy theories and urgent cries for arming schoolteachers.

Online, those same dark money forces unleash bot swarms and battalions of trolls, often disguising themselves as kooky leftists, pithy autodidacts or "concerned citizens" in order to spread confusion and stir distractive debate among netizens who already know better but can't resist interjecting to make their presence known. All that ever results from such wasteful back-and-forth is louder amplification of right-wing messaging. I'll tell you something, if I were working for Charles Koch or some other right-wing arch-fiend who hired me to create a gigantic bot swarm to keep the composite left hopelessly distracted by infighting instead of banding together and mobilizing, a lot of the divisive tweets and posts I'd program my rotten little automated monsters to post in response to basically any left-slanted social media messages would be drawn from simple templates, viz: "The nonsense you just posted proves you have no idea at all what it really means to be a true [choose one: Democrat; Green Party member; gun control advocate; Black Lives Matter activist; socialist; Bernie Sanders supporter]!"

It always works. People love arguing with others on the internet, but no one gets sucked into it like people whose ideologies lean leftward. There's so much to be angry about, too much disinformation to unravel, too many fires to put out. They'll start fights over anything. I've seen it first-hand. On Twitter and Facebook, I've had people hurl angry words at me for stating my views on a wide range of things: Libertarians, Christian rock music, Olive Garden's marinara sauce, and the fact that I flatly refuse to eat guacamole. But that stuff is nothing. All-out flame wars break out in left-leaning spaces when someone questions any popular online pundit's motives, regardless of whether anyone ever took a few minutes to study the rabble-rouser's posting history to determine for themselves whether that person might be a troll, a certified kook, or a bot. As Sun Tzu wrote in *The Art Of War*: "If you know yourself but not the enemy, for every victory gained, you will also suffer a defeat."

And beyond all that lies the question I'd ask anyone who chooses to "defend their bubble" by attacking or "dogpiling" on inconvenient naysayers: Is that person patently, demonstrably correct in their criticism? If so, it might indicate that the group's doctrines are a little screwy and a minor adjustment might be in order. Alternatively, if the criticism is based on nonsense, why bother responding to them at all, especially if it's evident that they're only there to waste other people's time? If people asked those questions before allowing themselves and their groups to indulge in unproductive exercises in angry posturing and finger-pointing, the online left might find a way to—horrors—cohere, collaborate and strategize.

Being civil to one another and targeting the natural "enemies of democracy/socialism" and whatnot doesn't mean you have to have brunch together every Sunday. It only means you're more committed to fostering positive change than getting Likes and growing your online brand.

Again, many hardcore Democratic voters who post on Twitter and elsewhere have indeed worked in political organizing and question some of the party's strategies, but many haven't. The latter are usually the loudest, angriest participants (when they're not trolls, I mean). Their unswerving faith in the Democrats has made them immovable and closed-minded about leftist third-party candidates because they see them as spoilers who take votes away from Democrats and "hand them to Republicans." Their fixation on harm reduction, inflamed by a corporate-sponsored liberal mainstream press that's become more like a Home Shopping Network of altruistic outrage than any reputable news dissemination service, has, some contend, nudged the party faithful to the right a bit, often causing them to heap as much scorn on progressive political parties as they do on the right-wing contingent.

Some find that mindset singularly discouraging. As one democratic socialist podcaster histrionically noted, and I'm paraphrasing, "the Democrats aren't there to defeat the Republicans; they're there to crush progressives." That's harsh, but liberals do have some annoying habits, including their reckless willingness to believe that "never-Trump Republicans"—right-wing pundits and ex-politicians who've done no small amount of harm to Democrats in the past—can change their stripes and "switch teams" from, say, Fox News to MSNBC. In other words, liberals are often too quick to forgive Republican rat-finks like David Frum for their past ravings and accept them into the mainstream liberal media fold, which they did en masse after Donald Trump became president.

I suppose voters who get all their information from MSNBC and CNN can be forgiven for believing that a few notorious Fox News fixtures had changed their stripes, but the speed with which liberal Twitter welcomed their formerly least-favorite media figures was a nauseating sight for progressives to behold. Memes depicting Lucy pulling the football away from Charlie Brown's kick at the last second were everywhere you looked.

But again, it wasn't entirely out of bounds. The Republican Party had split in half, fracturing with a resounding snap after Trump and his posse of cancerous elites hijacked it. Suddenly, two distinct sides were jockeying for positions in the party's big top. On the one hand were the party's sniveling old-guard chickenhawks, and on the other was a clown carload of Trump suckups, political opportunists who jumped at any chance to con voters into believing that they and Trump sympathized with their hatred of the system.

A new feel-bad era had dawned for the Republicans. In the wake of the Trump tsunami, the Halliburton-backed Republicans of old, along with their pundit class, were displaced. Thinking quickly, nerve-grating supervillains like former Sarah Palin puppetmasters Bill Kristol and Nicolle Wallace stole aboard Never-Trump Trojan horses to win talking-head gigs on liberal networks MSNBC and CNN without so much as reciting a few Fatima Prayers. And there they stayed, as the networks hornswoggled their viewers into believing that providing seven-figure salaries to a few former Bush propagandists was some sort of win.

One of the most embarrassing examples of liberals playing themselves for suckers was the endless drizzle of 280-character encomiums they posted to Twitter in praise of the daughter of former Vice President Dick Cheney, Elizabeth Cheney, who, after being one of only 10 Republican representatives to vote in favor of impeaching Trump over his alleged role in the 2021 Capitol fiasco, was instantly forgiven for every bad thing she'd ever said about the Democrats, like the time she called them "the party of anti-Semitism and infanticide." The capper came in March 2024, when NBC added as an on-air contributor none other than Ronna McDaniel, former Chair of the Republican National Committee, whose support for Trump had been ferocious (she hosted Trump's "Fake News Awards" show). NBC News host Chuck Todd had a kitten over that one on air, and eventually the network rescinded their offer, dropping her like a live tarantula.

This isn't merely tilting at windmills, mind you. I'm quite aware that it would be naïve to suggest that the political duopoly's most prominent media players are anything more than boggle-eyed Muppets working to advance the interests of the morbidly wealthy. It's the enfeebled emptiness of it. MSNBC couldn't find anyone more on-brand than *Bill Kristol*?

But to be fair, 24/7 cable news isn't about news anymore; it's about marketable, ad-supported show business. When a right-wing pundit suddenly appears in one of MSNBC's round-table chairs spouting anti-Trump platitudes, it doesn't mean the GOP is "cleverly infiltrating the Democrats." Chalk it up instead to good work on the part of the pundit's talent agent and a transparently phony intention on the part of the liberal media matrix to infer that the pundit is wholeheartedly abandoning ship: "Look guys, even [former George W. Bush strategist] Steve Schmidt thinks the GOP sucks now!"

Anyhow, as we've seen, there are other differences between staunch Democrats and voters who lean farther leftward, but for now, I'd again urge both sides to cease fire and consider what the aggregate left could accomplish if it presented a unified front online.

Of course, "online" is where real egalitarian, progressive thought flourishes these days, unlike mainstream media spaces. But the internet does have its problems.

2

The Decline of Corporate Social Media

I. Into the Rings of Dis: Political Twitter

In Dante Alighieri's *The Divine Comedy*, the city of Dis, aka Lower Hell, is mainly reserved for perpetrators of intellectual sins as opposed to sins of passion. Twitter and other corporate, bot-mollycoddled online arenas, where matters of progressive or Marxist-minded politics are discussed, can be an intellectual hell for any left-leaning pragmatist if they hope to attract a following for their work as a journalist, activist, freelance pundit, or whatnot. At some point (usually very early on), such a person will find themselves interrogated by someone who disagrees with something they posted or tweeted, which is normal. But somehow, this time, the conversation is awkward and unsettling: The inquirer comes off as vaguely hostile, incapable of expressing their dissent with any politeness, maturity, or intellectual curiosity, much less self-deprecating humor.

When that happens, it can be intimidating to someone who's new to the platform, especially if it quickly becomes evident that the questioner is more interested in humiliating them than engaging them in healthy, constructive, light-hearted debate. The inquisitor rattles off sardonic, smart-ass questions, one after another, like some nerdy shark that smells blood in the water. *Where the hell did that come from*, the victim wonders.

Who knows. Maybe the jerk is in a bad mood because they didn't have a nice breakfast or their mother was a little rough on them during their potty-training stage. Whatever the case, that kind of thing happens a lot online. When it does, things can get nerve-wracking for any well-meaning leftist who believes they have unique, valuable insights to offer the chattering masses. To those poor souls, the simple, innocent act of discussing politics on any corporate-operated social media platform—Twitter especially—can indeed be hell.

But such is the nature of intellectual confabulation in this life. Misunderstandings and miscommunications are to be expected when people talk politics, which, along with its brother, religion, is one of the two topics to avoid when chatting with strangers. We do it all the time online anyway, though, without any real fear, because at least the person we're debating can't throw their coffee cup at us.

As things stand, the online world is a mess, especially within its splintered left. Many longtime users of social media and various other chat spaces would say without hesitation that America's political left is the most efficient circular firing squad ever to appear on Earth. Marxists and atheists bash each other; Bernie Sanders supporters and liberals usually can't go more than two "reply cycles" in an exchange before one party blocks the other to ensure they never encounter them again, niche-famous Fifth Estate pundits go at it in endless feuds in which the most heartbreaking casualty is always common sense.

You could chalk up all the online infighting to lots of things. But after spending way too much time on Twitter for journalistic purposes, I'd say one obvious problem with the platform is that it's not conducive to honest, animated, deeply nuanced debate with others, mainly because tweets are limited to 280 characters (at least for non-paying users, which is a whole other can of worms we'll pry open later).

Unfortunately, pragmatism and unique, edgy political insights don't usually lead to "political Twitter" popularity. Well, okay, they can, but usually not for new or casual users who want to bask in the dopamine rush (dopamine is an important neurotransmitter that, in short, makes us feel good) of having their innermost thoughts go a little viral with the help of a good group of "pocket friends" (that's what some of us call the relative strangers we constantly chat with on our phones' Twitter apps).

Twitter's stock-in-trade is devilishly clever brevity, given that tweets are so limited in length. Some would say the most worthwhile non-journalistic, "philosophical tweets" are like fortune cookie-sized Reddit posts. Not everyone has a knack for that, and even if they do, there's no guarantee that their tweets will be seen by the right people. Getting retweeted by just one of those "right people" can lead to some measure of Twitter popularity, respect, and the dopamine rushes that come with that cachet.

That's not to say that every political Twitter user has a desperate yearning for dopamine—you can get plenty of it from exercise, listening to music, hanging out with a pet, getting an adequate amount of sleep, etc.—and in fact, there are plenty of people who simply use it as a micro-diary or personal blog and don't care what anyone thinks. Plenty of folks claim they use Twitter simply to "scream their rage into the void" when they become upset over some news story or journalistic revelation. They claim not to care if they get many (or any) Likes, retweets, or comments on their outbursts. I don't completely believe that; after all, the "social" part of social media is about, you know, socializing, in a virtual sense. But it's certainly true in some instances, so, you know, *salud.*

What I mean is that as humans, we want to feel connected to others. We want to talk things out and gather feedback on our thoughts, up to and including our quirky attempts at psychic expressionism, when we post the first things that come into our heads. We want to know for sure we're being seen by others. When we do feel seen and appreciated by like-minded individuals on social media, we experience dopamine highs similar to what we feel when indulging in online gambling, e-shopping and internet porn.[1] When our preferred social media platform deprives us of dopamine and we don't get it somewhere else, it brings lows, making us moody, forgetful, anxious, depressed, and unable to sleep (which can lead to further lowering of dopamine levels). At its most extreme, dopamine deficiency is linked with schizophrenia, Parkinson's disease, and major depressive disorder. Toward our ends, it can be easy to tell when an online acquaintance is depressed over the lack of "engagement" (Likes, replies, etc.) on their social media posts: Occasionally, a sufferer will post a note asking whether anyone can see their posts in their "feeds" (continuous streams of new posts displayed to users).

Sleep is the first physiological need people sacrifice when they become deeply addicted to their chosen social media platform. I found that out first-hand when, in February of 2021, I decided to undertake an experiment: For an entire year,

I would post at least four sociopolitically geared tweets a day on Twitter, every day, whether I felt like it or not.

II. My Descent into the Inferno

I imposed a few rules on myself. First, my tweets would not express any sentiments that were openly hostile to any contingent of the online left, meaning anything that would anger liberal Democrats, socialists, progressives. This required me to bite my tongue approximately 2,500 times a day.

Second, if I felt myself getting addicted to Twitter and/or the experience became depressing, alienating or generally awful, tough noogies for me; I still had to post those four daily tweets. Spoiler alert, I did get addicted to it, partly because it was fun, partly because I wanted to "meet" as many new people as possible in order to learn from them, and also because every time I thought I'd gotten the place figured out, something wacky would always happen, a bolt of lunacy out of the blue, usually the sudden materialization of someone who had consciously chosen to become incensed over something I tweeted.

That leads us to rule number three: If someone became upset over something I tweeted and started "yelling" at me, I would deal with it in a calm, friendly manner, not start a fight with them. I would be a Nice Person. A Serious Sociopolitical Analyst. In other words, not me.

Spending too much time on political Twitter turned out to be one of the stupidest things I've ever done, near the top of a list that's grown long over the years. But I did make a lot of friends. Privately I called the project "Supersize Me Twitter" in homage to Morgan Spurlock's 2004 documentary "Supersize Me," in which he embarked on a self-enforced diet of nothing but three meals of McDonald's food every day for 30 days, capturing all the horror on videotape, including episodes of barfing and footage of his doctor's appalled reactions to the effects the diet was wreaking on Spurlock's physical health (after finding out Spurlock died of cancer in May 2024—possibly because of that McDonalds binge, I assume—I upped my therapy schedule).

My experiment wasn't anything any psychologist would ever recommend, but I'll admit that Twitter didn't make me barf (very often). For the record, I sent a note to Spurlock in 2021 asking him if he'd be interested in having a hand in the project. He never replied, probably because mine is not a household name, and besides, who would want to become even peripherally involved with someone who spends way too much time on a social media app?

The project was something I undertook partly for experimental purposes, to see what would happen if I forced myself to tweet like a seriously dedicated Twitter user. Admittedly, I also wanted to grow my own platform as an obscure author who, unlike my more well-funded competitors, didn't have the luxury of hiring interns or assistants to take on all the perfunctory, repetitive tasks required to maintain my personal social media presence. Thomas Frank has interns helping him with research, and Chris Hedges has an intern handling his Twitter. Must be nice, but then again, I did come to rely on my Twitter readers to idiot-check some of my ideas for this book: I'd occasionally tweet takes that felt a little harebrained and wait to see if anyone yelled at me.

I knew the experience was going to suck at first. I'd only used Twitter sporadically in previous years, posting only infrequently when I was trying to get a little attention for *Russian Nazi Troll Bots* during 2018 and 2019. This time, I was going all-in, forcing myself to tweet constantly—well, every morning at least—like all the popular people.

I was working a day job, so I had to get all my tweets out before 9 a.m. every single day, seven days a week, including weekends. I wanted to become the "Morning Man of left-leaning political Twitter," waxing sociopolitical, telling boneheaded jokes, and being nice to everyone, in the vein of your basic quirky morning rock radio deejay who says dumb things between playing Pearl Jam and Kings Of Leon songs. We had a saying in the troll groups I frequented during the late 1990s: "If you can't make the Who's Who, try for the What The Hell Was That." I set out to do exactly that.

For the most part, I avoided expert-written, antiseptically polite books and articles loaded with patently obvious tips on "the best times of day to tweet for maximum reach" or "using the right hashtags" and all that stuff. Who even *pays* those people?

For the first several months, I received almost no engagement. I expected as much, given that by my own rules I wasn't allowed to make jokes about Biden's unbeatable streak of physical and cognitive pratfalls or the prefigurative stances taken by certain staunch communists (we'll get to it), but it took so long to accumulate a meager following that it did get discouraging. It was as if I, along with my endless stream of lukewarm, harmless, but (I thought) valuable observations, were invisible. It bummed me out, but I refrained from asking, "Can anyone actually see my tweets," because that would've been the first step toward admitting defeat, as inviting as that was.

I started the project with no active Twitter followers at all. While half-assedly pushing my first book, I'd accumulated a decent number of followers, a few thousand or so, but unfortunately, nearly all the "tweeps" (habitual Twitter users) I'd bonded with in 2018 had abandoned Twitter and scurried back to Facebook, Reddit or environs unknown. One thing you can always count on when using Twitter is that you'll see many people you click with come and go, mainly because no one "talks" to them or Likes their tweets. They give up, even if their tweets are brilliant. As the experiment dragged on for months, I found myself getting more upset that my friends were being ignored than I did about the fact that *I* was. I mean, my tweets weren't just circumscribed to tediousness; they were designed to project an air of emotional stability, which will get you nowhere fast on the platform (the more unhinged you seem, the more people like it), and as well, I physically couldn't stick to one subject and tweet 30 times a day about it. Unlike me, some people can stick to one pet subject and tweet their asses off about it. One guy lasted a couple of months, tweeting at least 10 near-identical tweets a day in which he hollered at the sky for student loan forgiveness. Aside from my patronage, he received almost no engagement on them at all until he finally quit Twitter in disgust.

Time for a pro tip. If you've accumulated a good number of followers on Twitter and all you really want to do is grow a little sewing circle with a few people who post there, try spilling your guts about something that's bothering you and turn it into a multi-part story, like a little tiny soap opera. Going through a horrible divorce? Post a series of tweets about it and watch them come running. The general population might—okay, definitely *will*, unless you're inexcusably good-looking and have the selfies to prove it, which is a golden ticket on social media—ignore you at first. But if you keep at it for a couple of weeks, a few shy strangers will eventually offer a thought or two and "Like" some of your babblings. Trust me, they'll show up sooner or later, unless of course you sound certifiably crazy (like I said, Twitterfolk do gravitate to crazy talk, but it's bad strategy to sound like you're posting from a rubber room).

As well, I'm sure I would have had more success if I'd stuck to one Twitter bubble and tweeted nothing but variations on the group's current favorite hate topics. But as I said, that wasn't the idea. I wanted to engage with every breed of leftist on the platform, from MSNBC-glued liberals to the really feisty armchair-communist-revolutionary types, aka "tankies," a group whose members blurt out random things for shock value, such as non-sequiturs about how Chairman Mao was "based" (really cool) because he killed anyone who questioned his leadership. The tankie space mainly comprises younger people with relatively small numbers of followers (typically less than 300, if not much fewer), but we'll get into that later.

I also probably would have had a much easier time of it if, from the beginning, I'd confined my tweets to subjects and ideas that actually appealed to me instead of sticking my nose in anything that looked vaguely interesting. If I had been there strictly to chat with like-minded folks, I might have adopted an unsmashable facade of casual nihilism that goes over big in most non-Democratic leftist bubbles. But if I'd done that, I would have been entirely out of the loop with what was happening elsewhere within the hivemind. I did want to fit in somewhere, yes, but fitting in wasn't my objective. I wanted to know the thought processes taking shape on *all* the bubbles. Unfortunately, by the same token, I didn't want to be bored. I wanted to make a lot of friends. So I followed a ton of people, most of whom followed me back.

Now, none of the above is meant to imply that racking up

vast numbers of Twitter followers is existentially fulfilling in any real way, but it feels like it when you're trying to take Twitter seriously. And in truth, accumulating lots of followers doesn't automatically mean those people will ever chat with you. Even after my Twitter follower count had reached 10,000 people, I found myself mostly "hanging out" with a small, widely diverse group of five to 30 people on an irregular, ever-shifting basis. I made friends with all types of leftists and center-leftists, even the odd conservative here and there. Unfortunately, my affinity for underdogs resulted in my gaining many followers who gave up after a few months of being ignored by all the other kids.

One thing that probably dissuaded a lot of political types from taking me seriously on Twitter was that I enjoy "comedy Twitter" and "cute Twitter," spaces inhabited by funny people and other lost souls who post random, hilarious things. Being the easily distracted magpie that I am, I dabbled in that as well, posting one-liners every three or four tweets (for instance, "Look, if all you're going to do is cite proven facts and provide web links that support all your statements, this argument is stupid and a waste of my time"). Other than that sort of stuff and the ultra-rare selfie, everything I tweeted was sociopolitically relevant, intended to spark engagement with my mutual followers on such subjects as the "class war" and the indiscretions of corporations and such (other protip: If you want people to engage with you, always end your tweet with a question. For example, "IBM has a long history of outsourcing good jobs overseas and cutting retirement benefits. From 2008 to 2015, IBM avoided paying $17.8 billion in taxes by operating subsidiaries in 16 offshore tax havens. What a bunch of scumbags, huh?" I think proprietary social media algorithms like question marks a lot and promote any posts that have them).

I also could have forced myself to post nothing but serious tweets while appearing to be implacably angry all the time, which is always a surefire way to keep tweeps coming back for more, but I couldn't bring myself to do that either. For one thing, it's hard for me to take American politics seriously enough to project a consistently angry persona when the lowest tier of our country's "politically engaged" intellectual pyramid took seriously the idea that drinking human urine could prevent COVID-19 infection.[2]

Besides, I didn't want to spout angry rhetoric in every tweet. Spending all one's spare time wallowing in the anger-management mosh pit that is "serious political Twitter" and never deviating from its miserable vibe isn't healthy. I can't stay in po-faced, outraged character if I've just watched a video of someone running down the street chasing a pug dog holding its owner's bag of take-out sushi in its mouth.

And nothing in the Supersize Me Twitter rulebook said all 28 of my weekly tweets had to be emotionally revealing. That was a mistake on my part. I know for a fact that more than a few people "unfollowed" my Twitter account owing to my inability to portray a distraught citizen who believed Armageddon was just one more Lauren Boebert tweet away from being uncorked but I really didn't care about that. I wasn't on the platform to win a Twitter Award (there are no Twitter Awards). Unlike many Twitter users, I had no illusions about the platform's influence on society at large, given that only 22 percent of Americans use Twitter at all, eighty percent of tweets come from 10 percent of the platform's users, and the bottom 90 percent of Twitter users barely ever participate. On average, those very casual wallflowers only create around two tweets per month, "Like" one tweet per month, follow 74 accounts, and have 19 followers, all of which means that the "Twitter consensus!" cited in mainstream media pieces is reflective of the thoughts of only a very tiny fraction of Americans.[3]

There's no denying that my so-called "Twitter career" was cursed from the start. Having a few real-life friends with whom I could've bantered on Twitter would have helped me, of course, but (and I got the sense that this is the case with the vast majority of Twitter users, many of whom are only on Twitter because they can't be themselves on Facebook, where if they revealed their true beliefs it would send their grandmothers straight to the cardiac unit) I only knew a couple of people in real life who spent any time at all on Twitter: A travel author/journalist who basically hates it and much prefers Facebook, and another buddy, a conservative who writes horny science fiction novels and tweets mostly about big giant boobs. We rarely communicated on Twitter, and I didn't blame them. I made plenty of new, sometimes very close acquaintances on Twitter, though, which increased my addiction to it.

I've had a few encounters with celebrities on Twitter, which is always rewarding. The most delightful instance was when I had a little back-and-forth with my favorite comic book writer, D.G. Chichester, whose credits include *Daredevil* and my personal all-time favorite, the hilarious *Terror Inc.* There was also joke-U.S. presidential candidate Vermin Supreme, who spends a lot of time on Twitter; he (or a bot he runs) replied to a few of my tweets when I mentioned his name in passing. Another hero of mine, actor Ken Wahl (from the '90s TV show *Wiseguy*), gave me a couple of Likes for my fluttery praise. Gloria Estefan from the band Miami Sound Machine contributed to a Twitter thread I started and still owes me a happy birthday tweet.

The funniest thing that ever happened to me on Twitter was the time a famous, recently retired porn star sent forth her entire fan base to attack me. Somehow, the starlet had caught wind of a snarky conversation I was having with a lady friend about people we'd dated, during which the porn star's name came up in an unflattering context. A hilarious flame war ensued, during which my friend posted some photos of the actress in her element, stuff that was decidedly "not safe for work." Oddly, the niche-famous thespian blocked my friend but never blocked me, which led me to believe that we'd had something special, brief though it was.

Magic happens on Twitter, folks; I'll attest to it without the most fleeting hesitation.

III. Welcome to Twitter, Now Get Out

There is—or was, as the case may be, depending on whether or not the company has been sold for scrap by the time you're reading this—no place like Twitter. With all its hustle and bustle and baked-in randomness, it's the New York City of social media.

As stupid as it seems to normal people, accumulating a decent-sized following on Twitter is a prestigious accomplishment for us "very online" types. It's different from platforms like the more family-friendly Facebook (which generally tends to evoke "your life as a Hallmark card," bubbling over with superficial, polite positivity and very little originality; nearly all the memes that appear on Facebook are stolen from other platforms) and the more topically regimented Reddit.com, an infinite collection of coffee-klatch chat forums resembling the siloed Usenet newsgroups of the

1990s. Some of Reddit's "subreddits" (individual sub-forums) are so tightly moderated that they're almost unusable. Nine times out of 10, if you're a very sporadic user of the site and post a simple question on a topic you presumed was under a particular subreddit's purview, either a bot or the subreddit's moderator will curtly inform you that you're posting your question to the wrong subreddit and you need to post it elsewhere on the site. It's like being Dorothy in *The Wizard of Oz*. Just when you thought you'd finally found the perfect group of people to answer your question, you get the speakeasy door slammed in your face.

By contrast, "political Twitter" is the Wild West, where you never know if some rootin' tootin' galoot is going to come gunning for you. It often feels like the viral multiplayer video game Fortnite, the object of which is to survive without getting zapped by any of the other anonymous players who want to be the last one standing. On Twitter, it's your reputation that gets zapped if you say the wrong thing to the wrong someone, because everyone can see your screwup. In other words, like all social media platforms, Twitter has a virtual-reality aspect to it that can be unnerving at first: You're a stranger in a strange, hostile land, where many of the people you encounter would like nothing better than to prove to the "crowd" that your thinking is off-kilter (or even bigoted) somehow, which, they hope, will lead to your getting "canceled" (mocked and pilloried until you're too humiliated to show your cyber-face on the platform ever again).

As I said, people often don't personally know anyone on political Twitter when they start using it, so the going can be a little rough at first if your goal is to sound off about certain politicians or other things that make you nuts. In that, it's go big or go home. Invariably, if you appear to be the slightest bit reasonable, someone will have the opposite opinion and let you have it. It's sort of like prison in that way. That endless dance of dominance is common to corporate social media spaces, of course, but where Facebook and Reddit are like county jails, Twitter is Attica and the air conditioner's down for maintenance.

One thing that attracts people to Twitter is that their thoughts can be seen by every user of the platform. If you tweet something about raccoons, for example, any Twitter user who types "raccoons" in the search box might find your tweet and engage with it without having to be in your "followers" list. In other words, tweets are, by default, visible to the public, unlike Facebook posts, which, for the most part, only one's "Friends" can see (since 2014, new Facebook users have the privacy level of all their posts set to "Friends only" by default, as opposed to "Public," which is Twitter's default. In both cases, most people leave the setting as is).

Twitter's default "publicly viewable" setting for tweets assuredly helped lead to the perception that the platform is "the village square of the internet": Posting to Twitter can feel like walking around on the streets of Manhattan, wonderfully random in terms of the types of people you might encounter. One minute, you're hanging out with a longtime acquaintance; the next, you're talking to actor Mark Ruffalo about how much Trump sucks and he actually *sees* you.

The "online trends and happenings" that receive breathless coverage by the Fourth Estate don't always originate on Twitter, of course, even if the mainstream media focuses almost exclusively on it. People discuss and debate politics on other social media platforms like Facebook and Reddit; they stomp their feet and bloviate on streaming video platforms like YouTube and Twitch.com; they operate podcasts; they write opinion (and sometimes well-researched journalistic) pieces for publication on sites like Substack.com, etc. But the establishment really only pays attention to Twitter.

Building a successful platform on any corporate site, social media-centric or otherwise, is challenging, but "Twitter popularity" is particularly difficult to achieve. Being that tweets are limited to 280 characters, there's little room for ambiguity, nuance or error. Every character you type counts if you want to make a compelling statement, which can be tricky if the statement has any complexity. If a tweet is too cryptically worded, too loaded with obscure acronyms or shibboleths, or isn't otherwise crystal clear, its intention can get lost on readers. Adding related web links, pictures or memes to a tweet can help alleviate confusion, but it can also exacerbate it. Despite all that, one could say that the extreme brevity of tweets makes them indispensable to life in our hypersonically paced Information Age, emblematic of the "blip culture" Alvin Toffler prophesied in his 1980 book *The Third Wave*. Tweets are compact and practical, perfectly suitable for people and public figures who want to express their consensus on matters without editorializing or presenting it as "writing" in any real sense. As habitual Twitter user Margaret Atwood, author of *The Handmaid's Tale*, once explained, "It's not writing, it's signaling. Put it in the same category as the telegraph, the semaphore flags, the smoke signal."

Over the years, there've been many Twitter success stories, like that of screenwriter Justin Halpern, whose comedic Twitter account "Sh!t My Dad Says" led to a book and a TV show featuring William Shatner. There's also Sohaib Athar, an IT consultant from Pakistan, who accidentally "live-tweeted" the Navy SEAL raid in which Osama bin Laden was killed in

2011. As well, there are plenty of mini-celebrities who became Twitter-famous by maintaining non-political accounts on the platform, such as Jason Scott, whose cat, Sockington (now sadly deceased), "tweeted" his way into the hearts of over a million followers (sample: "You call it a litterbox and I call it a screensaver for cats").

Humor has always been a prime component of Twitter; it's fun to challenge yourself to write amusing one-liners, which was pretty much all the platform's early users had room for when they felt like blowing off a little steam. In the first version of Twitter, tweets were limited to a paltry 140 characters (the same size as Short Message Service [SMS] messages, the cheapest and most common form of text messaging used today, which reveals the core technology behind the site when it debuted in 2006). Back then, along with status updates sent by various professionals to their colleagues, a good percentage of tweets consisted of goofy, nonsensical gags. "Comedy Twitter" is an art form, really, part Tetris and part joke writing. There's twice as much room to do that nowadays; the maximum size of a tweet was extended to its current 280-character limit on November 7, 2017. That development caused some Twitter users not to celebrate but complain that giving users more room to write things would "make Twitter more like Facebook."[4] (In one of the worst moves he made after buying Twitter, billionaire and amateur alt-right troll Elon Musk gave "Twitter Blue" subscribers the capability to post unlimited-sized tweets, which undoubtedly led to many longtime users hitting the exits.)

Either way, the idle, esoteric fun and games of Twitter's early days didn't last forever. Twitter saw its first uncontrollable, 100-megaton explosion of activity after Michael Jackson died in 2009. Millions of people took to the platform to offer bite-sized messages of condolence, among other sentiments. So massive was the outpouring that it overloaded Twitter's then-meager servers and caused the site to crash.[5] And just like that, a tradition was born: Ever since then, celebrity deaths—even relatively obscure ones—are pretty much guaranteed to bring Twitter to a standstill, not so much owing to the platform's hardware's inability to handle the load but to the fact that the overall depth and quality of the posted content are reduced through an overabundance of platitudes. It's like sitting in a restaurant when a busboy drops a tray full of dishes: The universe stops as thousands and thousands of people feel compelled to express their "shock and sadness" over the loss of someone whose relationship to them was, if anything, purely parasocial. Instantly, the platform is buried in itty- bitty requiems aeternam mourning the loss of the famous person, be they the Queen of England or an actor who specialized in playing the token crazy henchman on every network television cop show during the early 1980s.

That's not to say that the untimely (or, let's face it, timely, depending on the person's age) death of a human being isn't tragic. Still, social media does tend to bring out the (often insincere) mawkishness in people. As one tweep put it, and I'm paraphrasing: Every time a celebrity dies, Twitter turns into 5,000 people trying to flush the same turd down the same toilet. Like I said earlier, we want to be seen.

IV. Social Media Influence as a Capital Asset

Of course, many social media users really, *really* want to be seen, so they work at it, tweeting, posting and/or uploading videos to streaming services like YouTube every day as if it's a proper job. And for some users, it *is* a job. Top YouTubers—content creators whose videos typically get many thousands of "views" from their fans and followers—make around $5 for every thousand views. That may not sound like much, but it adds up when the number of views climbs into the millions.[6]

A lot of work goes into making someone internet-famous. According to the aforementioned books and articles that offer advice on the subject, achieving "success" on any social media platform—growing a sizeable following whose members engage en masse with one's every post and regale each one with Likes, comments and shares/retweets—comes down to a combination of consistency (i.e., posting every day, more or less without fail), quantity (posting many posts or tweets, the recommended number of which depends on who's giving the advice), and the quality of the messaging, reporting and/or writing. Quality is often low, but only because internet-popular people need to keep their fan bases coming back to check on their opinions and doings, so they're often forced to "phone it in," presenting repetitive, "microwaved" content just to make an appearance.

Of course, monetization of individual social media platforms doesn't begin and end with YouTube. Instagram "influencers" can make astonishing amounts of money (in 2022, Portuguese professional footballer Cristiano Ronaldo made an average of $2.3 million per Instagram post).[7] Budding authors and journalists can earn a few pence (or much more) for posting articles to sites like Substack, a platform that helps itself to 10 percent of a writer's subscription revenue (typical subscriptions are billed at around $5 to $15 per month for each creator's account). Those "neo-bloggers" employ cross-platform strategies, building fan bases on Twitter, Facebook, etc., where they post links to their primary platforms.

And all of that's fine if a content creator's stock-in-trade is cute animal videos or makeup tips. But the same monetization schemes apply to independent political commentators and video bloggers, many of whom find that the easiest way to increase their fan base is by occasionally erecting (and vociferously defending) gratuitous ancillary positions often rooted in conspiracy theories that don't accomplish much more than solidifying their bubbles while simultaneously keeping more-or-less-like-minded people feeling too alienated to engage with (much less support) their platforms.

You look slightly confused (suspicious?), and I don't blame you. Let's back up and talk about what a "conspiracy theory" actually is. To begin with, it's a theory, meaning that there usually exists some evidence and/or historical precedent to support it, but to date, no irrefutable evidence has surfaced to confirm its validity beyond all doubt. That means it's nothing more than an assumption. In Sir Arthur Conan Doyle's 1890 book *The Sign of the Four*, Sherlock Holmes utters the immortal line, "When you have eliminated the impossible, whatever remains, however improbable, must be the truth." That sounds nice and smart, but the quote appeals to a fallacy known as "arguments from omniscience," meaning that the proponent believes they know "literally everything there is to know in the universe," or, at least, everything about the subject under discussion. Since that's impossible, it means that any theory involving, say, accusing the government or some other organization of engaging in some horrifying plot without being in possession of irrefutable evidence must, by definition, prove that it can't be dismissed as a "Holmesian fallacy," which RationalWiki.org defines as something "believed to be true on the basis that alternate explanations are impossible, yet not all alternate explanations have been ruled out."

Here's an example. In 2023, owing to stupidly reckless investment strategies whose collapses led to a massive herd of customers hastily withdrawing their money from its rapidly dwindling coffers, California's Silicon Valley Bank, the 16th largest bank in the United States, failed. The disaster was complicated, but online pundits immediately weighed in with bizarre "explanations" for the disaster in no time flat. Various crackpots alleged that the bank had failed owing to its "woke culture" or an act of financial aggression perpetrated by actors within the murky jillionaire class, who were purposely working to collapse the financial system to gain a whole lot of assets from it. The best one of all was the allegation that the bank's failure was just the tip of the iceberg in "the Great Reset," an ever-morphing conspiracy theory presented by kooks as a plot cooked up by billionaires and other members of the World Economic Forum: They were using the COVID-19 pandemic as an excuse to reorganize the world's societies and economies, after which they intended to install a global totalitarian regime that would punish refuseniks by putting them in detention camps.[8] (Diving into the deep end, conspiracy theorist Spiro Skouras released a YouTube video on June 7, 2020, in which he spouted claims that one component of the Great Reset would be a "trans-human agenda," an operation that would involve turning people into cyborgs that would be easier to control. The video had received over 400,000 views as of early 2024.)

At any rate, while the internet was busily flipping out about the Silicon Valley Bank panic and blaming the meltdown on everything but SpongeBob SquarePants, Scottish economist Mark Blyth took to Twitter on March 13, 2023, urging the distressingly outnumbered 90,000 pairs of eyeballs that fell on the tweet to exercise a little caution. "I've been getting a few DMs [personal Twitter messages] saying 'why are you not weighing in on the bank run?' The answer is simple. I don't know what's going on and neither does anyone else. Here's why: We live in a world where opinion is instant and analysis takes time."

How true. Pragmatism isn't a hot commodity online, not when millions of social media users are more focused on increasing their platform capital than engaging in mature, level-headed debate and examining every available fact. That's par for the course, though; people generally respond more energetically to emotionally delivered, morally charged verbiage than unexciting truth. One study found that the presence of "moral-emotional words" in online messages increased their viral spread by a factor of 20 percent for each word.[9]

Some Fifth Estate content producers have readily admitted that, in a way, their sphere has fallen prey to the same sort of "if it bleeds, it leads" mentality that makes Fourth Estate media untrustworthy. In a June 2022 episode of his YouTube program *The Majority Report*, titled "How To Spot A Grifter On YouTube," host Sam Seder voiced his concerns. "For many, many years I have said on this program that I think YouTube is problematic." Checking his swing a bit, he continues. "We try and do this show in a responsible manner and try and be as transparent as we can. I know in some of our YouTube [segment] titles we use all caps [capital letters] and can be flamboyant, [but] we do not attempt to shape the show based upon the clicks that we're going to get."

He then imparts his thoughts on "grifters," i.e., Fifth Estate figures who try to wring controversial topics for all the clicks they can get. "You want to know what the definition of a 'grifter' is?" Seder asks aloud. "Look at the topics that they start to cover and then [compare them to what's currently viral on] Google Trends ... they are chasing this stuff, and they don't care what it is. You don't go out there and push [controversial COVID-19 remedies like Ivermectin] because you all of a sudden have become, like, you know, 'Alternative Medicine Guy,' or, you know, 'I have been for years secretly concerned about the injustice in Ukraine and their refusal to accept their Russian heritage.'"[10]

Anti-war activist and underground journalist Abby Martin expressed similar concerns during a November 2017 edition of *The Jimmy Dore Show*. "Unfortunately, you have a lot of grifters because it's so difficult [to succeed] that we need to brand ourselves. We need to become a brand, you know, to survive. And we have our Patreons [paid subscriber sites that feature exclusive content] and we have this and that. It's just unfortunate that that's the way it is. I do [however] have a lot of [faith in] citizens' journalism and 'people's media.'"[11]

Not all citizen's journalism is trustworthy, of course. Sometimes it's nothing more than "fake news," which tends to spread astonishingly quickly owing to its emotionally charged nature. In 2018, MIT Media Lab researcher Deb Roy noted that when a new item of fake news first splashes into the social media waters, its initial reader reactions are visceral, enhancing its virality. That's because expressions of "surprise and disgust" are much less forgettable than lukewarm "thumbs up" reactions. From there, social media users rush to tell their friends about it (and earn a little platform capital for themselves). That suggests that humans, not bots, are the prime movers of viral things, including fake news.

Angrily tweeting about politics on a constant basis can become as lucrative an endeavor as tweeting about cats, culturally ignorant dads, or Navy SEAL raids. Take for example the center-left-leaning, anti-Trump tweets of Majid Padellan (@mmpadellan, better known by his Twitter handle Brooklyn Dad Defiant), whose online efforts in support of the Democratic Party led to his amassing more than a million Twitter followers. A New York-based art director who supports, among other things, feminism, racial equality, and the anti-Republican "#Resistance" social media movement, Padellan met his wife through Twitter and became such a popular figure on the platform that he decided to release a book, titled *The Liddle'est President*, comprising cartoons mocking Trump.[12] Padellan's good fortune didn't come without controversy, though. In 2021, it was widely reported that he was paid more than $57,000 the previous year by liberal-backed super PAC Really American, which works to spread anti-Republican and pro-Democratic-establishment propaganda.

Progressives leaped on the story like starving wolverines, reminding their bubble buddies that Padellan had heckle-tweeted at Bernie Sanders to drop out of the 2020 presidential race to help Joe Biden and, in a move that even some liberals viewed as being rather nauseating, posted criticism of Tara Reade, a woman who, during the 2020 presidential campaign, accused then-Senate-candidate Biden of sexually assaulting her back in 1993, when she'd worked for him as a staff assistant in his Washington, D.C., Senate office. (Padellan never denied the payola accusations and only addressed all the fuss by reminding onlookers that his Twitter profile clearly stated that he's a senior adviser to ReallyAmerican.com.)

Padellin isn't the only pro-Democrat "resister" suspected of benefitting from tweeting enthusiastic support for the party's candidates. In late 2022, a group photo surfaced featuring 24 well-known Democratic-supporting Twitter personalities (including Padellan) posed in front of the White House. It appeared that they (along with other mini-celebrities from TikTok and other platforms, many of whom weren't active in online politics at all) were invited to gather at the White House on October 9, 2021, to participate in a social media summit. A meme featuring the photo, captioned "The Democracy Posse: Paid Social Media Influencers," went somewhat viral, generating lots of rage. In response to accusations that the people in the photo were all getting paid by a Democratic-affiliated organization to mobilize their collective millions of followers, one of the pictured influencers, Allison Gill (whose Twitter handle is @MuellerSheWrote), tweeted, "This is the most hilarious shit I've ever seen. Yes, we like democracy. No, we are not paid."

Whether that was true or not, the fact that they were invited to the White House did increase their online "clout," cementing their credibility in the eyes of their social media followers. In the meantime, it helped boost the sales of any companion products (books, podcasts, etc.) they might have been offering.

But in the end, who cares, really? We're talking about a horse that's left the barn and relocated someplace sunny. Until further notice, social media influencers are here to stay, having become movers and shakers of anything related to American culture, including its politics. They're no longer limited to helping companies sell overpriced clothes and muscle-building snake oil in their videos; they're getting hired by political consultants to urge their fans to vote for specific candidates. Curtis Hougland, CEO of the liberal-leaning company People First, partners with influencers to saturate social media spaces with political messaging. In 2022, he disclosed that a study by his company revealed that 43 percent of the people polled on the matter trust influencers more than they do traditional political campaigns. But that's not the best part: By funneling their messaging through influencers, campaigns easily sidestep bans on political advertising on platforms that disallow it altogether, including Twitter, TikTok and Instagram.[13]

Any way you slice it, it's a sneaky trick, pointing to yet more evidence that online influencers aren't subject to the same rules of etiquette as mainstream media celebrities, owing to the simple fact that the system at large isn't quite sure what to do with them. For instance, it's basically unheard-of for a local TV network's weatherman—much less someone like *Today* show meteorologist Al Roker—to quip, "Can't wait to vote for Joe Biden next week" before handing the spotlight back to the anchor team. Stuff like that isn't done, partly due to tradition but more to FCC rules about ensuring candidates are given "equal time" and such. In general, Fourth Estate figures watch what they say in public but do occasionally push the boundaries. "As a reporter," Elex Michaelson of Fox News' Los Angeles affiliate TV station gingerly tweeted in January 2020, "I don't endorse candidates or policy positions. But as a human being, I like @BernieSanders and have always enjoyed working with him."

Professional athletes also generally refrain from endorsing politicians, although Red Sox pitcher Curt Schilling's off-the-cuff remarks urging fans to vote for George W. Bush after the club had won the 2004 World Series was one rather boorish exception.

Not that I have any real problem with it (aside from the fact that progressive third parties don't have the funding to compete at the Democrats' level), but the practice of hiring influencers to push Democratic candidates does give the party something of an unfair advantage, since voters age 18 to 29—a demographic that is of course ferociously online—chose Biden by a 26-point margin over Trump in the 2020 presidential election, and Democrats over Republicans by 28 points in the 2022 midterm elections.[14]

That said, it's not as if the Democrats are the only political faction that deploys influencers to spread their messaging. On July 11, 2019, Donald Trump held a "Social Media Summit" at the White House that was attended by such fringe right-wing figures as Ben Garrison, a cartoonist who'd faced accusations of being anti-Semitic; radio host/QAnon conspiracy theorist Bill Mitchell and an array of others.[15]

Even the progressive, social democratic wing of our political sphere has cached a history of passing off targeted political messaging as innocent, spontaneous opinion. Syndicated columnist David Sirota, who co-wrote the screenplay for the 2021 climate-apocalypse film *Don't Look Up*, chose not to disclose that in 2019, he was in talks with the Bernie Sanders presidential campaign to sign on as a high-level team member at the same time he was writing fiery, pro-Sanders pieces for *The Guardian* and posting tweets that bashed pretty much all of Sanders' Democratic-establishment-backed rivals (a list that included Beto O'Rourke, Kamala Harris, Cory Booker and Joe Biden). Thousands of Twitter users demanded an explanation, and after popping off a few angry rebuttals, Sirota deleted 20,000 tweets.[16] It was all quite awkward, because Sirota's acts of aggression didn't jibe with the tightly measured, Gandhi-like messaging of Sanders himself, who'd scolded in 2018, "Negative attacks on Democratic candidates just continues the process of debasing the Democratic system in this country, and is why so many people are disgusted with politics."

That sort of thing is fair game now, but it's probably just a matter of time before influencers will be legally compelled by their Big Tech platforms to reveal what political organizations are paying them for "stating their opinions." There are already precedents outside of the political arena, for instance the 2023 case of French reality TV star Nabilla Benattia-Vergara, who was fined €20,000 for promoting Bitcoin to her millions of Snapchat minions without revealing that she was paid to do so. The "advice" she and other influencers imparted to their fans led to a class action lawsuit filed by more than 100 victims who lost money by following it.

What's my personal take on all this? Well, as we'll discuss shortly, anodyne politics aren't my thing, so I'm inclined to forgive Sirota for giving progressivism a boost, regardless of his methods. In the meantime, what intrigues me about the "Democracy Posse" story is that Padellan's role as an (arguably) overt operative whose actions lined up with his (apparently) long-held beliefs is something farther-leftists should consider emulating rather than repudiating out of hand simply because the tactic is being employed by "the wrong team."

I hope they do, and with that, it's probably a good time to confess that I'm a casual, eternally disappointed supporter of Bernie Sanders and his small but growing contingent of progressive-minded Congresspersons, often referred to as "The Squad," an improbable handful of politically altruistic House representatives.

V. Chasing Political Rainbows: The Social Democrats

Ostracized by a Democratic establishment that's forgotten they're even there, the "Squad" includes in its informal number Alexandria Ocasio-Cortez (commonly referred to as "AOC," the U.S. Representative for New York's 14th Congressional District since 2019) and Representatives Ilhan Omar of Minnesota, Ayanna Pressley of Massachusetts and Rashida Tlaib of Michigan.

The Squad stands as proof that with enough determination and hard work, populists can come into political power directly from nothing, or at least from backgrounds your typical deeply funded politician would consider poverty level. The Squad's dooming problem is that there aren't many of them, which stymies them when they're faced with politically volatile situations. Notably, there was the 2021 "Force The Vote" snafu, when the group's support base demanded that they refuse to vote to confirm Nancy Pelosi as Speaker of the House unless she pledged to bring a "Medicare For All" vote to the floor of the House. It was a lose-lose proposition that would have resulted in either a flat rejection of the bill and a sharp reduction of the Squad's political capital if they went for it or a lowered standing in the eyes of progressive voters if they didn't. They chose the latter to avoid wholesale shunning by their corporate-owned establishmentarian "colleagues" and live to fight another day.

Blowback for that move came swiftly from well-known Fifth Estate figures, such as former Sanders press secretary Briahna Joy Gray and Jimmy Dore, a Morton Downey Jr.-reminiscent pundit-comedian. They and many of their peers went right to work, filling hours of their respective talk shows' time scolding the Squad for not doing the right (but politically suicidal) thing. At first I wasn't pleased that the Fifth Estate was going after the Squad with such venom but I later realized that if they had forced the vote it would have been a long overdue demonstration of populist power. Holding Pelosi's speakership hostage to force establishment Democrats to reveal their "true feelings" regarding Medicare For All probably would have resulted in future election losses for the Squad, but it would have, among other things, strengthened the resolve of their supporters, inspired other progressive citizens to consider running for office, and shown the Democratic establishment that they needed to start taking the populist Fifth Estate seriously as a media force.

Of course, the members of the Squad have their work cut out for them, starting with the fact that they aren't fully aligned with Democrats (despite the Squad's somewhat discouraging voting record, which has delivered to their critics a truckload of rotten tomatoes to throw at them) and are thus treated like dirt when the "grown-ups" are plotting to make things worse for working people and client nations. Despite the Squad's growing pains, I believe that our (thoroughly screwed up) politics can—or at least could—bring change for the better if the group expanded. That stance doesn't make me one of the popular kids now but it did during the 2016 and 2020 presidential races, when Sanders' political rallies filled sports stadiums with young voters who believed in his messages of hope for a better, more egalitarian country.

Unfortunately, those days are gone. Banished to the back of the chamber, Ocasio-Cortez and her crew nowadays do little more than hawk their ideological wares to the few press people who still cover them, that is when they're not busy being strong-armed to surrender to the whims of the Democratic establishment or getting hammered by progressives.

Sanders and the Squad identify as "social democrats," an

ideological demographic defined as one that supports "a government system that has similar values to socialism but which operates within a capitalist framework." Social democrats support a competitive capitalist economy but one in which people's basic needs—food, shelter, healthcare, etc.—will be met even if their jobs don't pay enough to afford them.

Point of order. If you're ever chatting with a staunch leftist on social media, never use the term "democratic socialist" when you're actually referring to a "social democrat." You see, technically, there's a big difference, and if the person at the other end of the exchange is in a pedantic mood, they might jump down your throat over it. Democratic socialism is, according to Brittanica.com, a political ideology whose proponents work toward the *eventual* establishment of a decentralized, democratically run socialist economy. In other words, they desire a socialist system in which workers share in all the profits generated by the companies they work for. In contrast, social democrats like Sanders condemn the economic inequality that comes with capitalism, but, you know, if you can't beat 'em, join 'em, more or less, as long as people are properly cared for.

Sanders, whose ideas are widely interpreted as nothing more rebellious than the New Deal programs of Franklin Roosevelt, is often purported to be a democratic socialist, mostly because he says he's one. Technically, that's dead wrong, at least in the opinion of Marxists, who've yet to hear anything specific from Sanders about how he'd seize control of America's profit-distribution system from the wealthy. That's fair; invariably, his criticisms of "the system" have been campaign-stump-bait, anecdotal grenades lobbed at certain aspects of the rather bestial form of capitalism practiced in America (and which is quickly spreading to Canada, Australia and other countries), as opposed to the economic philosophy itself. In the meantime, everyone from right-wing Fox News host Tucker Carlson to Joe Biden has condemned the greed of capitalists, if not with Sanders' abandon, which, truth be told, hasn't been completely unchecked. Indeed, until the release of his 2023 autobiography *It's Okay To Be Angry About Capitalism*, Sanders never spent a lot of campaign time railing against capitalism itself or demanding that workers share in the ownership of the "means of production" and so forth.

In the end, Sanders and the Squad are populists, which, as *What's The Matter With Kansas* author Thomas Frank would attest at the top of his lungs, is the proper term to use when describing them. The group is a humanitarian political detachment descended from the William Jennings Bryan-led Populist Party (1892-1909).

Along with delivering a history of populist movements, Frank's 2020 book *The People, No*, made a valiant (if ultimately failed) effort to stop people from using the word "populist" to describe Donald Trump or any other labor union-hating Republican wolf in sheep's clothing; Trump and his henchpeople are "anti-populists" if we're going to be accurate about it. But like all ideas born from good intentions on this increasingly hostile planet, journalists from basically all walks ignored Frank. They insist on describing Trump as a "populist" or a "right-wing populist," either of which is lazy and unprofessional, not that we've never seen such a thing from the scatterbrained Fourth Estate.

In 2020, Bernie Sanders took another run at the presidency. It would not be American socialism's (nor populism's) year, it turned out. Scores of progressive voters threw up their hands in frustration after Sanders announced he was withdrawing his bid for the 2020 Democratic presidential nomination and throwing his support to Joe Biden, the eventual winner. Sanders' supporters felt angry and betrayed, convinced that he'd given up the fight too quickly.

On face, the optics bore out those sympathies. On the strength of small political donations only, Sanders had won Democratic presidential primaries in California and eight other states and boasted frontrunner status until after the March 3, 2019, "Super Tuesday" primaries, the traditional day on which approximately one-third of all delegates to the presidential nominating conventions are decided. Sanders—whose most costly mistake was, according to *Atlantic* reporter Edward-Isaac Dovere, mistakenly counting on "a divided opposition to let him coast to victory without securing the vote of the median Democrat"—lost the Super Tuesday battle when Biden, suddenly rocket-boosted by support from dropout candidates Pete Buttigieg and Amy Klobuchar (both of whom had just quit the race after frantic calls from former president Barack Obama and other major Democratic players), walked away with 10 states in his back pocket.

Super Tuesday was a crushing blow to us Sanders supporters. It felt like Sanders had been kneecapped by the entire liberal "Matrix": the Democratic establishment, the mainstream liberal media, Hollywood celebrities, the whole smash. To his credit, Sanders did stay in the running until April 7, 2019, when he lost Wisconsin, but by any measure, the race had been over long before that; the centrist Democrats had finally consolidated behind Biden as their candidate, and the only person still standing in their way was Sanders. By all rights, Sanders' extra effort should have counted for something in the minds of leftists, but it wasn't enough to dissuade a sizable segment of the progressive left from cursing his name. He could have pushed a (completely hopeless) write-in candidacy, which his supporters urged him to do, but he didn't, which made them mad. Many saw his surrender as a fig leaf to the Democratic establishment (his Democrat-aligned voting record didn't help matters). Others accused Sanders of committing a selfish act of political self-preservation.

It was likely a combination of both. After all, Sanders is a U.S. senator, which makes him one of the 103 most powerful politicians in the Western world. Most senators wouldn't give up that amount of power for anything. While the average age of a senator is around 64 years, many serve into their 70s, 80s and 90s, perpetuating an out-of-touch gerontocracy that doesn't sit well with most people. Too often they serve until death, which is unsettling; since 1990, at least 13 U.S. senators have died while in office. All of them but John Heinz III (R-PA, plane crash), Paul Wellstone (D-MN, ditto) and Paul Coverdell (R-GA, stroke) were well past retirement age when they died.

I don't mean to promote ageism against senators. Sanders is in his 80s at this writing, and I'll give him a hall pass because it's my book. But meanwhile I completely understand the disappointment felt by his voters over his dropping out of the 2020 race and backing Biden, whose lifetime record is nothing I'd ever be proud of. However, considering the horrific spectacle of Sanders' 2019 Super Tuesday gang-mugging by the Democratic establishment, I think it should be kept in mind that when Custer knew he was about to be scalped, he probably said something like, "Okay, okay, we were just kidding." Whether it can be chalked up to dirty political dealings, the forces of dark money, or the shadow of Count Dracula himself darkening every door in the Capitol, the votes for progressive measures just aren't ever there, which is as much our collective fault for not getting more votes for progressives in the primaries as anything else.

But yes, it was Sanders' fault, too. If his people had paid more attention to what their wisest progressive critics were saying on the internet, they might have realized that their strategy of turning a blind eye to the center-left wasn't working all that well. At the same time, the pro-Sanders crowd was under constant attack on Twitter, not only from Democratic establishmentarians but also from bot swarms and troll squads operated by groups working for both the right and the left. Among other things, those disparate forces combined to perpetuate the myth of the "Bernie bros," a fictitious online brigade of rabid Sanders supporters who, it was claimed, were ruthlessly attacking his Democratic establishment opponents (while simultaneously dividing the left, which brought joy to the conservatives).

The ferocious pushback against Sanders' online supporters clearly indicated that both sides of the duopoly were nervous, and with good reason. On Twitter, the vociferous support Sanders was receiving drowned out any love the other Democratic candidates were getting. That helped lead to the perception among some Democratic voters that the "Bernie Bros" were part of some sort of sinister, robotized force, especially given the fact that during the run-up to the 2016 election, other Democrats, including Elizabeth Warren and Hillary Clinton, had accused Sanders' Twitter followers of being "uniquely cruel," an accusation that, like the existence of any "Bernie Bros operation," has since been categorically disproven.[17]

After Sanders' unconditional electoral surrender, progressive-leaning independent media figures let their disappointment be known far and wide. Kyle Kulinski, host of the million-subscriber YouTube channel *Secular Talk*, called Sanders a "cuck" who should have stayed in the race until the bitter end. Jimmy Dore echoed Kulinski's sentiments, branding Sanders a "coward."

Whether or not Kulinski's and Dore's criticisms were performative (possibly) or overdone (definitely), it wasn't conducive to solidarity. It wasn't the Fifth Estate's brightest moment.

VI. Independent Media vs. Legacy Media

Fifth Estate media can be viscerally compelling, but the time has come when its top content producers need to exercise a little restraint when informing their audiences. Slowly but surely, the space is growing as strapped consumers drop television from their car-payment-sized cable-internet bills. A lot of eyes are falling on them as news cycles accelerate faster and faster and the Fourth Estate ignores the economic majority's concerns.

A lot, but by no means all. Habitual mainstream media consumers (people who generally avoid news and political commentary that doesn't come from network and/or cable TV channels, corporate news websites, demographically targeted social media feeds and/or newspapers) are often shocked to learn that by any measure, the era of independent media as a reliable news delivery system has arrived and needs to be taken seriously.

Naturally, the independent media renaissance is arriving with no mainstream media fanfare. Surely the statistics seem terrifying to legacy media companies as they watch consumers get more and more of their news from internet-based sources. According to numbers cited by *Adweek*, the

Pod Save America podcast—a liberal-politics-oriented talk show hosted by four former Barack Obama presidential aides—averaged, during August 2022, 1.5 million listeners per episode, beating CNN's *Anderson Cooper 360* (950,000 watchers per episode) by half and thrashing MSNBC's *The Rachel Maddow Show* in the coveted 25-to-54 age demographic.[18]

Meanwhile, the Fifth Estate's cognoscenti are realizing that they're in the driver's seat. On the April 20, 2023 episode of his *System Update* video-streaming show, American journalist Glenn Greenwald, whose 2013 series of *Guardian* articles on whistleblower Edward Snowden's American global surveillance disclosures resulted in a media firestorm, could barely contain his glee while reporting that *Buzzfeed News*, a mainstream liberal news outlet that routinely ignored progressive causes and was often accused of not paying contributors for valuable online content, was going to stop posting new content as part of a staff reduction initiative across the company. To Greenwald, it was a direct cannonball hit to the mainsail of the mainstream media. "This is [symptomatic] of a very long process of failures from this [corporate] digital media culture," Greenwald crowed while running down a list of setbacks the legacy media had experienced in previous months. *Insider* (formerly *Business Insider*) had begun cutting 10 percent of its staff to keep the company "healthy and competitive." NPR canceled four podcasts and fired 100 people as part of an initiative to reduce a reported $30 million deficit. Disney's broadcast news division was laying off 50 people at ABC News, with more layoffs to come. (Incidentally, to cover all the bases, we should note that *System Update* is exclusive to the Rumble platform, which many on the left dismiss as a right-wing alternative to

YouTube. The Canadian company powers the back-end technology of Truth Social, a Twitter-like platform owned by Donald Trump's Media & Technology Group. That doesn't mean Greenwald suddenly "turned MAGA" somewhere along the line; quite the contrary. Like journalists Matt Taibbi, Seymour Hersch and others, Greenwald has been cruelly snubbed by the mainstream media owing to his anti-establishment journalism and thus can't be blamed for diffusing his work through any high-capacity platform that will take him.)

Frankly, it's somewhat puzzling that corporate news media has survived this long. We could blame some of that on stubbornness or apathy on the part of the news-consuming public, but the establishment's "consensus manufacturing system"—cable television, spiffy corporate newspaper sites, etc.—can indeed be easier for people to absorb than spending minutes or hours searching Google or YouTube for the facts and opinion they may be curious about. Given that many news consumers are accustomed to the mainstream media's dishwasher-safe, glitzy feel, they likely feel put off by independent media, viewing it as a mysterious, dangerous information-jungle. And for that matter, some news consumers don't *want* to know the unsettling but well-documented truth about things (personally, I get a little annoyed when someone on social media posts something like, "I stay out of politics." It makes me want to ask them, "Where exactly do you think all your existential struggles are coming from, someone yelling 'jinx' at a crayon drawing of you?").

Independent media provides regular citizens the chance to grow their own journalistic/opinion/thoughtfluencer brands. Its opportunities will only multiply exponentially in the years ahead (in my last book, I pointed to blockchain as a technology that will, in time, provide individuals with "virtual citizenship," interacting with social media platforms, banking sites and everything else they do on the internet under a single user ID, or avatar. The days of keeping track of passwords, getting randomly hacked, and dealing with bots and trolls will be all but over. Independent journalists and thoughtfluencer will be able to grow their brands seamlessly across multiple platforms).

Until then, though, citizen journalists shouldn't get overconfident. Not only is the corporate media well-funded, but many independent journalists depend on only one online platform, meaning they can find themselves out of business if their preferred platform changes search algorithms or bans their work outright, regardless of its wide reach. In 2022, the careers of activist/journalist Abby Martin and progressive author Chris Hedges were upended when hundreds of broadcasts they'd produced for RT (formerly *Russia Today*, an international news television network funded by the Russian government) were removed from YouTube and most of its other outlets in the wake of the Russian invasion of Ukraine. It happened during a U.S. intelligence crackdown on "content that might foster radical discontent."[19] The takeaway is that the corporate platforms will allow rebelliousness, but only up to a point, and always subject to governmental approval.

The major platforms won't be able to keep a lid on "radical discontent" forever, though, given that things are just getting worse and worse all the time for legacy media, a situation the corporate platforms can't (or won't) stop. After all, they have a symbiotic (and very profitable) relationship with the Fifth Estate.

There's a caveat to all that, however. The Fifth Estate can falsify its audience numbers much more easily than legacy media. Internet-streamed news shows on YouTube, Twitch, Patreon and other platforms record millions of views, but those numbers can be misleading. Ratings for cable and network TV news shows are based on single, one-time broadcasts, as opposed to online shows, whose cumulative view totals increase over weeks or years. Also, "view numbers" for online content can be fudged through trickery: Any enterprising independent media personality can hire an outside firm to unleash a swarm of bots to engage with their online videos for enough time that the platform records official "views" of the content. We know that vast bot hives are commonly purchased for mass deployment by influencers and others who have their bots carry out tasks such as clicking "Like" and/or even posting vapid, cookie-cutter comments on their "employers'" videos to make them appear to be more widely popular than they really are.

Bot swarms working to manufacture consensus are ubiquitous in these times. Not only can they be purchased, they're easy to make if you want to do it yourself. All that's involved in creating a small bot swarm is to create a bunch of free, brand-new email accounts, sign up for individual social media accounts under each email address and then use one of many free programs to loose them upon the unsuspecting public. Bots are everywhere, but the companies that own and operate the major social media sites don't necessarily want to get rid of them, since the more users a platform has, the more enticing their stock looks to investors. If that stuff bothers you, you can always report suspected bots to the platform's moderators (most of whom are bots themselves) when you see something that's generally considered bot behavior: An unusually large number of banal, strikingly similar remarks posted in response to a video or social media post by users who have screen names (aliases) like "Sally52916" and "RickSmith329108." In that case, it would be natural for you to be suspicious; it could very well be that those "users" were automatically assigned their name-plus-number-style usernames by the platform when they signed up.

Of course, not every social media user who gets on people's nerves is a bot. There are trolls, too, real live people who may or may not believe in the nonsense they dispense. Sometimes, they want attention, or they're bored with or annoyed by what other people are writing, and want to disrupt the discussion. Sometimes they're working for political groups or other interests. Regardless, for the most part, you'll never know their motivations, thus, it's bad practice to run around the internet accusing people of being bots or trolls. Only "clueless newbies" do that. That said, if you've ever done it, I absolve you of any and all responsibility. If you misidentify a troll or bot, it doesn't mean you should leave the internet. No one has a perfect record of posting pure consistent brilliance. Creating an online persona for yourself and building a history of stuff you've said online is like having an only child: You won't get everything right all the time, so don't beat yourself up over a simple mistake.

I could go on, but there's no need to. Most people already have a vague idea of trolls' and bots' methods, tactics, goals and origins. And if it's all news to you, my last book goes over any basics with which you may be unfamiliar.

So, at this point, it's probably best to try to answer the most pressing question about online activism: Can it really help drive political and/or cultural change?

I believe it can, or I wouldn't be here. The fact that you're reading this suggests that you think our "virtual society" does have some potential for driving progressive change.

And why not? Where else other than the internet do millions of citizens from all over the world gather together daily to discuss and debate the state of our current political and socioeconomic conditions with others? Sure, any activist working to organize a labor strike or increase turnout at a climate protest will tell you that, pound for pound, engaging with people on social media pales in comparison to seeing new members in attendance at a rally or even just holding a face-to-face chat with a stranger who's suddenly interested in hearing about what their organization wants to accomplish. As labor organizer Jane McAlevey (pronounced "MACK-uh-lee-vee") once put it, "Social media is very different than when a worker looks another worker in the eyes and helps them work through fear, ambivalence, and all the normal things that happen when a union buster shows up."[20]

As we've seen, however, online activism has helped to empower movements. It could do much more, of course, but it's constrained by corporate social media platforms, whose hostile, divisive environments divert the online left's energies away from building solidarity and toward individualist success. There's a way out of that whole unsightly morass, though.

3

Twitter is Dead, Long Live the Fediverse

I. The Way Out

The problem with American social media isn't that the people who use it are bad; it's that the corporations that own, operate, and work to monetize social media platforms want us that way. They want users to be self-centered thrill-seekers chasing individual achievement, not dedicated to establishing socioeconomic and cultural equality and fostering solidarity between activist movements. One way to improve social media, however unrealistic under the present circumstances, stands out. Ideally, our social media spaces would be public utilities, not carelessly managed playthings owned by wealthy people and corporations bearing dubious intentions and ever-expanding lists of bad ideas for "increasing the site's profitability."

Of course, removing the profit angle from corporate social media would require the same seismic level of change as replacing the bald eagle with the vulture as the more appropriate national bird. But we can always dream, work toward a better future, yadda yadda, and in the meantime, the next best thing to a public takeover of the top corporate social media platforms has already launched, namely the "fediverse," an infinite association of small, interconnected social media sites powered by individuals and groups that use their own computers and other equipment to act as social media data servers. Its programming code is "open source," meaning its look and functionality can be tweaked by site owners. Today, the fediverse is widely used by people who are fed up with corporate social media and all its pitfalls: Obstructive algorithms, intrusive ads, the constant hacking of user accounts by bored troublemakers, etc.

You can think of the fediverse as an ever-expanding collection of thousands of mini-Facebook.com sites connected as if they were one entity. If you're signed up at one fediverse "instance"—the fediverse's term for a single computer server (a computer or collection of computers containing software and hardware that offer shared services, such as applications, to other computers, aka "clients," that are permitted to use them)—you can easily find and interact with people who are using other instance(s).

The most widely known section of the fediverse is Mastodon, a "galaxy" of more than 13,000 instances serving over six million users. The most popular Mastodon instance is mastodon.social, an anything-goes instance focused on general socializing, a la Twitter or Facebook. As with Reddit's subreddits, there are instances available for whatever you're into, like chemistry, pet ownership, etc.

A fediverse post is called a "toot," as opposed to a tweet. Usually, toots are limited to 500 characters by default when the instance is created, nearly double the size of a Twitter tweet. However, some instances allow for larger toots. The right-wing social media sites Gab and Donald Trump's Truth Social were allegedly (there was a legal kerfuffle) built using Mastodon's code, so they also have 500-character-length posts (Mastodon doesn't allow posts from those platforms on their slice of the fediverse).

Like most of my Twitter friends, I didn't become aware of the fediverse's existence until October 2022, shortly after the news broke that Elon Musk was trying to purchase the site. Musk's takeover was not hostile by any means, quite the opposite. He'd signed a contract, presumably against the wishes of his accountants, and was thus legally forced to go through with the purchase. Had that not been the case, there's no way he would have gone through with it, not if we assume he possessed a kindergartener's accounting knowledge. Profit-wise, since its launch in 2006, Twitter has been a money-loser every year, save for 2019.[1]

Whatever the case, as the date for Musk's takeover drew closer, he began constructing a schizoid, vaguely Trump-like bully pulpit focused on "free speech," an issue that had suddenly and inexplicably become of paramount importance to him. Upon catching wind of that, liberals and other leftists began hurriedly abandoning Twitter for different social media platforms, including the fediverse, which, owing to things like its relative longevity (it first appeared in 2008 as a single instance, identi.ca, just two years after Twitter was born), its predominantly user-supported fundamentals and its infinitely wise decision to keep the running number of "Likes" posts receive an extra click away from user view, appealed to veteran Twitter users. Over the years, they'd grown to dislike a lot of things about Twitter even before Musk showed up (it seemed as though veteran users had just been waiting for the final straw before bailing out of Twitter. Google searches for "Twitter Alternatives" increased by 258 percent globally in October and November 2022, when Musk had finalized the purchase, according to a study that based its findings on data drawn from Google Trends).

When Musk finally did take charge, he immediately began alienating leftists and long-time advertisers alike, babbling incoherently about the right of free speech without ever mentioning its limits or clearly condemning hate speech. It was a constant stream of mixed messaging. Musk reinstated many alt-right and proudly racist personalities who'd been banned from Twitter during the preceding years. Not only did Musk un-ban Trump's Twitter account (Trump never returned to Twitter, preferring instead to post on his self-owned platform, Truth Social), he also reopened the accounts of other controversial figures, including Andrew Anglin, arguably the alt-right's most vicious, over-the-top troll, who'd founded the neo-Nazi website The Daily Stormer.

In reality, Musk seemed less concerned with supporting "free speech" than with ridding the site of liberal do-gooders and generally making Twitter a safer place for anti-labor billionaires like himself. In 2023, in an incident that exposed Musk's union-busting mindset, a federal appeals court ruled that he unlawfully threatened Tesla employees with the loss of their stock options if they voted to be represented by a union. Musk delivered the alleged threat by way of a May 20, 2018, tweet, a fuckup that had come to plague him ever since the case first arose. Along the way, one Tesla employee had allegedly been fired for union-organizing activity. The National Labor Relations Board finally ordered the stock options tweet deleted and the worker reinstated with back pay.[2] With that in mind, maybe Musk thought that if he owned Twitter, he wouldn't be inconvenienced if a similar scenario arose later. (Musk isn't renowned as the most conscientious boss in history, especially concerning employee safety. Hundreds of employee injuries, including one death, have been reported at Musk-owned Tesla, SpaceX and tunnel-drilling startup The Boring Company, allegedly owing to a "consistent disregard for employee safety."[3])

Many veteran Twitter users had assumed that Musk's sudden obsession with free speech would result in an army of trolls invading Twitter from the notorious 4chan.org and elsewhere, constituting a force that would gleefully spread racist messaging all over the site once Musk took charge. That did happen to some extent, although I didn't happen upon much of it myself, apart from a few xenophobic memes featuring "Pepe The Frog" (4Chan's de facto mascot).

As many had feared, chaos took hold quickly. The volume of hate-filled tweets targeting the LGBTQIA+ community rose noticeably.[4] Restrictions against spreading disinformation about COVID-19 were eased.[5] Aping Trump, Musk fired nearly every engineer who'd been keeping Twitter's systems running, along with scads of sales personnel who'd built strong relationships with advertisers over the years. Within a month, panicked over Twitter's hard-rightward turn, half the site's top 100 advertisers had fled.[6]

The loss of advertising dollars was a lethal blow to a corporate ship that was already sinking. To finance Twitter's acquisition, Musk had taken on $12.5 billion in debt, which ballooned the company's yearly interest loan payment to over $1 billion from an almost manageable $51 million in 2021, a typical year in that 90 percent of the company's revenue had come from advertising. Suddenly, the slew of bills that began conga-lining their way toward Twitter's Accounts Payable inbox appeared to be basically unpayable, except of course by a ketamine-microdosing, easily distracted billionaire like Musk, who, according to some observers, seemed to have no real idea what he was doing financially, technologically, nor toward his stated dream of free speech uber alles.

Apparently convinced he was a real-life Joker, Musk seemed to want to turn Twitter into a gigantic 4chan (a site he probably could have bought for a few million dollars, if that), but with occasional puzzling exceptions, as if to remind the world that the Clown Prince of Crime had taken over Gotham City's Arkham Asylum. By the same hand with which he'd reinstated the accounts of dangerous wackos like Trump, Musk refused to lift Twitter's ban on spittle-spraying conspiracy theorist Alex Jones, who'd lost his Twitter account after leading a pro-NRA disinformation campaign against some of the families of the children who'd been killed in the 2012 Sandy Hook Elementary School gun massacre in Newtown, Connecticut. Jones claimed the event never happened and that it was simply a plot carried out by the government so they could start seizing guns. Some of Jones's followers harassed and threatened the Newtown families to such a monstrous extent that some of them were forced to move out of town. In the end, Jones was successfully sued for nearly $1 billion, but even after that, Jones continued to push the envelope, telling his audience in late 2022, "I don't really know what really happened there," referring to the massacre.[7]

Whether or not Musk feared having similar lawsuits thrown at him if he allowed Jones to come back to Twitter,[8] his upholding the ban on Jones was all the evidence the far-right needed to determine that Musk wasn't the die-hard "free speech absolutist" he claimed to be, that he was okay with limiting it to some extent. The troll corps at 4chan's most outrageously xenophobic board (chat group), Politically Incorrect (/pol/), derided Musk for keeping Jones' ban in place, as well as renewing his early promises to maintain a zero-tolerance policy for tweets that spread Holocaust denial misinformation. Even so, as time went on, those types of tweets began trickling into Twitter and were even monetized when Twitter's algorithm placed them next to ads for such corporations as Nokia and *The Wall Street Journal*,[9] which led to a fresh outflux of advertisers dropping Twitter like a live grenade. As well, although Musk isn't Jewish, the Nazi trolls at /pol/ flung handfuls of anti-Semitic bile his way, posting unfounded accusations that Musk was helping to reinvigorate the online presence of the similarly gentile Trump to "promote Semitism." Many of the /pol/ posts incorporated the group's old triple-parenthesis in-joke, meant to indicate they suspected Musk and Trump of engaging in a secret Mossad operation or whatnot, as in this sample /pol/ outburst from November 18, 2022: "(((Elon Musk))) buys Twitter to shill for (((Donald Trump))), which amounts to Israel [sic] meddling in yet another U.S. election."

Lunacy aside, some 4channers celebrated the departure of liberals to the fediverse, where, they bragged, they could troll and "drag" (hurl insults at) them mercilessly. (Any attempt to do that was put down quickly. Owing to the fediverse's instituting more sensible moderation policies than Twitter had ever had, any attempt to cause trouble on the platform would have failed. I never heard about such a thing ever occurring, but it's a given that coordinated troll attacks were launched against certain fediverse instances and put down instantly.)

(My apologies for the technical stuff I'll be going over for the next page or so. It won't be on the exam, but it does relate peripherally to this section's focus.)

Musk's purchase of Twitter was a bizarre little soap opera that many of us "very online" and techie types tried to puzzle out. At first, I had assumed that the whole thing was an act, that the 50something libertarian billionaire wasn't really going to go through with the purchase. I figured he'd simply been trying to impress a posse of young groupies by portraying a political sphinx who "understood" the internet's darker spaces and characters, as if he were some "Master of 4Chan." For what it's worth, Musk's trolling style is amateurish, much like Trump's; I'm 99 percent sure he has a secret 4chan account and isn't one of the popular guys.

I put a lot of idle thought into the mystery, at one point going so far as to give Musk the benefit of the doubt: Maybe he really did want to "fix the internet" by allowing "free speech" to have free rein on Twitter. Perhaps the idea was to bring 4chan's faux-xenophobic troll culture into the mainstream because it would somehow fix everything, that the well-off, upstanding, Generation X soccer parents who represented one of Twitter's most busily active demographics would suddenly, somehow experience a Zen moment and learn to love their least favorite people, young "meme culture" internet addicts who enjoy pissing off normies.

Of course, only Musk will ever know what really motivated him to offer to buy Twitter. The move could have been driven by his own Twitter addiction and a hunger for attention from the "cool kids," i.e., the vast population of experts, pundits, celebrities, and other figures maintaining presences on the platform. Or maybe he wanted to disrupt all the liberal-slanted, anti-Republican discourse that dominated the site (which some attribute to pressure from Democratic bureaucrats and intelligence groups, as author Matt Taibbi has written about extensively in his "Twitter Files" series of articles). In his 2024 book, *Battle For The Bird*, Kurt Wagner of *Bloomberg* contends that Musk's frustration with the site's omnipresent bots was what prompted him to buy the place (Musk did remove free access to Twitter's API technology, which got rid of bots, even, unfortunately, the really funny ones, like @RealDonnyBot, which automatically reposted old Trump tweets every hour of the day, ex: "Yesterday's and Today's Nightmare Bill Kristol!").

I'd also guessed that it was all a money-making megascheme: Perhaps Musk had bought Twitter to initiate a test run of features and monetization schemes that are or will be seen in the company's spin-out project, Bluesky Social, a social media platform that offers a new networking protocol (specifically, parent company Bluesky's own Authenticated Transfer protocol, or "AT" protocol, which uses the "@" symbol in user addresses to contact users of different social media platforms, for [hypothetical] example, JohnSmith@facebook.com). If that was the plan, maybe Musk was planning to pour money into Twitter to make it—or Bluesky—the go-to site for "decentralized" social media, making it the central hub of the fediverse.

That theory died quickly on the vine, though. No individual social media site can "rule" the fediverse. Put (more or less) simply, in a truly decentralized social media network, no independent site is accountable to a single set of tyrannical "host" processes dictating the entire network's content. In other words, it isn't a centralized platform like Twitter; it's simply a network that allows users of different social media sites/servers to communicate back and forth with each other. By the same token, Bluesky may eventually accommodate communication between itself and more mainstream platforms like Twitter and Meta's Threads (Facebook itself probably won't ever be integrated into the fediverse, but Threads [Facebook chief Mark Zuckerberg's Twitter competitor] did dip its toe into the space in early 2024, with Threads users communicating with users on Mastodon. One hawk-eyed observer wrote that Meta may be planning to become the center of the fediverse and sneakily rebrand it as "the Metaverse,"[10] but I don't see that happening. It's too geeky a thing for politically ambivalent, brunch-selfie-snapping Facebookers to want to bother with, and even if they did, it's a sure bet that instance owners would rebel, probably in some pretty nasty ways).

Bluesky's technology is very similar to the fediverse's underlying "ActivityPub" protocol, a technology that connects separate, standalone social media sites (Threads is also adopting it). In short, like the VHS vs. Beta video cassette wars of the 1980s, Bluesky's AT protocol and the fediverse's ActivityPub are jockeying to dominate the decentralized social media universe. All of this could lead to the purchase (and subsequent modification and/or replacement) of ActivityPub's technology by Twitter/Bluesky, a scenario that's been foreseen by fediverse proponents who are concerned that such "advancements" would lead to unpleasant things, such as an oversaturation of content from Twitter/Bluesky and/or their commercial advertisers, which, they attest, would spoil the experience of participating in the decentralized social media universe.[11]

The upshot is there's a danger that someone like Musk or Mark Zuckerberg would have too much control over the technology that undergirds the fediverse. That wouldn't be good. The whole point of decentralized social media is allowing users to interact with others while nestled in a relatively safe (caveats apply) social media environment that isn't wholly privatized.

As Musk's Twitter takeover rolled out, techies sought clarification about whether Musk owned both Bluesky and Twitter. It eventually emerged that Bluesky is independent of Twitter. Developed under former Twitter CEO Jack Dorsey, Bluesky was originally a spin-out project owned by Twitter, which meant that for a time, by virtue of Twitter's financial backing of Bluesky, Elon Musk did indeed have control of Twitter's biggest potential future competitor, which made exactly zero sense unless one suspected Musk of trying to discover what might work in the area of financing Bluesky Social without relying on traditional advertising revenue. Theoretically, after all the self-financing data had been analyzed and Bluesky was ready to launch, Musk could have Twitter declare bankruptcy and transfer most or all of its assets to the new venture.

But like I said, that wasn't to be. Bluesky sailed off on its own, and when it had safely launched, Dorsey burned his ships by skeeting (Bluesky's term for tweeting/posting) a barb or two at Musk. It was now on Dorsey and his small board of directors to shape Bluesky as a better Twitter: If there were ways to remove the features and algorithms that made Twitter's users refer to it as a "hellsite" that engendered so much angry divisiveness, it would be a success. Its users would happily skeet away and just, you know, get along and debate issues maturely without worrying about how many Likes they got on their posts, how many Followers they accumulated, and so on.

Dorsey promised to keep those harmful "social validation" elements out of Bluesky. Problem was, he didn't do that. From the start, Bluesky was little more than a Twitter clone, albeit without Musk's constant meddling and trolling. "Bluesky's development teams have already recreated some of Twitter's most toxic elements," Dave Lee wrote in Bloomberg in May 2023.[12] "The like and follower counts are there. The quote-tweet function, too. Under the 'What's Hot' tab, viral posts take center stage, creating the same incentives to drum up divisiveness or offense."

Reading that and a few other depressing paragraphs was all I needed to grasp the unfortunate truth: Bluesky was a Loot Crate version of the fediverse with Twitter fungus growing all over it. But even before Lee's piece came out, my stomach had lurched at the sight of thousands of Twitterfolk—including many of my friends—begging half-jokingly for an invite to join the app, as if it were a Willy Wonka golden ticket out of Musk's ongoing campaign to scuttle Twitter or whatever the fuck he was doing. As Lee noted, *Rolling Stone* magazine had boneheadedly declared the first batch of highly limited invites—only 100,000 were issued at first—to be the "hottest club online." Thus the very rollout of Bluesky was toxic, remindful of LeBron James's "The Decision" TV special ESPN broadcasted in 2010, in which the elite NBA player announced that he'd be leaving his hometown Cleveland Cavaliers team for the Miami Heat. Only the cool kids were getting those golden tickets to Bluesky. Gag me.

I eventually joined BlueSky in mid-2023, reconnecting with a few Twitter friends who'd bailed out of Twitter the minute they had the chance. I didn't have fun there, mostly because I had no interest in it. It was very much what Dave Lee had described, just another cliquey Twitter (but with funnier jokes).

I looked at Zuckerberg's Threads, too, but didn't join. It struck me as a repressed, less sophisticated Bluesky, eager to spread pro-establishment doctrinarianism far and wide. In my brief engagement with the platform, after it first launched, I noticed lots of posting activity coming from DNC-obeisant mediocrities like serial virtue-signaling actress Alyssa Milano and MSNBC show host Ari Melber, whose street-cred-begging name-dropping of corporate hip-hop artists is always unintentionally funny. I like that Threads is "federating," but its future is bleak (and a bit menacing): If Threads fully integrates with the fediverse, its family-friendly standards will clash with any R-rated content coming from Mastodon or whatnot. There will be problems. Big ones. Threads will likely end up being nothing more than a bit player in the fediverse, its user-base tolerated but not welcomed by users of other instances, similar to how longtime Usenet users shunned America Online (AOL) users when Usenet was added to AOL's suite of available services in the 1990s.

But who knows. Companies are and have been spending billions of dollars trying to become the new, undisputed "town square of the internet," but to date, all that's been accomplished is that the online left has been splintered worse than ever.

I'm sure plenty of bot/troll skullduggery was and is afoot, meant to dissuade people from joining the fediverse en masse. In the meantime, I'll admit that using a fediverse instance might take a little getting used to, especially if one wants to view just one single dumb-stupid list of posts instead of the set of three or four thin, scrollable columns users see by default in the main window of their fediverse user session. That busy-looking window can confuse users who are more accustomed to Facebook, Twitter and all the other corporate platforms, all of which present the user with only one scrollable list of posts or tweets.

Luckily, the look of your main "home" fediverse screen can

be changed so that you only see one list of posts filling most of the screen. That is to say, if you want your home fediverse window to look more like Twitter or Facebook, click the menu button (usually three small, stacked lines next to your name), choose "Preferences," and then click Appearance. In the Appearance Options frame, un-check "Enable advanced web interface," then click "Save Changes." That's it. Now, the main window of your Mastodon interface is as plain-looking as Twitter's or Facebook's, but there are far fewer distractions. And best of all, for the most part, you won't be subjected to any advertising (although some instances do run ads).

Some users prefer the default multi-column view, which actually works to the users' advantage, I'd say. From within a single window, a user can choose to scroll through either a list of posts from people whom they're friends with, or a list of all posts from people on the instance they're registered with, or a broader, more fediverse-wide list, commonly titled "Explore." Whichever column you're reading, the contents of each post you select will show up, squished into a little box, fitted into the column. But like I said, some people don't like that.

Either way, there's no sneaky algorithm dictating which fediverse posts you see. More or less universally, the posts in your feed(s) will be shown in chronological order, with the most recent post at the top, regardless of whether they're viral or were posted by your friends. If you like, you can donate to fund your "home" (or any other) instance through Patreon, Paypal, or other electronic payment apps. In many cases, you can pay with Bitcoin or another cryptocurrency if you're comfortable using them. (Reddit, Twitter and Meta have already added "crypto wallets" to their payment method types, and some anticipate that Bluesky will be very crypto-centric. Oh, and while we're on the subject, crypto wallets can be hacked, but really only if their owners don't follow strict guidelines for keeping them safe.[13])

It should be noted that the fediverse does have its detractors, mostly in the mainstream, who dismiss it as a niche, impossibly nerdy platform that no one should bother with. In early 2023, a clutch of technology journalists pronounced it a failed experiment, misreporting that it was bleeding users when in fact its actual user-retention rate was "astonishingly high," according to a May 2023 *Techdirt* article.[14] As one reader observed, "Mastodon may not get a hundred million users overnight just because Elon has no idea what he's doing and opened Pandora's box to let out all the Nazis. It'll grow slowly, steadily, getting an influx of users every time Twitter and/or Facebook do something else horrendous, and as the people developing it smooth down the rough edges to improve the overall user experience."

Hope springs for that. The fediverse is a vitally important step in the evolution of social media platforms owing to its relative imperviousness to corporate corruption. This makes it the best microblogging platform for keeping the Fifth Estate flourishing and honest, something the corporate platforms cannot do.

Earlier in this book I agreed that there was truth to the epithet "The revolution will not be tweeted," but when Malcolm Gladwell wrote his same-titled article, there was no fediverse. The fediverse is by no means "just another Twitter." I don't believe any centralized corporate social media platform like Twitter, Facebook or Reddit would ever allow its users to propagate and organize a game-changing act of civil disobedience—like a national general workers' or college-debtors' strike—without interfering with it in one way or another. But in the fediverse, it could be possible. If some person or group wanted to mobilize people to participate in an action and the idea went crazily viral, with a planned launch date and signifying hashtags and such, the government or whatever corporation was being pressured couldn't simply "make a call to headquarters" the way they can with Twitter and Facebook, because each instance owner in the fediverse would have the option of "quelling the rebellion" (by automatically deleting any posts that made reference to the action, or banning the "offenders," etc.) or not. So, even if half the fediverse's servers blocked or made invisible any posts that mentioned the action, the other half's users could still spread the information around.

I'm painfully aware that the fediverse is too obscure and underpopulated now to attract the masses to it. But if it keeps up its growth, it may supplant Twitter sooner than anyone thinks.

Yes, Twitter could disappear at any moment. At this writing, Musk has been surreptitiously floating the idea of charging all the platform's users a monthly fee to use it. That effort would fail. Social media is a barter arrangement: the sites get our personal information, and we get to use their technology for free. Any platform that breaks that compact will disappear very quickly.

It's all but guaranteed that Musk will suffer massive losses from his investment when all is said and done. Twitter has a lot of users but doesn't have much in the way of physical assets. Computer hardware-wise, there wouldn't be much for Musk to sell if Twitter closed, or at least not as much as one might imagine. In 2018, before Musk entered the picture, Twitter moved a sizeable portion of its data infrastructure (including hard drives where people's tweets are stored) to Google Cloud rather than continuing to manage and maintain everything in-house. Then, in 2020, after the company was forced to delay the full implementation of its Facebook Stories-like "Fleets" short-video feature owing to system overload, the company signed a multi-year deal with Amazon Web Services (AWS) to have them handle Twitter's server-hardware needs (the machinery that stores and manages tweets, etc.). This means that much of the computer hardware that runs Twitter belongs to Amazon's Jeff Bezos and principal Google shareholders Larry Page and Sergey Brin. Since Musk couldn't simply break those hardware service contracts on a whim without facing legal problems, in November 2022, he gathered his underlings and demanded they present him with ideas for a billion-dollar infrastructure cut, which they did, advising Musk to lay off a ton of employees. Around half of Twitter's staff was told to box up their cubicle oddments, and later, so were an unknown number of contract workers, primarily folks whose roles were focused on content moderation, you know, doing stuff like keeping hate speech and other pleasantries out of people's Twitter feeds.

Musk then proceeded to cut more infrastructure costs. He downsized the company's data center in Atlanta, closed their Sacramento, California data center, and slashed whatever he could from the Google Cloud bill. Spoiler alert, all those drastic moves resulted in a partial outage of the site for several hours on December 28, 2022. That too did pass (somehow), and the site ran fine after some adjustments were made (but not before a few wiseassed blog articles made the rounds, begging Musk to pretty please bring back the beloved, long-discontinued "Fail Whale"—a cartoon whale being lifted out of the ocean by a flock of orange birds—as the default graphic to be displayed on-screen when informing visitors that the site was currently shut down owing to technical difficulties[15]).

Those fixes proved to be insufficient, however. The site crashed for hours at a time, seemingly every week during one 2023 stretch. Liberals hit the deck laughing after one such incident: Musk persuaded Florida Governor Ron DeSantis to announce his 2024 presidential bid live on Twitter, and when the big moment arrived, the site froze, delaying the announcement for an hour.

Aside from the fediverse's "independent franchisee" approach, there are ways to finance a humongous social media network without corporate advertisers. I mean, miracles can always happen: maybe Musk tires of playing with the site, sells it to a group that meets his price through a fundraising effort and then takes Twitter public, selling shares not to investors and hedge funds but instead to its end-users, similar to how the vast majority of shares in the Green Bay Packers football team are owned by its fans, a base comprising more than a half-million "Cheeseheads."[16]

I'm pretty sure that if Musk were willing to hand the ownership of Twitter over to its die-hard user base in a Packers-like scenario, the public would have the will and the money to make it happen. After all, corporations aren't the only entities that want to keep Twitter alive. Celebrities, public relations firms, book publishers, TV and movie studios and other entertainment-industry-related entities rely on Twitter for exposure, so a genuinely well-run, trustworthy Twitter would entice a lot of accounts, large and small, to pay more than they already do for things like "Promoted Tweets" (Twitter posts that appear within users' feed, just like ordinary tweets, regardless of device), "Promoted Trends" (which appear at the top of the list of trending topics for an entire day in a particular country or everywhere on Earth), and the like. For his part, Musk tried several revenue-generating approaches that didn't require advertisers, such as offering premium "Twitter Blue" subscription packages (most platforms, including Facebook, currently offer such things). Again, though, people don't want to pay to use social media. In 2023, an expert reported to Bloomberg that Twitter's subscription business was on track to bring in less than $120 million annually, barely putting a dent in the more than $2 billion it lost in ad revenue.

And the competition keeps coming. Aside from Bluesky, many new companies have been and still are offering "sane alternatives to Twitter." Some may have gone belly-up by the time you're reading this, but here goes. There's Tribel, a "bigotry-free" social media platform that some believe blew it out of the starting gate by requiring users to authorize a "terms of service" agreement that granted the platform far too much ownership of users' posted content (they walked that idea back relatively quickly, but the damage was done in the minds of many, and if that wasn't a big enough screwup, a March 2023 update of the app was hampered by a horrendous bug that prevented many users from accessing their accounts). I tried Tribel when it first launched; it was okay if uninspiring.

Post.news, another liberal-slanted site primarily owned by American media conglomerate Chatham Asset Management, is aimed at people who prefer bovine, easily digestible corporate media. It's basically a glorified version of Buzzfeed's comment sections, offering mainstream, pro-establishment-skewed news stories from *The Washington Post* and such while doing little if any journalistic probing into mainstream news' imperial/free market bias. I wasn't fond of Post's vanilla, often clickbaity content and aggravatingly slow signup process.

I also opened an account on Counter Social (counter.social), a liberal/left-slanted platform built with Mastodon technology. Counter Social was banished from the Mastodon alliance for blocking any post whose IP address indicated that the sender was posting from Iran, North Korea, Syria, China, Russia, or Pakistan, all of which are countries known to harbor troll farms. To me, that does seem a bit overprotective, but then again, Counter Social was launched not by a money-minded team of corporatists who don't care who posts on their platforms but by a hacker known as The Jester, who apparently wanted to have an easy time keeping troublemakers out of the site. It's a fun, enjoyable, easygoing platform, like a cross between Mastodon and Facebook. Last I checked, The Jester was posting a lot there and was pretty friendly.

In the end, the fediverse is the closest thing to a public social media sphere that—on paper at least—can't be completely spoiled by the presence of one corporate or moneyed interest. In an ideal world, the fediverse would be the social media space where most people waxed sociopolitical. Activists could plan hashtag campaigns, post-storms (timed, coordinated posting campaigns powered by multiple users) and other viralizing efforts, and it would be in one place. At present, activists are forced to spend a lot of time posting the same messages to Twitter, Facebook, and other platforms from which they operate.

I should also mention that for now, fediverse servers don't usually require each new user to provide a verifiable phone number to register on their instance. I assume that will eventually change so that bots and secondary "sockpuppet" troll accounts are essentially barred from entry, but in the meantime, people whose paramount concerns are privacy and security—journalists, government officials and such; basically anyone who wants to assemble in small-ish groups to hold private chats—might want to consider using the Signal app (https://signal.org/). Recommended by National Security Agency whistleblower Edward Snowden, the free, donor-supported messaging service rose to prominence in 2021 as an alternative to WhatsApp after the Meta offshoot announced that all its users' personal data was going to be shared with its notoriously intrusive parent company. Signal features end-to-end message encryption and supports groups of up to 1,000 users at this writing; you can think of it as a hyper-secure version of Discord (if you have no bloody idea what I'm even talking about concerning any of that stuff, consider yourself lucky, and besides, I'm sure that by the time you're reading this, at least a dozen similar apps will have popped up out of nowhere to challenge it).

Of course, I can advise you on what social media site you should use until the moon turns purple, but expecting people to cohere and settle on one social media platform is a pipe dream at first blush. For starters, science tells us that plenty of people are literally born to defy even the most sensible consensus, owing to variations in human brain structures. I'm not kidding: in 2012, neuroscientists at University College London proved the existence of a spectrum of hard-wired rebelliousness in humans that causes some people to refuse to "follow the crowd" if they have an underdeveloped lateral orbitofrontal cortex, an area of the brain associated with social behavior and decision-making.[17] Point being, for every idea there will always be rigid naysayers, owing to human nature.

And there will always be new platform choices. The possibility of striking it rich will always compel people and corporations to launch their own social media spaces to get a piece of the pie, so the question of "which site should I use" will often come up as time passes.

As an advocate of the fediverse who's expended a good deal of cyber-breath on it, I don't think most people understand how important and groundbreaking it is. I submit that it's social media's answer to the Do-It-Yourself (DIY) punk-rock phenomenon of the late 1970s and early 1980s, when bands and artists fought the stranglehold the major record companies had on the music business by releasing their own records and promoting them through mimeographed fanzines and other underground means.

It's past time for a similarly determined "people's takeover" of the social media sphere. But for that to happen, it's helpful to understand what the internet is and what it isn't.

4

Digital Divides

I. The Demon-Haunted Internet

Obviously, online communication is simply a method of, you know, communication. But its ethereal form—ghostly images magically appearing on one video screen or another—is still relatively new. We're accustomed to it now, but in the beginning, our getting news, information and *communion* over the internet was a breathtaking leap forward. It has reduced its predecessors to near irrelevance, from Mesopotamian tablets to daily newspapers. And it happened fast. We entered the Information Age basically overnight. The pervasive, ubiquitous presence of the internet has, by now, all but forced us to trust it to some extent.

Yet, people distrust much of the information they read online. That's natural, I'd say, owing to all the hacking and trickery that goes on and because the sheer volume of information that's available seems overwhelming. The internet is no longer relegated to a handful of news and chat spaces that can only download a few thousand bytes of data at a time through modems; it's everywhere. In 2021, it was forecast that the amount of data available on the internet in 2022 would total around 79 zettabytes (79 trillion gigabytes, or 79 sextillion bytes) and that by 2025, that amount would double. To be sure, there's a lot of redundancy in all that data; out of all the data in the world, only ten percent is genuinely new, non-redundant data,[1] but that's still a lot of data. To put it in perspective, a (purely hypothetical) 79-zettabyte hard drive could hold over 17.5 trillion copies of the entire Encyclopedia Britannica (the current size of which is 4.5 gigabytes), a number that easily dwarfs the number of stars in the Milky Way galaxy (100–400 billion), as well as the number of cells in a human brain (86 billion). Nothing readily visible on Earth exceeds the internet's 79-odd sextillion (and counting) number of bytes, not even the estimated total number of grains of beach sand on the planet (5 sextillion).[2] In the meantime, of course, not all digital data is stored on the internet. As I described in *Russian Nazi Troll Bots*, the Utah Data Center is assumed to store yottabytes (a thousand zettabytes each) of data at their Saratoga Springs, Utah, facility. Purportedly closed at one point by order of Congress, the Center was originally launched by the National Security Agency after 9/11. Allegedly, every single digital thing people do—make cell phone calls, pay bills, post to social media, etc—was, or still is, on record there.[3]

The human brain isn't equipped to comprehend such impossibly huge numbers. In fact, humans have difficulty keeping track of more than three random things without requiring some sort of device to help them keep track.[4]

What I'm getting at is that "future shock" has set in, as futurist writer Alvin Toffler predicted in his 1970 book of the same name. The internet has grown to a size that the human mind cannot grasp, and it appeared in the blink of an epochal eye.

January 1, 1983, is considered the official birthday of the internet, owing to the ARPAnet's adoption of the TCP/IP protocol, which made it possible for separate computer systems to communicate with each other using a set of standardized "rules." Cut to now, just 40-odd years later, to a world that's been changed forever by this human-to-human communication breakthrough: Our brains are still adjusting to it. Many millions of people who lived in an internet-free world during their early to mid-adulthood are still alive, which some would say has fostered an unbridgeable generation gap. But I'd argue that the internet, with its constantly expanding, all but immeasurable size, as well as its invisible, electronic form, is now so alien that any non-technical person, young or old, might view it as something of a godlike entity to some varied degree.

"Fear of things invisible is the natural seed of that which every one in himself calleth religion," wrote Thomas Hobbes in *Leviathan*. Despite the mysterious nature of its workings, we love the internet because it gives us all the information we want on demand. Yet, by the same token, we fear (or even despise) it for its omniscience and omnipresence. And so it is indeed godlike in many ways, not the least of which is that only a fraction of its human users have any idea what makes it tick. Yes, we see text and images on our devices, but what made them, and should we trust them?

Indeed, do people trust technology itself in general? In his 1995 book *The Demon-Haunted World*, legendary astronomer Carl Sagan reminded us that, along with all the convenience technology has provided, it's also given us terrible things: thalidomide, chlorofluorocarbons and Agent Orange, just to scratch the surface. Its spreadsheet and financial programs work directly and insidiously to enable the unstoppable growth of all but unregulated industries whose products are ruining the planet's climate.

More recently, the rise of artificial intelligence (AI) programs has given observers night sweats, and not just over the increasingly real threat of their replacing artists, music composers and writers. In the area of global finance, there's Aladdin, an electronic system built by the risk management division of the world's largest investment management corporation, BlackRock, Inc., which, as of 2020, was managing $21.6 trillion in assets, more than the gross domestic product of every country in the world other than the United States and China. The software, also used by other fund-managing behemoths like Vanguard and State Street Global Advisors, gathers and collates real-world data, evaluating what-if and worst-case scenarios to calculate risk for investors large and small. Experts have warned that Aladdin could destroy the world's economy if the system were hacked, suffered a glitch or encountered some other unforeseeable problem. In January 2020, the UK's Financial Conduct Authority gently warned that the failure of Aladdin or a similarly all-powerful analytical system "could cause serious consumer harm" or even "damage market integrity."[5]

"There's a *reason* people are nervous about science and technology," Sagan offered. I share his belief that people have a natural aversion to technology; it's perhaps attributable in part to inherited genetic memory. As much as we try to appear comfortable using the internet to communicate with each other over matters of politics, current events and such, there's an air of unnaturalness to it that keeps many if not most of us feeling reluctant to be completely forthcoming. *Who's actually seeing all this?* we wonder.

Computer technology changes so quickly that it sometimes makes us feel out of the loop, even obsolete. Programmers and users alike can't keep up without constantly, doggedly studying the latest changes, regardless of how old we are chronologically. Every few years, Microsoft releases a new version of Windows, forcing users to learn the ins and outs of new features, some of which wreak as much inconvenience as software bugs. And yet, users are expected to adapt to those adversities, regardless of how abandoned they feel.

"Future shock," Toffler wrote, "is the shattering stress and disorientation that we induce in individuals by subjecting them to too much change in too short a time." Regarding today's computer technology, the phenomenon is perpetual, affecting all generations. Despite their constant use of tech devices and having "grown up on the internet," younger people are as prone to experiencing fears of technological obsolescence as older people.

We've all seen young people portrayed as omniscient tech gurus on television and in movies. The kid says, "Here, let me see your phone, Grandpa," and suddenly, like magic, whatever Grandpa wanted is working correctly. With tropes like that around, older people automatically assume that members of the younger generation are more deeply aware of how computer technology works than they are. But there's a difference between technology users and programmers. Not that it's of earth-shattering importance, just saying: people who know how to use *information appliances* like smartphones or tablets or whatnot to navigate the internet are a lot more common than people who know what systems their devices are accessing, how they're accessing them, or anything about the technologies that make that information presentable to users. They don't know how data is sorted and stored on relational databases, large network servers and various interdependent files on hard drives; how it's sent through electronic exchange methods after connecting through layers of security and programmatic translation; how web browsers format information into readability, etc.

None of that stuff will be on the quiz, folks. The point is

that, for the most part, people of all ages don't care how the internet works; they just want it to work, hence the media-propelled notion of there being an unbridgeable "tech generation gap" is only partly true, if that. Unfortunately, that perception has become a source of cultural divisiveness that's worked to hobble cultural and sociopolitical solidarity: younger tech-savvy people may assume that the tech knowledge of older people is hopelessly out of date, whereas older people reveal a little insecurity when they scold the young for "having it too easy" owing to advances in technology.

Meantime, however, modern-day workers of all ages are slowly becoming more tech-savvy by osmosis, through constant immersion in software and hardware systems that automate their most dreary tasks. Today's college graduates become trained in the basic disciplines of their careers and then are "upskilled" through immersive training in computer programs and other digital systems that help them automate tasks, instantly collaborate with their colleagues, etc. Some refer to this new breed of worker as the "T-shaped" graduate.[6]

Not every young person enters the workforce well-versed in new or old technology. Indeed, only a fraction of today's high school kids are interested in computer science enough to want to learn its ins and outs. In 2021, a report issued by Code.org's Advocacy Coalition and three other computer-education agencies revealed that, in 37 states that disclosed data on computer-class enrollment in their high schools, only 4.7 percent of students had taken any computer science courses.[7]

While all this is happening, there's a tactile factor present: In the end, a smartphone is a digital entity, not an analog device like a typewriter, printing press or stone tablet; it doesn't "feel real" in more ways than one.

I don't want to belabor too much the question, "Is online stuff real?" but it does lurk behind many non-technical people's mindsets. It must be addressed because many people don't believe it is "real" to any notable extent. People who gravitate to Fifth Estate and online left spaces—people who, ironically, tend to spend their social media time talking about "real things" like income inequality and climate change—are vastly outnumbered by people who don't spend much if any time on "serious" social media and view it as idle, disposable chatter.

Whether everything we read on the internet is entirely reliable or not, it's all quite real to plenty of people. Edward Bulwer-Lytton's 1839 adage, "The pen is mightier than the sword," is as true today as it was then, probably more so: the internet is a collection of millions of virtual pens that, when united by purpose, often form an especially formidable sword.

Take for example the Arab Spring protests, a wave of civil disobedience during which citizens of various Arab countries pushed back against authoritarianism and absolute monarchy. It began in 2010 when 26-year-old Tunisian fruit vendor Mohamed Bouazizi set himself on fire to protest the police harassment that had made his life miserable and menaced his livelihood for years. A band of activists on Twitter shared a video of the event, after which thousands of disgruntled Facebook users spread the word, boosting the movement. "Social media was absolutely crucial," Khaled Koubaa, president of the Internet Society in Tunisia, told *The Guardian*. "Three months before Mohammed Bouazizi burned himself in Sidi Bouzid, we had a similar case in Monastir. But no one knew about it because it was not filmed. What made a difference this time is that the images of Bouazizi were put on

Facebook and everybody saw it."[8]

"Everybody saw it" is one of social media's unique powers, a double-edged sword. In recent years, we've witnessed the ruination ("cancellation") of famous media and entertainment figures who were caught doing or saying bad things. When word got out about their misdeeds, their reputations were washed away by floods of vitriol posted by pitchfork-and-torch-bearing "netizens" bent on pillorying them. You know their names, the various celebrities—mostly powerful, famous males—who stepped way out of line in real life and lost their online platforms when vengeance-wreaking hashtags such as #MeToo went to work on them, guys like Harvey Weinstein, Kevin Spacey, Anthony Weiner and a Macy's parade of others.

Such negative virality reveals the dark side of online mobs, but it's not just celebrities who get pilloried. Plenty of regular people have been cyberbullied until they broke psychologically and ended their own lives, such as Ryan Halligan, a Vermont teenager whose 2003 suicide was examined in an episode of PBS's *Frontline* television series titled "Growing Up Online." Virtual ostracization was very real to him, as it was to such others as K-Pop singer Choi Jin-ri, Missouri teen Megan Meier, Japanese actor Haruma Miura and 14-year-old Australian Dolly Everett, all of whom committed suicide, allegedly after undergoing relentless cyberbullying.

There's a winners-and-losers feel to online life. A small percentage of users new to this or that platform fit in right away and are immediately regaled with positive reinforcement, whereas others gain widespread acceptance after a time. But most, try as they might, never quite make it into the Cool Kids' Club, which can lead to depression or worse. There's plenty of evidence that social media use by children should be monitored by their (usually similarly distracted) parents.

Social media use has been the source of much concern in academic and scientific circles, owing not only to its history of spreading disinformation and whatnot but also its proven addictive qualities. Books, papers, and articles examining internet addiction abound, some pronouncing it a compulsive behavior akin to alcoholism or drug use. Some people can't control their use of social media and fall into bad habits, such as putting aside things like school, employment, and personal relationships. Before her passing, Pennsylvania psychologist Kimberly Young wrote several books on the subject, including her seminal work, 1998's *Caught in the Net*, in which she offers pragmatic solutions to people whose lives have been adversely affected by overuse of the internet (you can still gauge your own level of internet addiction by taking the short survey at her website, netaddiction.com).

Anecdotally, my own "Supersize Me Twitter" experiment led to obsessive-compulsive behaviors that hindered my ability to perform daily functions. I'd look on hopelessly as all my spare time (and more) disappeared into thin air. But per the rules of the experiment, I allowed myself to become irretrievably addicted. I did as much virtual socializing as I could fit into a day, checking in with mutual followers, Liking their posts, chatting and getting quite close to many of them on a personal level (which of course I don't regret at all). I would bolt out of bed unusually early most mornings, excited and simultaneously terrified to see what was going on, worried I'd discover that someone had gotten upset with something I'd posted, or no one had Liked my last few tweets, etc. The addiction stuck with me after the year expired, but luckily, around a year and a half in, my virtual social circle had widened to the point where it was (and still is) consistently enjoyable without my having to tend to it every minute. The addictive aspect is long gone; nowadays, I feel like one of those impossible people who can smoke one "special occasion" cigarette and not have another jolt of nicotine for months (okay, weeks) (days?).

Social media may be making people miserable, but we've seen it coming for many decades. In the final scene of the 1940 film *The Great Dictator*, the "Jewish barber" (played by Charlie Chaplin) delivers a speech in which he urges humanity to change the harmful ways in which it has (mal)adjusted to all the "advantages" technology has bestowed. "Our knowledge has made us cynical," he glooms, "our cleverness hard and unkind. We think too much and feel too little. More than machinery, we need humanity."

Nowhere has this crisis, our losing battle with the myriad psychic disorders that have come with hyper-advancement, ever been more evident than on our corporate social media platforms. In those "places that aren't actual places," the compulsion to appear at once omniscient, depthlessly hip and emotionally invincible too often leads people to feel intellectually orphaned, lost and friendless. Richard Seymour alludes to the syndrome in his 2019 book, *The Twittering Machine*: "Whatever we write has to be calibrated for social approval." We all do it. Whenever we type a public post, we alter ourselves, performing for anonymous crowds, becoming less and less familiar with our true beliefs.

Feelings of inadequacy and loneliness are endemic on social media. Instead of being alone with our loneliness, we often can't help indulging in social comparison, where we tend to view our own lives as more or less fulfilling in comparison to others'. It's not uncommon to see posts from popular social media users who, upon noticing apparent drops in their engagement numbers, abandon their disaffected façades and publicly address the issue, asking the faceless crowd, "Where are all my people?" or "Am I invisible?" Despair creeps in like a sickly green fog, regardless of whether or not the lull in interpersonal engagement is attributable to a lowered interest in the user's usual messaging, the hivemind's suddenly becoming distracted by a breaking news story, or deliberate manipulation of the user's visibility by the platform itself (such as through changes in what the platform's search algorithms "decide" other users should see, or, most unsettling of all, "shadowbanning" of the user's account, meaning that the person's posts have been deliberately hidden from view through programmatic means, which is assuredly a lot rarer than people believe).

Whether you call it internet addiction, compulsive computer use, pathological internet use, or internet dependence, if you think you have a problem, there's help available from therapists, who tend to classify it as an obsessive-compulsive disorder or impulse control disorder. That's not to say that the psychology community considers social media a serious threat to mental health in general; it doesn't at present. But that's probably coming, considering that since 2022, the American Psychiatric Association has regarded "Internet Gaming Disorder" as a condition warranting more clinical research, which could eventually lead to social media addiction being likewise listed as an "official" disorder in the industry's bible, the Diagnostic and Statistical Manual of Mental Disorders. If it ever is, Young's research on internet addiction will have likely informed the debate, which could lead to its being taken more seriously.

It's probably just a matter of time before that happens.

Studies are piling up, all providing irrefutable proof that the internet might need a warning label. A 2017 Sage Journals study of a half-million 13-to-18-year-olds found that the number of kids exhibiting high levels of depressive symptoms rose by 33 percent between 2010 and 2015, coincidentally the same period during which social media had an exponential growth spurt, the speed of which closely matched an explosion in smartphone sales, which peaked in 2021.[9] Also in that time frame, the suicide rate for girls in the same age group increased by 65 percent.[10] As for how adults hold up, a 2021 study funded by the U.S. National Institute of Mental Health concluded that Snapchat, Facebook, and TikTok were the most depression-causitive social media platforms for adults ages 18 and up. In (undue, I think) fairness, some experts advised caution in putting a lot of stock in those findings.[11]

To many of its users, corporate social media is a significant stressor in modern life; I don't care if the American Psychiatric Association is too cautious to find that out for itself or not. But by far, the worst thing that its toxic, manipulative, disinformation-soaked environment has wrought is the atmosphere of paranoid negativity that permeates it, crushing even the faintest hope for sociopolitical progress. As such, it falls upon us as citizens to stop wasting time arguing with trolls and naysayers, to agree that certain undeniable sociopolitical truths are, in fact, truths; and to find a way to leverage corporate social media platforms—or, more preferably, the fediverse—toward efforts to organize against the forces that control our politicians and deny citizens all the things that would make their lives more livable. Oh, and save the planet.

I highly doubt that the major corporate social media

platforms will ever be of much help. As an industry, they've spent a lot more time studying internet user habits than the American Psychiatric Association could ever dream of, albeit not toward the goal of making their products less addictive but toward increasing the addiction's severity. To cite just one ugly revelation out of many, in 2021, Frances Haugen, a former data scientist at Facebook who turned whistleblower against the company, attended a Senate hearing on Capitol Hill in which she revealed the mechanics behind some of the more vicious, user-addicting tactics practiced at her former workplace. She depicted the brass at Facebook and its subsidiary, Instagram, as being so focused on growing user counts that they had little to no concern for the mental health of their users. They'd blithely ignored internal studies showing that Instagram was causing 32 percent of its teenage female users to feel worse about their bodies. Also, internal analysts had discovered that Facebook was fully aware (and had done nothing about the fact) that organizers of the "Stop The Steal" movement (led by right-wing extremist groups that had spread agitprop claiming that Donald Trump had actually racked up enough votes to win the 2020 presidential election) had easily dodged Facebook's AI surveillance processes, allowing them to rally their troops to lay maladroit siege to the U.S. Capitol in January 2021.

If Facebook's human "moderating team" were much bigger and more well-directed, maybe staffed with real people acting in Reddit-like "regional moderator" roles, the space would see a lot more constructive, even-tempered debate. As is, moderation is primarily handled by sloppily programmed bots and other obtuse AI processes, rendering it a virtual mosh pit where, too often, simple disagreements spiral into wasteful squabbles marked by childish displays of finger-pointing and mutual disrespect.

At present, the AI used by the corporate social media giants is more a hindrance than a help. It's unable to differentiate between harmless in-jokes and actual death threats, which often results in users' unfairly losing their posting privileges temporarily or permanently without warning. Of course, managing trillions of online conversations in a monolithic, centralized space like Facebook or Twitter through primitive AI methods is a recipe for continued disaster, and some point to that as proof that, for all intents and purposes, both companies should be broken up and/or converted into public utilities.

They've obviously grown too big to be housebroken. Communicating through social media has become so ubiquitous that it's made the phone call obsolete. We must admit defeat and take the next step: admitting that "internet accountability by decree" is no longer feasible. As YouTube commentator Kyle Kulinski asked in early 2023, "If a mafia person calls a hit-man to go kill somebody, does anyone blame Verizon?" That's an interesting question. Given that the sheer daily volume of tweets and Facebook posts literally cannot be managed by those companies, whose only guardrails comprise deeply flawed artificial intelligence processes and (in Facebook's case) a paltry staff of overworked "content moderators" (some of whom contract Post Traumatic Stress Disorder by constantly getting subjected to disturbing images popping up for their split-second review), haven't the corporate platforms proven that they can't be trusted to promote the public good in any capacity?

By law, they aren't compelled to. In 1996, Section 230 was added to the Communications Decency Act. That legislation provided immunity for web platforms that offer third-party content. In short, platforms aren't held responsible if a user posts something that causes harm. Of course, it's logical for such a law to be on the books in our free market system, which, as often and irrationally as possible, protects businesses regardless of how much harm they might cause (Facebook was accused of fomenting genocide in Ethiopia[12] and Myanmar,[13] respectively, owing to alleged gross negligence).

But it's all good. After all, it's a First Amendment matter. Isn't it?

VIII. Some Relatively Inexpensive Words About Free Speech

The politically theatrical "free speech debate" that's played out ad nauseum over the last decade or so is a bit tangential to our scope, but it does warrant some discussion, since changes in laws governing what's okay and not okay to post online would obviously come into play if a social media site were pressured by the government to shut down certain anti-establishment accounts or ban words or phrases whose virality might work to disrupt the system.

Most of the time, what does and doesn't constitute "freedom of speech" online is in the eye of the beholder. Depending on the circumstances, the door swings whichever way the orator wants it to. Right-wingers often represent the First Amendment as a law guaranteeing the freedom to say inappropriate things at inopportune times. In contrast, liberals can be found decrying its perceived near-total absence of limits.

Toward the latter, the First Amendment isn't and hasn't ever been an "anything goes, any time and any place" pass. It doesn't allow for obscenity, fraud, child pornography, or "speech integral to illegal conduct," for starters. As initially conceived 230-odd years ago, it was intended as a general rule of thumb—periodically amended with legal and/or morally sensible exceptions—preventing the government from silencing its critics.

Of course, you wouldn't think that the First Amendment had any caveats at all if you look at how our legal system handles *internet* speech, but that's par for the course. Too often, our hilariously tech-ignorant legal system seems incapable of equating "online things" with their "real-life" counterparts (not to sound snobby, but I sometimes wonder if any judge in the country even knows how to connect a monitor to a computer). There are plenty of examples, such as the system's failure to pass sensible labor laws regarding internet-driven "gig work" like ridesharing (Uber, etc.). And we won't even talk about whether or not Lady Justice understands the first thing about cryptocurrencies or the completely not-ready-for-primetime NFT (Non-Fungible Token) "copyrighted works" market (if you don't know what NFTs are, don't worry about it; I'd say they're about 10 years away from attaining legal viability at minimum). Similarly, the main reason "online free speech" is such a hotly debated issue is that the legal system hasn't settled on what internet speech actually *is* and what should be censored.

But behind the scenes, the U.S. government has decided what's okay to say online. The establishment and its Fourth Estate arm would have the public believe that the government should have the legal right to censor pro-Trump propaganda and other right-wing malinformation on social media, and that's as far as they'd ever take it. Many journalists don't believe they would stop there, however, including Glenn

Greenwald, Matt Taibbi and others, who've pointed to evidence refuting such mainstream media-driven fables as the "Hunter Biden laptop-tampering" story[14] and the "Russiagate" 2016 election-interference story,[15] and have raised the alarm about the government's bizarre, unwavering refusal to admit that the COVID-19 pandemic could have originated through a "lab leak" in Wuhan, China.[16]

Government overreach aside, we're still left with problems like online hate speech. In that regard, Kulinski's likening a social media post to a private telephone call is the wrong analogy. It's the "public" part of it: It's less accurate to compare a public, racist social media post to a private phone call between two violent racists than to compare it to, say, a racist message spray-painted on the side of a city building. The building's tenants would undoubtedly want to have the graffiti removed or covered up immediately, as would the building's owner, since it would detract from the appeal of the place. The only logical reason for the landlord to leave the scribbling alone (and take no steps to protect the same space from being defiled again) would be if they agreed with the sentiment or didn't think it was a big deal.

One would think that "dedicated free speech advocates" (unfortunately meaning, for the most part, right-wingers who commonly engage in xenophobic dog-whistling to keep Republican voters placing all the blame for their socioeconomic woes on immigrants and other minorities rather than the GOP politicians who craft most anti-labor legislation) would have been okay with keeping Section 230 exactly as it was. After all, as long as the platforms weren't worried about getting sued for hate-speech-inspired incidents, the freedom fighters remained free to spout their vituperative nonsense to their hearts' content. Easy peasy, right?

But Donald Trump—the most prolific spouter of vituperative nonsense in human history—had other ideas during his presidency. He wanted the platforms to "stop censoring conservative voices", and didn't care what they thought about it. So, on May 28, 2020—the same day on which riots erupted in Minneapolis, Minnesota, in reaction to the murder of George Floyd by police—Trump signed the "Executive Order [EO] on Preventing Online Censorship." The EO was intended to stop the platforms from removing offensive posts and banning users they didn't like. Unsurprisingly, Joe Biden rescinded the order four months after taking office while simultaneously and predictably vowing to remove protections that cut the other way so that the platforms' managers would be forced to manage the sites more carefully and sensibly. To date, nothing has been done in that regard and probably won't until the day we successfully colonize Alpha Centauri (according to Statistica, Meta alone spent nearly 10 million U.S. dollars on lobbying activities in the first half of 2023).

Section 230 has had a long, strange trip, but it seemed uncomplicated at first. The ruling, comprising just 26 words, goes like this: "No provider or user of an interactive computer service shall be treated as the publisher or speaker of any information provided by another information content provider." The rub is that it protects online platforms from lawsuits arising over content generated by users and posted to their sites while preserving the platform's rights to moderate any content as they see fit. One co-author of the legislation, Oregon Democratic Senator Ron Wyden, saw the futility of it, admitting, "[C]ontent is posted on their platforms so rapidly there's just no way they can possibly police everything."

Without question, that statement fortifies the platforms'

"too big to manage" argument. But by no means does it excuse their continued refusal to invest heavily and proactively to keep their users safe from misinformation and dangerous agitprop. It's outrageous that they don't do a better job of it.

Of course, the above mostly applies to people who spend a lot of time on corporate social media and are thus vulnerable to its myriad tricks and traps. But what about casual social media users? You know, the normies?

They couldn't care less, is what. My sense, gathered from years spent participating in and observing online discourse, from Compuserve's forums and Usenet's newsgroups in the 1990s to the Facebook, 4chan and Twitter spaces of today, is that people with hectic personal lives don't take social media all that seriously.

And why would they? All the sociopolitical drama is too convoluted for casual social media users to keep up with. That stuff's for others to handle, people who have time for it. My impression of people who have a deep sense of "real life" communal belonging—members of big, stable families or other types of large, close-knit social herds—is that they tend to view social media as something of a mindless, tiresome chore that's only peripherally relevant to their everyday lives. Mostly, they log into social media only to perform the occasional, perfunctory "check-in," posting pictures of the meal they just ate or the vacation spot they just visited. That may seem vacuous and tone-deaf to people who spend hours every day discussing and debating politics online, but, like they say, it is what it is.

Millions of people are disengaged from politics because their lives are too busy for it. Swamped with everyday social obligations, work demands or other responsibilities, they simply can't keep up with the latest news, much less the daily minutiae covered by the Fifth Estate. That may lead them to believe, often quite rightly, that they have little or nothing to add to the conversation. Maybe they don't, but whatever the reason, it's unconstructive for armchair activists to scold them for not knowing a lot of Political Stuff; it's like resenting a dog for being unable to solve a Wordle.

While all this is happening, many upper-class citizens—particularly "old money" types who've benefited from decades or centuries of generational wealth—tend to avoid social media altogether. They feel no need to flaunt their highly privileged lifestyles through posts that might make them appear gauche in the opinion of people who aren't as fortunate. To the rich, "social media participation, in general, is frowned upon," observed Denver-raised fashion influencer @madisonelsewhere in a 2023 TikTok video. She revealed what everyday life is like for her and her family, one that's blessed by generational wealth. There are unwritten rules in force when the rich decide to surface briefly on Facebook, like whales coming up for air. "Don't post pictures of you skiing," she cautions, "or on vacation, or doing pretty much anything at all other than bad, kind-of blurry photos of, like, toast and breakfast and your dog."

Whether rich or poor, most people don't participate in online political discussions for many reasons, including their feeling powerless to do anything about all the injustice. As Noam Chomsky told *Jacobin* in 2015, "[The U.S. is] a country in which about 70 percent of the population—the lower 70 percent on the income scale—are completely disenfranchised. Their opinions have no detectable influence on the decisions of their own representatives, which is ... a large reason why a huge number of people don't bother voting. They know that it's a waste of time. So is that a democracy? No, not really."[17]

IX. Nothing But the Truth

Like we talked about, when someone's social media platform starts receiving a lot of positive reinforcement in the form of Likes and such, their desire to get even more of it may override any desire to be entirely forthcoming with their audience. That goes double for the more popular Fifth Estate figures: Even when one discovers a glaring flaw in the narrative they've spent the last few weeks (or indeed their entire career) supporting, the last thing in the world they want to do is admit it since it could wind up costing them money and/or platform capital.

Here's the problem with that. Willfully disseminating misinformation isn't just immoral; it impedes progress, not only because it risks half-assed ideas going viral but also because the thought leader's followers may stop seeking deeper truths for themselves.

But the truth always emerges. The Fifth Estate won't supplant the Fourth until their reporters and journalists fully commit to a code of ethics that swears them to seek and report only the truth, however uncomfortable it is.

Ultimately, all truth is for the public good and should be of paramount concern to any self-respecting independent media figure. The Fifth Estate's audience never fails to discover that relevant facts are being withheld (or missed entirely) by misinformed do-it-yourself pundits and self-serving charlatans big and small. The online left never misses a trick, and as such, it keeps the Fifth Estate honest.

Some would argue that budding (even veteran) Fifth Estate figures can't maintain high standards of journalistic integrity. There's too much to do. Producing independent news and opinion content requires one to research every topic du jour exhaustively, often while handling many or all of their show's production duties. The tasks in the latter area can include deploying and maintaining broadcast equipment (microphones, cameras, lighting, etc.), scheduling guest speakers and editing audio and/or video recordings. Like full-time reality TV stars, the hardiest thoughtfluencers spend many hours in front of a camera daily. Maintaining a constant presence is essential to building a personal platform for their voice and attracting a dedicated fan base. That's because the algorithms used by YouTube and various other profit-driven media companies favor quantity over quality. Unfortunately, that can force thoughtfluencers to resort to a lot of repetitive messaging and a less-than-ideal signal-to-noise ratio. Accomplishing all of that requires seriously workaholic tendencies.

It's a similar rat race for the average person who chases online "clout" by maintaining one or more social media accounts. Obsessively seeking dopamine boosts, overworked users punch the clock to "scream at the sky," rarely if ever offering well-thought-out suggestions on how to solve anything. Such users spend too much of their social media time working to promote themselves—their own self-serving, personal brands—and not enough on more valuable things, such as researching the subjects they post about or improving their communication styles so that they can help build real solidarity within their networks.

That's not as easy as it sounds. Every serious online leftist should seek first to understand before attempting to be understood. We need to stop being so defensive, is what that means. If I ask an interlocutor the right questions in a respectful manner instead of immediately dismissing them out of hand and engaging in verbal swordplay, both of us might learn something and/or work out the bugs in our critical thinking. Too often, we react to honest questions as if they're angry criticisms of our ideas, and we respond by posting rude responses or reaching for the Block button (thereby conveniently removing the other person's thoughts from our sight) rather than engaging the other person in a little harmless debate.

That's a major problem with corporate social media discourse. It keeps people from understanding each other, which doesn't help anyone evolve. I'll only block another user if, after a few back-and-forth "reply cycles," they're stubbornly hostile, refusing to address my questions or points.

When dealing with people online, a good rule of thumb is to imagine that the two of you are face-to-face, not hidden behind protective screens and separated by miles or oceans. If the conversation were taking place in real life, I'd simply walk away from it if I sensed that the only reason the person was talking to me was that they were deliberately trying to get me worked up (which is, of course, a troll's raison d'être) or were bent on hammering me with brainwashed, hard-wired doctrinairism until I agreed with them.

As online leftists, we need to stop mistaking simple disagreement for random aggression and scrambling to hit the Block button. Blocking someone simply because they subscribe to a single, relatively minor point we find offensive—say, a misogynistic, culturally backward belief held by alt-lite "manosphere" hero Jordan Peterson—severs any connection that may have been building over things on which we agree. It's wasteful, leading to deepened division and intellectual petrification.

As for the part about seeking to be understood by others, that too gets tricky when discussing politics online. Over decades, owing to fears of appearing unhip or ignorant about whatever subject they're talking about, social media users have evolved the odd habit of eschewing social niceties when communicating online. Your mileage may vary, of course, and no, I have no interest in establishing a platform as some sort of "Emily Post of the internet," but really, flaunting one's "hipness level" by offering ideas (good or bad) in an opaque, terse, semi-obfuscatory fashion has become de rigueur, an essential ingredient in people's online branding strategies. It makes one appear less interested in communicating clearly than in being perceived as aloof and detached.

I mean, kidding around is different. I enjoy reading random silliness as much as anyone else, and the best time for that sort of thing is, well, most of the time, if one is chatting casually. But not everyone has a knack for humor. If you do, and you're debating someone who doesn't appear to want to lighten the atmosphere at all, there's nothing wrong with sticking to a rote script and stating your ideas as clearly as possible, using the exact phrasing you've used countless times before, including posting links to web pages that have relevant details. Anything's better than keeping people from understanding you by impatiently spouting your "crucial points" in a clipped, indecipherable manner. It turns people off and muddies your messaging. Keep in mind that many people come to leftist social media spaces looking for simple answers to complicated questions. When they don't get straightforward, intelligible answers, it does nothing to help your outreach. Ultimately, it hinders your efforts to recruit others to your cause.

Of course, not all online leftists are trying to appear confoundingly hip when they communicate in a terse, maddeningly obscure manner. Let's face it: Some people aren't good communicators, so they can't grasp the fact that imprecise, detached brevity isn't always strategically sound. For activists, there's nothing wrong with being receptive and pleasantly, agreeably enthusiastic with strangers who seem interested in your ideas. Try radiating a little positive energy. Who knows, maybe they'll eventually become useful cogs on your platform.

Anyone who's ever tried to organize anything, from a pickup softball league to a million-person march, will tell you that finding and recruiting just one person who's good with people (because they actually *like* people) and has a genuine love for their cause (and may thus have the makings of a potential fellow organizer) is more valuable than finding 100 unmotivated people who have no real idea of (or interest in knowing) what the fuss is about.

Whether operating online or off, serious organizers shouldn't spend much time commiserating with others who are already sold. The more important task is to engage with people who disagree with us, to encourage them to ask questions so that they'll know more. That slow-moving, case-by-case recruitment/conversion approach can be exasperating, but it's the key to organizing. It requires one to have a genuine interest in all types of people and an ability to put aside personal dislike for or prejudgment of those who seem least likely to have faith in our vision or methods.

Hard work, yes, but it needs to be done in the interest of building solidarity between movements. Despite its egalitarian, populist undergirding, leftism itself is in shambles, a near-hopelessly splintered movement whose durability has been debated even by the Fifth Estate's most well-known personalities. In December 2022, Chris Hedges and Marxist economics professor Richard Wolff were engaged in a workaday discussion on preventing fascism from taking permanent hold in America. Their chitchat led to a brief debate over whether or not a cohesive left exists in the first place.[18]

> Hedges: "We don't have a strong left. We don't have a counterweight to [the right's] protofascism embodied in figures like Trump, DeSantis, Pompeo and others."

> Wolff: "We don't? I don't know, it depends on your point of view, [but] if I were in the leadership of this country, I wouldn't put too much reliance on that."

That brief exchange between two of the Fifth Estate's most well-known icons would be Exhibit A for anyone seeking to prove the existence of a divide between fervent Marxists and politically pragmatic progressives. Neither of those guys felt any need to shift their position, mainly owing to personal experience but also, to a debatably lesser extent, a half-conscious impulse to defend their personal brand. Neither of them wants a divided left, of course, but their life experiences have been dissimilar. As they spoke, Wolff was riding a wave of adulation from fans who didn't mind that he hadn't done much if any on-the-ground activism, such as appearing at protests (he has, however, been very generous with his time, speaking at Occupy Wall Street's Open Forum and many other gatherings). Contrast that with Hedges, a frequent flier at protests, who'd been arrested in November of 2011 at a mock trial of Goldman Sachs CEO Lloyd Blankfein during the Occupy Wall Street protests.

Actually, Hedges has sacrificed a lot more than that. After spending many years embedded in war zones, investigating white supremacist enclaves and such, he was rewarded for his reporting and punditry by being fired by *The New York Times* and summarily banished by the mainstream media for daring to challenge America's imperial transgressiveness and speak truth to power. At the time of that particular exchange with Wolff, Hedges had settled into a platform that urged nonviolent civil disobedience as the only means of positive change. His funereal demeanor doesn't so much bespeak an explicit call to action as it does a patriot's last, deeply pessimistic hope for cohesion among all sides of the left.

That's not to detract from Wolff's platform by any means. He's undoubtedly had some unpleasant experiences while working in the oppressive environment of academia. From his days as a young economics student up to the present, it's certain he's had many tense conversations with peers and colleagues who ostracized him for gravitating to Marx as opposed to free market cultists like Milton Friedman.

Meanwhile, Thomas Frank would likely approach the question of whether the left has any strength from a different angle than both Wolff and Hedges. In *The People, No*, Frank exhibits some measure of faith that our problems can be solved politically, as long as the left's biggest arm, the Democrats—"the party of technocrats and consultants, smoke-filled rooms and calculating triangulators," as he chides them—can somehow get their act together and lead the way.

Hope springs, I suppose. Maybe the Democrats can forgive themselves for the neoliberal politics they've practiced over the past several decades and go back to their moderately progressive post-war roots, but I'd be mortally shocked to see it. Without intense public pressure in the form of strikes, walkouts and other disruptive civil actions, there's no reason for the Democrats to venture out of their smoke-filled rooms and do anything different than what they've been doing.

Of course, for the moment, the left is a scattered mess, so until further notice, the only path to a more humanist-minded future does run through the voting booth. Regardless of one's politics, everyone should vote, especially in primary elections, which are critically important. The field is as wide open as it'll ever get during the primaries, meaning you can help support independent candidates whose views are more in line with your own. Alternatively, you can express your disapproval for the whole lot of them by registering what is, in effect, a protest vote, in the form of an "undervote," in which one or more individual ballot choices are left blank to send a message to party and campaign organizations that you disapproved of all the candidates they offered up. Both camps of the red/blue duopoly do keep track of undervotes, and, although most times their numbers barely rate a footnote, undervotes can mean the whole ball game. In the 2020 general election, the number of Arizona ballots whose presidential choices were blank was greater than the number of votes by which Trump lost the state to Biden.[19]

No matter where you sit on the leftist spectrum, the Democrats aren't the only duopoly party with serious problems. We'd be remiss if we didn't spend a little time on the ideological divide that exists on the right and makes the Republicans as fragile a party as the Democrats. This schism could be exploited by Democratic activists and liberal media figures as easily as the right-wing press leverages the yawning neoliberal-vs-progressive divide that exists on the left.

Here it is: Where the left's state of disarray can be attributed to a feud between oft-vindicated cynics who have no faith in the Democratic establishment and liberals who haven't given up on it yet, the soul of the Republican Party is, similarly, engaged in a cold civil war, one that pits culturally repressed Christian fundamentalists against government-hating, free market-loving libertarians.

I've gotten guff for proffering this theory on Twitter, and I'll admit it's not a hill I'd want to die on. Still, I believe it's just a matter of time before the Republican Party cracks in half over its fundamentalist/libertarian incompatibilities. But first, a distractive countermeasure to hedge my bet.

There are, believe it or not, "Christian libertarians," conservatives who believe that the scope of the law "should be limited to acts of assault, theft and fraud." Such ridiculousness is par for the course with libertarians. Like hermit crabs from hell, they're so obsessed with "freedom" (a twisted version that always involves something that feels good to them but deeply harms someone else) that they'll "embrace" any jury-rigged bullshit ideology that might serve as a bony protective shell. Their first duty is to their own wallets; everyone else can either sink or pull themselves up by their bootstraps (if they have any). As a Quora.com user put it, a "libertarian Christian" would somehow need to possess a desire to "step up with some big-time voluntary charity toward those less fortunate than themselves ... Unfortunately, it is the rare Libertarian who is anywhere near as dedicated to voluntary charity as Christianity would require them to be."

Without a doubt, Christian libertarianism is an oxymoron, regardless of the two world views' overlapping preferences for, among other things, a planet governed by anything other than humans (God in the case of the Fundies; Scrooge McDuck in the case of libertarians). At its core, libertarianism is fiercely secular, which means that true libertarians don't care if God's laws are broken as long as it doesn't interfere with their freedom to make a buck. But that's precisely what happened on July 9, 2021, when trans figure Caitlyn Jenner, at the time a Republican candidate running for California's governorship, was chased out of a Conservative Political Action Conference (CPAC) in Dallas, Texas, by a camera-wielding man who heckled her unmercifully until she fled to a limousine. "Bruce," the dingbat hollered, addressing her by her trans-culture-associated dead name, "what do you think about the stuff they're teaching in the schools regarding the LGBTQs?" followed by, "Don't forget about Jesus!" The attack (obviously perpetrated by a Christian or a moderately talented liberal troll) was ignored by most Republican politicians and pundits, who just wanted it to go away.[20]

But not all of them. Alt-lite personality Tomi Lahren (famous for her bon mot "I'm not a big 'reader'") tweeted, "There's no room for your hate in the America First movement. We believe in freedom and we believe in limited government. The way she chooses to live her personal life harms you in no way!" Not to be outdone, former Donald Trump data and digital advisor Brad Parscale (who may have chosen the moment to try to redeem himself after video of his experiencing an unsightly personal meltdown had surfaced and gone as viral as something can get) tweeted, among other things, "Incidents like this create a dark cloud over the party." Well duh.

Naturally, voices of devout blockheadedness also chimed in, like Marjorie Taylor Greene, who commented ... well, let's not.

The Republicans' Christian contingent may have nodded their heads in agreement with the interloper, but there's no way any libertarian would have been happy about that little kerfuffle. In general, libertarians are haughty, solipsistic ideological chameleons who'll say anything to smuggle themselves into leftist groups and try to convert them to free market greedism. Jaws dropped worldwide when it was revealed that a "libertarian wing" had somehow materialized within the Democratic Socialists of America, a Scandinavian-economy-minded, Bernie Sanders-worshiping organization that apparently forgot to tape a "no libertarians" sign to their door (I don't have the patience to try to unscramble their, ah, ideas, but if you want to shed a few IQ points without chugging a gallon of Jägermeister, go marvel at them at https://dsa-lsc.org).

Anyway, back at the 2021 CPAC, you have to know for a fact that there were some "neutral" libertarian product vendors at the conference who would have loved for Jenner to stick around and spend some time with them, maybe chat with convention-goers in front of their display tables to get people's eyes on whatever they were selling, like books about how all-Dorito-diets provide inner-city schoolchildren's bodies with lots of newly discovered Omega-3 fatty acids or whatever. But no, she was gone, cast out by a self-appointed Witchfinder General. O Fortuna, opportunity (and liberty and stuff) lost!

The mainstream liberal media also lost an opportunity. MSNBC and CNN could have weaponized the incident against the GOP if they'd spent the subsequent few weeks sending microphone-wielding reporters out to pelt distracted-looking Republican lawmakers with questions about whether LGBTQIAs were welcome in their Tent of Freedom. If they had any brains, those news channels would have deployed their preferred weapon of the day, rallying their flat-screen-glued troops with preposterously hyperbolic "Breaking News" chyrons ("Tucker Carlson: 'Caitlyn Is Still My Favorite Male Athlete'") every 30 seconds.

But they didn't, not that there aren't still plenty of ways for the GOP to tear itself apart at the seams. Like the Democrats, the GOP has been a dead party walking for years since losing its intellectual leader, William F. Buckley Jr., in 2008. In the 1960s, Buckley, leveraging the powerful influence of his magazine, *National Review* (a publication that promoted the so-called "fusionism" of traditional conservatives and libertarians), was successful in banishing the most unhinged right-wingers of the era to the sidelines: Ayn Rand, the John Birch Society, George Wallace, etc. Upon retiring from the magazine in 1990, Buckley said that one of his greatest achievements was bringing about "the absolute exclusion of anything anti-Semitic or kooky from the conservative movement."

Nowadays, the lunatics are in full charge of the Republican asylum. The party, having been forced to accept its new role as the Cult of Trump, is currently led by demented liars like current RNC chair Michael Whatley (a South Carolinian who sat in on the December 2020 phone call on which Trump urged Georgia Secretary of State Brad Raffensperger to "find" the votes he needed to win the state), constant fixture Reince Priebus (Ronna McDaniel's RNC Chair predecessor, a major supporter of the anti-taxation Tea Party movement) and a supporting cast of hundreds who need no introduction, all of whom portray tertiary cartoon villains. Any half-informed liberal could rattle off a list of their 50 least-favorites.

In the end, however, regardless of how ideologically divided the right may appear on paper, it's only the left that fixates on its differences. Some believe that the rift in the left is partly a socioeconomic subclass thing.

X. The "PMC?" The "Brahmin Left?" The "Knowledge Worker Class?"

Your basic, off-the-shelf Marxist regards the proverbial "class war" as a conflict between two distinct classes, business owners (the bourgeoisie) and workers (the proletariat). Molds are made to be broken, though, and some leftist intellectuals believe it's important to go a bit deeper and examine the hierarchical subdivisions that exist within the aggregate working class. That subject comes up now and then in Fifth Estate media discourse.

Anyone who's ever put in a 40-hour workweek knows that most workplaces have pecking orders beyond the owner/worker dynamic. At the very top of the labor hierarchy is the upper management class, or "managerial class." The latter term comes to us from the 1941 book *The Managerial Revolution: What is Happening in the World* by James Burnham. A Trotskyist turned American conservative, Burnham described the managerial class as a subset of highest-level workers tasked with keeping businesses in business. They're responsible for such things as handling the tasks associated with the technical direction and coordination of all production processes and components, including the workforce itself. According to Burnham, the managerial class is paid to perform all the *workaday duties* of business owners while not actually owning the means of production. In other words, unlike the owner class, the managerial class of Burnham's day had precarity (job insecurity). They received nice paychecks but didn't own the places where they worked.

Burnham reasoned that all the baked-in worker uncertainty and the absence of owner-level authority would someday drive the managerial class to, as Burnham admirer George Orwell (yes, *that* George Orwell) interpreted, "eliminate the old capitalist class, crush the working class, and so organize society that all power and economic privilege remain in their own hands." It would be up to them to defeat the owner class, Burnham believed, because everyday workers were too disorganized to ever band together and pressure the ownership class into sharing profits with workers and such.

Burnham had become disenchanted with communism over the fact that the Russian Revolution had failed to produce a genuinely socialist work environment (in other words, one in which there are no class distinctions on shop floors, an environment where all workers share resources and profits). Instead, it had produced Josef Stalin's bureaucracy, which joined the rest of the world in growing a new managerial class that controlled the means of production indirectly.

Burnham was by no means the only 20th-century figure to abandon the left over the betrayals of Stalinism. As trans activist Sybil Davis noted, Robert Oppenheimer became so cynical over it that he joined the right, eventually building the ultimate tool of capitalist "lesser evilism," the atomic bomb.[21]

Predictably, today's right-wingers falsely prop up Burnham's perfectly understandable rejection of Stalin's "proxy capitalist" cabal of good old boys as proof that he was a born right-winger who never believed socialism could ever really work. Along with sneakily trying to conflate Marxism with "managerialism," Charlemagne Institute editor Edward Welsch offered as evidence this Burnham quote: "The 'managerial economy' is the basis for a new kind of [exploitive] class society."[22] That's true, of course, but come on, Stalin was the one leading the faux-socialist charge Burnham was complaining about, not Andrew Carnegie.

I view Burnham's "managerial class" as nowadays being incorrectly lumped in with the "Professional Managerial Class" (PMC), the highly skilled, college-educated, politically liberal-centrist segment of the general labor force. That subset has been examined and written about extensively for decades, which, as you'd expect, has led to confusion over exactly what it is.

The husband-and-wife team of Barbara and John Ehrenreich coined the phrase "Professional Managerial Class" in a 1977 essay for *Radical America*.[23] At the time, the Ehrenreichs viewed the PMC as an affluent group of laborers that included not just degreed, well-off specialists and assorted other professionals but also their upper management bosses. By that measure, there's a truckload of gray area in the PMC distinction, which has made for much discussion fodder in academic and Fifth Estate circles.

By and large, Marxists tend to view the PMC as being no different than any other subset of the composite working class and thus they hold that any time spent arguing about them or their motives diverts attention from the only class struggle that matters, the one between business owners and workers. In fact, some say that despite fitting the PMC description due to having advanced degrees and such, some PMCs aren't actually PMCs at all, such as low-paid public-school teachers. Workers in that group, Amber A'Lee Frost observed, "don't actually manage their students so much as provide a service for them, and are managed almost completely by non-teacher administrations."[24]

Mostly, the fuss over PMCs revolves around the fact that, as a class, they gravitate to mainstream liberal establishment groupthink and that their unshakable faith in the Democrats and center-left media propagandists (MSNBC et al) is a deterrent to labor solidarity. Accurate as that may be, Frost contends that they'd support pretty much any worker-empowerment movement that gained real traction, given that the class is, as Frost puts it, part of "the cart, not the horse."

That's a possibility; if a few MSNBC hosts were suddenly to shift their focus away from Donald Trump's boundless horribleness and toward the myriad discomforts suffered by anyone who spends most of their waking hours working for a paycheck, there's a good chance they'd take their low-fat salted-caramel cappuccinos and jump right on the bandwagon.

Like every other intellectual chew-toy eggheads chomp down on, the PMC is known by different names. Some refer to it as the "Brahmin Left," a label invented by French economist Thomas Piketty, whose major claim to fame is his 2014 bestselling book, *Capital in the Twenty-First Century*, a 700-page doorstop in which he comes to the mind-blowing conclusion that people who come into huge amounts of money usually invest it to increase their wealth instead of donating it to orphans.[25]

Since the passing of Barbara Ehrenreich (the most well-known of the couple), the tradition of analyzing and critiquing the PMC has been taken up by such figures as University of Pennsylvania professor Adolph Reed Jr. and Catherine Liu, a professor at the University of California, Irvine. Liu's 2021 book, *Virtue Hoarders: The Case Against the Professional Managerial Class*, expands on the Ehrenreichs' ideas, characterizing the PMC as a class of elite, well-paid workers who "labor in a world of performative identity and virtue signaling, publicizing an ability to do ordinary things in fundamentally superior ways."

Farther leftists view the PMC as a toxic component of the "neoliberal problem" and maintain that the PMC's role as the de facto "dictatorship of political correctness" is leading the country's left wing in the wrong direction. PMCs focus their rage on *symptoms* of the system's failure—issues of racial equality and such—rather than the political, economic, and legal causes of it.

Some would say PMCs are so content with their lot that they oppose any changes to the socioeconomic landscape. Their jobs are cushy, rarely if ever requiring them to perform manual labor. Life is good for them, so in the end, most PMCs don't feel any urgent need to "join in solidarity" with the broad labor movement.

That's a grave mistake on their part. In 2013, Barbara Ehrenreich revised her assessment of the PMC, conceding that times had changed since the 1970s. She noted that, as a class, the PMC is slowly being stripped of its power, a feeling with which workers in the US manufacturing sector have been agonizingly familiar for decades. She wrote, "[It] came as a shock to many when, in the 2000s, businesses began to avail themselves of new high-speed transmission technologies to outsource professional functions. Hospitals sent a growing variety of tasks—such as reading X-rays, MRIs and echocardiograms—to be performed by lower-paid physicians in India. Law firms outsourced document review, review of litigation emails, and legal research to English-speakers abroad. The publishing industry sent out editing, graphic design, and—for textbooks—even parts of content creation. Corporations undercut U.S.-based engineers and computer professionals by outsourcing product design and development."[26]

Note that Ehrenreich wrote those words long before the recent boom in artificial intelligence, which threatens to replace many professionals specializing in technical, artistic and other functions today. It's inevitable that no matter how well-paid they are or how secure they feel, more and more PMCs will be stripped of their duties, which will be performed by automated processes or sent overseas to be handled by low-cost labor. And there'll be nothing they can do about it. They are, after all, laborers, not capitalists.

In the foreseeable future, when the capitalists' money-saving tanks really get rolling, the PMCs' university pedigrees won't save them from feeling the numbing dread of precarity. As is, many older tech workers are familiar with it. Like the janitor who knows there'll come a day when they can't bend down to snatch a piece of trash off the floor, the techie PMC has an "expiration date." The moment they graduate from college, the clock begins counting off the minutes toward their degree's obsolescence, when their skill set will no longer meet the needs of their managers. At that point they must either abandon their career or undergo extensive "retraining," regardless of how little enthusiasm they have for doing so.

Let's not forget academia, as long as we're gazing into the blackest depths. For years, the tradition of tenure has been under assault by "free speech"-thumping conservatives. One upshot of that has been the widespread replacement of full-time faculty by low-paid adjunct professors, which resulted in double-digit declines in full-timers being offered tenure. That trend has prompted many non-tenured educators to give up their careers.[27]

Meanwhile, for employees in Burnham's "managerial class," the line between worker and capitalist is blurring. While precarity continues creeping up on the PMCs, the managerial class is fast transcending any "proxy capitalist" designation. Increasingly, they're workers who double as board members, turning Burnham's prediction of "the takeover of capitalism by the managerial class" on its head. As Ehrenreich explained, "College-educated professionals seem to have been fully integrated into their corporate enterprises—to the point where stock options have effectively transformed middle- and upper-level executives into 'owners.'"

Economic precarity isn't the only thing affecting PMCs negatively. Critics assert that PMCs become increasingly alienated just for blithely enjoying the peace that comes from their being culturally "woke" (and well-off). "People getting woke in twenty-first century industrialized societies often experience themselves as profoundly disconnected from others," wrote author-activist Cynthia Kaufman in 2019. "Coming to consciousness in a toxic culture of individualism and consumerism can make it difficult to find the next necessary steps to unraveling structures of power: engaging in effective action."[28]

I'd submit that genuine, effective action won't come without solidarity among all workers. Toward that, Liu doesn't fully concur with Frost's contention that the PMC would ever join the rest of the working classes under any circumstances (if the lower classes would even have them). It's all uncertain, I'd say, considering that the PMC has snubbed the lower classes for so long that Trump and his army of alt-right Borgs had no trouble assimilating them. "I think the alt-right appeals to working-class alienation and anger," Liu told me. "The PMC is alienated but uses self-discipline and liberal false consciousness to channel their outrage into hatred of working-class people, whom they see as irrational. The working class is the disorganized *majority* [my emphasis], and they respond to the status quo by rejecting liberalism and even democracy, which they see as hopelessly corrupted by special interests." So what's the bad news? "They're not wrong."

Culture war issues seem to have a dangerously narcotic effect on PMCs, distracting them from their own precarity.

The result has been that they appear to be more concerned with matters of decorum, such as Donald Trump's unsightly presence in the political arena, than the fact that his ascension was a cartoonishly predictable by-product of the system itself. Meanwhile, as they brandish the word "fascism" at anything they don't like, one irony escapes them: The system under which they thrive was initially put into place by the same sort of propaganda apparatus (and, more to the point, blindly supported by the same sort of liberal mindset) that didn't simply allow Benito Mussolini to come to power but, as economist Clara Mattei has posited, actively encouraged it.[29] Thus, many—by no means all—PMCs are ideologically adrift, imagining themselves to be "morally responsible citizens." Placing their faith in the mainstream media and adhering to the "capital order," they remain completely distracted from or willfully oblivious to the increasingly lopsided class war between the First and Third Estates.

Denying their own exploitation by getting into wars of words with people on the internet does allow PMCs to feel as if they've helped to accomplish something from time to time, such as when this or that minority figure is "allowed" into the upper echelons of the system by securing a position of power. Such victories—"the first trans person on such-and-so-state's Supreme Court"; "the first Black mayor of this former Jim Crow city"—are, of course, important advances. Still, some dismiss those rare "individualist capitalism" wins as Band-Aids affixed to mortal wounds, providing nothing more substantive than a fleeting opportunity for all the other members of the lucky person's demographic to celebrate for a moment before going back to their labors and economic uncertainty.

It can certainly seem as though persuading liberals to join

with the more socialist left would be as difficult a task as convincing white, working-class Fox News addicts that Donald Trump isn't really their friend. A lot of liberals will never forgive Bernie Sanders for what they perceive as his followers' having a hand in Hillary Clinton's loss in the 2016 presidential contest (it was actually overconfidence that did her in; Clinton assumed she had the states of Pennsylvania, Wisconsin, and Michigan locked up but lost them all by not spending enough campaign time in them). Moreover, some liberals are as opposed to socialism as card-carrying right-wingers. Their disdain for anything that appears vaguely Marxist assuredly extends to the class struggle. In my online travels, I quickly found out that liberal PMCs hate talking about their class's socioeconomic advantages more than just about anything. Where the socialist's battle cry is "No war but class war," the liberal's is "Don't engage in both-sidesism," meaning "don't foment conflict between different left-leaning coteries, even when the Democrats have just done something to prove once again that they don't care about the class war," which, the Fourth Estate dog-whistles, is an express route to Republicans' winning elections. They hate it. If you're on Twitter and feel like trolling, say, a liberal human resources director who fires lots of angry tweets at "communists" who refuse to vote for Democrats, ask them innocently why top Democratic lawmakers like Nancy Pelosi supported repealing the SALT (State and Local Tax) cap, which would disproportionately benefit high-income taxpayers (as well as violate the principle of tax neutrality). Prepare to be instantly blocked if you pull a stunt like that.

It's not the PMC's fault that they sometimes overreact when someone points out their level of privilege, given that terrifying levels of precarity are alien to them. For years, scientists have known that social class directly influences how deeply one cares about the well-being of others. It boils down to how free and independent we feel, as one study found: The less we rely on others for help to survive, the less we care about what others are going through.[30] The scale of selfishness (and greed) peaks at the billionaire class, of course, a group thickly populated by people possessed of disturbed personalities that psychologists have described as a "dark triad" of dysfunction combining elements of Machiavellianism, psychopathy, and narcissism.[31]

As well as occasionally revealing themselves to be a bit tone-deaf to the difficulties experienced by their fellow citizens, center-left PMCs are staunch believers in the pillars of the "liberal class" (loosely defined by Chris Hedges as a demographic whose members put faith in "liberal institutions," such as churches, the mainstream media, the Democratic Party, labor unions, and academia), so much so that it confounds people who only rarely consume news and political opinion from Fourth Estate sources.

At this point, Hedges should add America's intelligence agencies to his list of liberal class institutions, particularly the Central Intelligence Agency. PMCs began venerating the Agency in the wake of the 2016 presidential election, probably because the mainstream liberal media was working hard to convince them that the Agency's "top secret" efforts would lead to Donald Trump's arrest, which, of course, never happened.

That was an odd development. It's not as though the CIA has ever actually earned any respect, least of all from the college-educated liberal crowd. As Florida journalist River Page wrote in 2021, "Historically, the agency has been more adept at cultural manipulation than intelligence gathering (see the Bay of Pigs Invasion, the failure to predict the Iranian Revolution, the failure to predict the Yom Kippur War, the failure to predict the Soviet Invasion of Afghanistan, the failure to predict 9/11, the faulty intelligence pointing to the existence of [weapons of mass destruction] in Iraq, and most recently, miscalculating the strength of Ashraf Ghani's government in Afghanistan)."[32] One item Page cites is particularly revealing: the only American demographic that adamantly believes Lee Harvey Oswald acted alone in assassinating John F. Kennedy is white college graduates.

Another thing PMCs should consider regarding the CIA is that it's a redundant, unnecessary institution. Every time a microphone got anywhere near him, Chalmers Johnson urged that the Agency be closed[33] and its duties handed over to the U.S. State Department's Bureau of Intelligence and Research (INR). The INR's budget is open for public scrutiny (in contrast to the intelligence agencies, all of which have budgets that are kept entirely secret from Congress), and it's staffed by career government professionals (unlike the CIA, whose practice of hiring highly paid outside contractors led to the leak of intelligence secrets by Edward Snowden).

On the other hand, PMCs do have the CIA to thank for "woke culture." Page posits that the CIA *invented* wokeness as a "dialect of power," a way for upper-middle-class citizens to differentiate themselves from the rabble. That is to say, where upper-middle-class citizens in the mid-20th century took to affecting a faux-British accent to signal their privileged status, today's upper-middle-class citizens speak fluent "woke," often using phrases like "cultural appropriation" and neologisms like "microagression" (defined as an interaction between people of different races, cultures, or genders in which a member of a "victim group" is subjected to subtle but powerful attacks that the attacker is unaware they're carrying out).

Indeed, since at least the 1950s, the CIA has insinuated *itself* as a model of diversity and wokeness by doing such things as investing heavily in the Congress of Cultural Freedom, a German-born propaganda effort that journalist James Petras has described as "a kind of cultural NATO" that was "completely free to defend Western cultural and political values, attack 'Stalinist totalitarianism' and to tiptoe gently around U.S. racism and imperialism," all toward an anticommunist, pro-free market effort.[34]

It's funny; many well-enough-heeled liberals jump on the spy stuff like puppies to a trough of Hamburger Helper, rarely if ever stopping to think about why the intelligence agencies might want the liberal media to "let citizens know" about a particular thing in the first place. The script has flipped: the educated liberal class, a segment of humanity that at one time stood as a Keep On Truckin' hippie vanguard denouncing imperial chicanery in general, has become a chimerical petit-bourgeoisie that trusts the Central Intelligence Agency more than it does Ralph Nader, its former hero.

Anyway, despite their being CIA-approved and mildly rich, most PMCs do indeed feel some sense of precarity, but the dread they experience is elusive. For PMCs who fancy themselves as capitalists, the television comedy series *Schitt's Creek* is at once comforting and terrifying: wealthy married couple suddenly find themselves flat broke, they're forced to resort to drastic measures to survive, mortally embarrassing high jinks ensue. At some level, all high earners can relate. While earning big bucks at the height of my software programming career, my concerns mostly revolved around unimportant things, such as, "What restaurant should we try next," never anything remotely like, "Will we be able to pay the rent this month." But precarity bubbled underneath, manifesting in my subconscious. Many nights, just before falling asleep, I'd be jolted into full wakefulness by hypnagogic hallucinations in which I suddenly imagined myself sitting at the edge of a city skyscraper, with no exit in sight and nowhere to go but down. I have severe acrophobia, and those sudden, vivid panic attacks jolted me out of near-sleep more times than I can count. But past that stuff, the "worries" that haunted my waking life revolved around trivial "rich people problems." Even so, back then, my political sensibilities didn't revolve around "woke" issues as much as systemic ones. I was always big into underground journalism, punk-culture agitprop (any SubGeniuses out there?) and gravitated to books like Bob Woodward's *Veil: The Secret Wars of the CIA*, so I didn't trust the CIA as far as I could throw it. To be honest, when all the culture war drama got into high gear on Tumblr and whatnot in the 2010s, I didn't get worked up about it, figuring it was all just a CIA operation intended to keep people distracted and divided.

But is wokeness really such a terrible thing?

XI. "Wokeness" and Prefiguration

The term "woke" first appeared in a 1962 *New York Times Magazine* article written by William Melvin Kelley, who intended it to mock the appropriation of African-American Vernacular English (AAVE) by privileged white beatniks. Nowadays, it denotes intolerance of intolerance, demands made by white liberals for respect and equal rights for any citizen who doesn't typically reap any of the benefits enjoyed by straight white males.

That's obviously an admirable position. However, many on the farther left challenge its seriousness. Author Chris Hedges criticized wokeness in his 2010 book *Death of the Liberal Class*. "[T]he campaign for cultural diversity," he wrote, "does little to perturb the power elite. It does not challenge economic or political structures that are rapidly disempowering the working class."

More pointed complaints have come from elsewhere. In a January 15, 2020, YouTube discussion of her book on labor organizing, *A Collective Bargain*, Jane McAlevey (who more or less replaced Saul Alinsky as the leader of the labor movement and, like Alinsky, isn't/wasn't a devout Marxist by any stretch) complained that one of the audiences she wanted to see becoming more class conscious was "liberals in America who think we can solve the problem [of the declining presence of labor unions] by empowering everyone *but* workers in the workplace."[35] She quickly added, "By the way, I'm not denigrating the topics [addressed by wokeness]. All of that is essential." The message, however, is clear: liberals, in her judgment, appear to be more interested in virtue signaling and maintaining political decorum than working toward universal equalitarianism.

That's a variation of the same complaint lodged by progressives for decades. In their 1972 book *A Populist Manifesto*, Jack Newfield and Jeff Greenfield remarked, "For a generation we have watched liberals gain more power and display less liberalism. It began in the early 1950s as liberal politicians and intellectuals dropped everything else to prove their anti-communism. Later in the decade, exhaustion and boredom set in, and political issues were subordinated to sociological concerns with affluence, organization men, suburbia, and mass culture." Cut to now, when some view the woke, pro-Democratic mindset as a lazy, socioeconomically oblivious one that's only a few degrees more "leftist" than that of the average Trump voter.

However. Comfortably situated liberals shouldn't be rudely accused of being insincere in their support for equal rights for minorities, and they're not bad people simply because they thrive in America's economic system. The fact is that they're like any other economic demographic in that they obsess over the things to which they're exposed every day, which, in their case, is, in the main, propaganda diffused by mainstream news outlets owned by corporations and oligarchs who'd prefer that their own misdeeds go unnoticed. Some liberals watch MSNBC all day long, the way sports fans keep their TVs tuned to ESPN whether it's broadcasting a football game or a cornhole tournament. Distractive chyrons (actual example: "Ted Cruz: I Don't Think We Should Have Grown Men In Bathrooms With Little Girls") serve up a bottomless banquet of anger-riling gruel, their random outrage-nuggets examined ad infinitum on-screen by dweebish, anachronistic political celebrities and retired, long-out-of-the-loop experts whose only talent is the ability to riff forever on the minutiae surrounding all the "troubling developments."

But past all that, if we look at wokeness more closely, we see that it's a form of "prefiguration," which has, ironically, become an important staple of progressive and socialist movements.

Loquaciously defined by anarchist writers Paul Raekstad and Eivind Dahl as "the deliberate experimental implementation of desired future social relations and practices in the here-and-now," prefiguration, or "prefigurative politics," is the practice by which ideological or sociopolitical groups engage in a "dress rehearsal" for everyday life in a future America where the system's workings are informed by equalitarian, as opposed to neoliberal, philosophy. Prefiguration is endorsed by such thinkers as "social movement historian" Chris Dixon, whose 2014 book *Another Politics* gave a name to the set of principles and traditions observed by a broad, intersectional cohort of such anti-authoritarian protest movements as Occupy and Black feminism. Commonly seen online in spaces like Twitter, the practice addresses the question, "Which needs to be transformed first, society or people?" Prefiguration points to the latter, advising us to *be* the change, to recognize and honor the strategies, methods and challenges activist movements have in common while we wait for real-world change to come.

Prefiguration is a power- and solidarity-building method, encouraging movements to function and interact as though their mutual enemy—the system—is a lot less hostile than it is, so their members can eventually step outside their bubbles and share what they've learned with other movements. When they feel confident doing that, movements will learn that they all have many things in common. They'll come to realize that the trade unionist is no more the enemy of the trans activist than the climate activist is the enemy of the prison abolitionist. No movement is more important than another. The left cannot cohere until most or all movements agree to cooperate with each other.

We're seeing more prefiguration every day. For example, worker-owned businesses, which, by definition, prefigure socialist workplaces while existing within a capitalist framework. There's also the now-common practice of "mutual aid," in which strangers contribute financial support to people in need without expecting anything in return. That custom prefigures a society where the social safety net focuses on real, immediate needs, not how much money a citizen has in the bank or paid into Social Security over their lifetime.

Prefiguration has also been applied to money. Members of Rohan Grey's Modern Money Network are expected to contribute some of their time to the organization, working on various projects or everyday tasks. The hours they spend on those labors are paid for in credits—not dollars—that reduce their membership fees and/or come with other perks.

As much as people may disdain wokeness, it too is a prefigurative mindset. It expects and demands tolerance for people whose race, ethnicity and/or gender identification or sexual orientation differs from ours. And it has succeeded to some extent. In the real world, women and minorities still live with systemic unfairness, but you rarely find such ignorance tolerated in online spaces. It simply isn't done. Blowback and/or shunning are instantaneous. For that reason alone, one could say that perhaps the culture wars of the Aughts weren't fought for nothing.

Along with prefiguration, many other pragmatic ideas for "fixing the system from within" can be found online and are worth investigating. Plenty of concerned citizens would jump at the chance to get more involved and see all the time they spend discussing and debating politics and such on social media result in Actually Accomplishing Something. Since that's the case, the next thing to explore for our purposes is whether all the debate and interpersonal interaction that are conducted online could lead to a unified left.

The short answer, if you're speed-reading this, is yes. But perhaps the most important step toward solidarity is the broad left's coming to understand the mechanics of our socioeconomic system so that we can understand its true nature and spread the truth about it everywhere. "Know your enemy," Sun Tzu said. At the moment, collectively, we don't know it at all. Let's work on that.

5

It's Really, Truly, Madly The Class War, Folks

I. Economics: It's a Hit!

"Macroeconomics" (the branch of economics that takes a helicopter view of the performance, structure, behavior, and decision-making of an economy as a whole) became a white-hot topic within Fifth Estate circles and the online left in the early 2020s. A phalanx of economists and other experts emerged from the woodwork, constructing platforms to explain (or at least try to explain) their thoughts on what historical events and precedents led to our increasingly miserable era of "austerity capitalism" (a term proffered by Italian economist Clara Mattei, describing America's current economic system; she avoids using the word "neoliberalism" because it implies that there's ever been such a thing as a "good version of capitalism"). Some offered radically sensible ideas on how to make the economy more livable for all; others presented compelling research they'd conducted that revealed the thinking that guided the construction of the system. Collectively, their efforts helped usher in what I'd call the Fifth Estate's current "golden age," a period during which independent journalists have enjoyed free rein to report on uncomfortable truths to which the mainstream Fourth Estate turns a blind eye.

Most of the rebellious, anti-establishment economists we'll look at here are or have been frequent guests on popular podcasts, video streams and the like over the last few years, rarely if ever receiving mainstream media coverage. Whether we call them "Fifth Estate economists," "punk economists," or the more traditional "heterodox economists," their views of our economic system differ greatly from those of mainstream economists. Some host their own independent media shows, like Jennifer Doleac's *Probable Causation* podcast (focused on "the economics of crime and discrimination, with particular interests in prisoner reentry and on policies that affect public safety"); Mark Blyth's *Rhodes Center Podcast*, in which the personable Scot interviews various experts on a broad range of economic history and thought; and Richard Wolff's nationally syndicated *Economic Update*.

Until recently, leftists generally operated under the vague understanding that all but our wealthiest citizens are routinely exploited and that's simply how things are. But as the corporate-greed-crazed 2020s dawned and the need for change grew more urgent, many leftists felt the need to understand what actually makes the system tick and what might be done to improve it. The people's desire for deeper knowledge was of course driven by an ever-escalating onrush of horrors: a government-bungled pandemic, signs of imminent climate collapse, and increasingly absurd levels of inflation and wealth inequality among other economic injustices. Suddenly, en masse, the "too online" hoi polloi held their noses, overcame their aversion to the (not horribly) complicated subject of economics (the "dismal science," as Scottish essayist Thomas Carlyle once described it) and became grimly determined to understand its components, mechanisms and history.

The Fifth Estate's reporting on those economists fascinates many online leftists, particularly progressives. They've looked on helplessly as their economic power—in terms of both negotiating for fair wages and, axiomatically, the ability to buy the goods and services they want and need—has been drastically reduced.

People are broke, in other words. Consumer debt and bankruptcy filings began skyrocketing during and after the COVID-19 pandemic's spread. But even before COVID, the writing was already on the wall for heavily indebted consumers, given that debt becomes inescapable once it's gotten out of hand (according to American economist/historian Michael Hudson, even the ancient Babylonians knew that any debt that's loaned at a 20 percent compound interest rate doubles in five years, quadruples in 10, and so on). And while we're at it, "after" is the wrong word to use when discussing COVID-19.

Unsurprisingly, electing a new U.S. president in 2020 didn't solve the COVID problem. Obviously forbidden by his corporate donors to shut down America's economy completely for a couple of months (nor mandate that all wage labor be performed by employees at home when and where possible) until COVID could be controlled and eliminated, Biden followed Trump's lead in surrendering to the virus, allowing it to run rampant and become endemic. At this 2024 writing, it's as common a fatal risk to American workers as car accidents during daily commutes.

Citizens were and are aware that COVID has never been properly managed by the U.S. government. In July 2022, Gallup found that 70% of Americans believed the pandemic wasn't over. Despite (or perhaps because of) Biden's vow to bring things "back to normal," that number fell to only 51% in February 2023.[1] That's of course a slippery statistic, given that when a disease is still in its "pandemic" phase—whether through its "novel" (still-misunderstood and possibly mutative) status or through the absence of any vaccine (like dengue in Pakistan and chickenpox in Mexico)—there's still hope for controlling it. COVID, however, has reached its less sexy sounding "endemic phase." It's become a permanent, everyday threat, which is partly our own fault as citizens. Most independent epidemiologists believe that if most Americans had been vaccinated against COVID-19 when the vaccines first rolled out, it might not have become endemic. But as of May 2023, 18.7 percent of Americans had still not received a single dose of any COVID vaccine.

Popular consensus on how COVID-19 should be handled was and still is roundly ignored by the country's leadership. But in the end, the virus has become just another unsettling item to add to what's grown to be a very long list of citizens' grievances regarding the establishment's handling of economic matters.

II. And Now, Here it is, Your Listicle of Doom

American citizens' dissatisfaction with the country's economic system has risen to the boiling point owing to many factors. Consider:

– In a February 2023 poll, Gallup found that no group of American voters was satisfied with the government's efforts to deal with poverty and homelessness. A paltry 11 percent of Democratic voters expressed approval with their handling of it, Republican voters 17 percent, and independents 16.[2]

– In 2018, Gallup revealed that 66% of Americans were very (43%) or somewhat (23%) dissatisfied with the way income and wealth are distributed in the US, as opposed to 32% who replied that they were very (7%) or somewhat (25%)

satisfied.³ In the meantime, regardless of how screwed up the economy is, Americans do have their priorities straight: According to a 2023 Gallup poll, 52% of participants said that solving the climate crisis is more important than working to expand economic growth (43%).⁴

– The US federal minimum wage, adjusted for inflation, is around 40% lower than it was in 1970.⁵ Many events transpired during the 1970s and 1980s that went on to greatly reduce the quality of life for working families in America, the Powell memo being just one of them.

– American consumer debt is presently at crisis levels. Student loan balances are particularly burdensome on Millennials; they're a stressor with which Generation Z is also becoming alarmingly familiar. Seven percent of US citizens with high levels of college debt have considered committing suicide over it.⁶ Meanwhile, college is free in Finland, Denmark, Ireland, Iceland, Norway, Sweden and Mexico.

But wait a minute, stop the listicle. How did a student loan crisis happen in the world's richest country?

III. School's Out (of the Question)

Whether or not you believe that the Democrats' efforts to lower college tuition costs and/or forgive student debt are maniacally blocked at every turn by Republicans, the Democratic Party hasn't done much to convince younger voters that it sympathizes with their concerns.

They've laid a few eggs for sure. During a 2018 interview with Patt Morrison of the *Los Angeles Times*, an overly comfortable Joe Biden uttered a remark that was as recklessly divisive as Hillary Clinton's 2016 blanket dismissal of Republican voters as a "basket of deplorables." The subject had shifted to the financial challenges young people face concerning college costs. Instead of mindfully sympathizing with the cohort—which was trying to wrap its head around education costs that were, along with the costs of health care and housing, five times higher than they'd been just a few decades ago—Biden sputtered, "I have no empathy for it. Give me a break." He then immediately (and oddly) began touting the activism of the Vietnam era, implicitly urging young people to become more politically involved or something. "Because here's the deal guys, we [the baby boom generation] decided we were gonna change the world. And we did. We finished the civil rights movement in the first stage. The women's movement [came next]." That was a bit of an exaggeration, as *Newsweek*'s Summer Meza pointed out; the struggles for civil rights and women's rights are far from over.[7]

There's been no shortage of debate over whether the U.S. government could or should forgive student debt. The fact is that it could be zeroed out owing to the *nature* of America's currency, which we'll get into later. But even without that advantage, all but a tiny percentage of federal student loan debt is already figured into the national debt, meaning that its total would rise only slightly, mostly in the long term, if all federal student loans were forgiven.[8]

Yet, both sides of the duopoly refuse to take that step, citing economic dangers that don't exist. Researcher Indigo Olivier diagnosed the problem in *The Guardian*: "The US's partiality toward abstract economic concepts like 'deficit' and 'inflation' ignores the reality of protracted human suffering and boils down to how economic health is measured."

One rather alarming macro issue this all brings up is that neither side of the duopoly seems eager to cultivate an educated workforce. While the Republicans have been anti-education since at least Reagan's time, the Democrats since the election of Bill Clinton have mostly offered empty platitudes, advising citizens to obtain college degrees "somehow" while doing almost nothing at the political level to make them affordable.

In 2023, three years into his first term as president, Biden finally acted on a 2020 campaign promise to forgive up to $20,000 each on all student loans, but his executive order was promptly blocked by the Supreme Court.[9] Biden's delaying the process (as well as the program's convoluted maze of "means testing" hoops) was puzzling to many. Critics brought up the time in 2005 when, as a Delaware senator, Biden himself voted to pass the Bankruptcy Abuse Prevention and Consumer Protection Act, which made it nearly impossible for student loan borrowers to have their debts settled and erased by declaring bankruptcy[10] (in fairness, Biden stated that he never liked the bill; he'd offered amendments to it while being fully aware that it was going to pass regardless of his vote).

Either way, as the weeks and months of the early 2020s dragged on, with Biden canceling only a tiny fraction of student debt, some observers were dumbfounded by the administration's hesitating to act with any of the authority it possessed. "They actually have immense power to do the right thing," Astra Taylor, co-founder of the Debt Collective, a debtors' union organization, told the *New Republic* in June of 2022. "I think it would be good for the soul of the Department of Education if it actually was about education and it wasn't actually one of the country's biggest banks and biggest debt collectors."[11]

IV. The Old Folks Need Homes

The Millennial generation isn't the only age demographic mired in despair. The baby boomer generation (born 1946–1964) has its own financial nightmares, the scariest of which is a retirement catastrophe that's likewise set its sights on Generation X (born 1965–1980).

It's generally thought that the chunk of money needed to finance an adequate retirement (80% of yearly income) is nearly double what it was just a few decades ago. As of 2022, a woman born in 1967 and hoping to retire in 2032 will need to have saved 11.5% of their net pay, year in and year out from age 25 on and invested those savings in a target-date fund to enjoy a retirement comparable to what a woman born in 1950 was able to achieve by having saved only 5.8% of their pay. Obviously, the current figure is contingent on nothing unusual happening to affect the woman's average income, such as their paycheck failing to keep pace with a 3.3 percent increase in the median wage, a less-than-eight percent increase in the S&P index, etc.[12] Saving is even more urgent for younger people today. Someone born in 1998 would need to save 14 percent of their current income every year from age 25 onward to retire on 80% of what they earned during their working lives. Commenting on the thought of millions of already woefully self-deprived, politically unrepresented young people practicing such an unbearable level of austerity, one Twitter user quipped, "On what planet? I'm a Millennial, and if I thought any of my friends had this much cash saved I would rob them myself."

The retirement reality for too many of today's U.S. workers is grim, to put it gently. According to the 2017 U.S. Census Bureau's Survey of Income and Program Participation, about 50% of women aged 55 to 66 have no personal retirement savings at all, compared to 47 percent of men.[13] That, along with a growing crisis in affordable housing, has led to dire circumstances for retired people living on Social Security, including an explosion in the number of older citizens living in their cars and trucks and such. Those citizens, euphemistically referred to as "car dwellers" or "vehicle dwellers," are casualties of an ever-devolving economic environment more closely resembling that of a failing third-world country than the world's number one superpower.

Homelessness is an accelerating issue that's already gotten out of hand. To cite statistics from one area alone, the Los Angeles Homeless Services Authority reported that in 2020, more than 20,000 people were sheltering in cars, vans, and campers. In fact, vehicle-dwelling, a lifestyle featured in the 2020 reality-based drama *Nomadland*, has become so commonplace that in 2022, a vehicle dwellers' advocacy group appeared, the National Vehicle Residency Collective ("NVRC," whose website is vehicleresidency.org). Describing itself as "a network of vehicle residents, social service providers, and legal experts joining forces to support people living in their vehicles," the group has objectives that include fighting laws that prohibit vehicle-dwellers from parking in public spaces (public lands, such as National Forests and Bureau of Land Management spaces, have become increasingly restrictive against the lifestyle, leaving those citizens few choices aside from living in campsites or the parking lots of big box stores like Walmart).

"It's in times of crisis that the fragility of our systems are [sic] laid bare," Graham Pruss, a scholar with the University of California, San Francisco's Center for Vulnerable Populations, told *USA Today* in February 2021. "We have seen more people moving into vehicles and more restrictions on public parking for them over the last decade, and then COVID hit," he said. "I am concerned that we may be facing a population increase in mobile sheltering and vehicle residence at unprecedented levels."

As the crisis spreads, one housing option that's recently emerged for aging citizens is "co-housing," a communal home-sharing lifestyle made available through apps like Cirtru, Spareroom and others; think of those platforms as housemate-matching services for the over-50 set.

V. Ladies and Gentlemen, The Precariat

I could go on, rattling off an alphabetized list of economic troubles various groups of American citizens are facing under our current system. Americans of all ages are finding it difficult to survive, let alone thrive. For many, America has become a techno-Dickensian hell, its despondent casualties dreaming of expatriating from the United States, where imminent threats of financial disaster and ensuing homelessness loom over workers' heads each time their employer's board meets to decide on their next profit-churning move.

So describes the socioeconomic class that's faced the toughest survival challenges under our neoliberal "trickle-down" system, the economic philosophy Ronald Reagan and Margaret Thatcher foisted on the Western world in the 1980s. That class, comprising most people in the country, is often referred to as the "precariat."

The phrase, which came into wide use after the publication of British economist Guy Standing's 2014 book *A Precariat Charter*, is a portmanteau of "precarious" and "proletariat." It specifies the economic majority, citizens who sell their labor—often too cheaply—in exchange for wages that provide them with nothing more than the stuff of basic survival. Their lives are made unbearably miserable when emergencies such as major medical bills or car repairs come up. Deprived of a heartbreaking number of things that would provide them with acceptable levels of material, psychological and self-actualizing comfort, the worst-off members of the precariat are often "food-insecure," a weasel-worded euphemism for "starving" that could only have been invented by someone who's never experienced it.

The precariat isn't relegated to the United States. In 2019, a European Council on Foreign Relations survey revealed that only a third of Germans and a quarter of Italians and French had any money left over for discretionary spending at the end of the month.

It stands to reason that at some point, in some country, the precariat will demand an end to its economic suffocation. The online left could be an indispensable asset toward that effort, but it must concur on what specifically is wrong with the American economy, its original design flaws, and what could be done to make it more livable for all citizens. That's the point of this exercise. Time's running out, pointing to a future predicted over a hundred years ago by Rosa Luxemburg: "As things stand today, capitalist civilization cannot continue; we must either move forward into socialism or fall back into barbarism."

One could say we live in a "barbarian capitalist" system already, but no one really seems to know exactly what to call it. It's been variously described as "corporatocratic," "neo-feudalistic" or, more recently, "techno-feudalist," which is how Greek economist "Yanis" Varoufakis brands it, referring to the notion that Big Tech is largely to blame for the economy's being so unbalanced these days: too much wealth and market power has been concentrated in the hands of a few large technology companies (Google, Apple, Facebook etc.) that control how we access information and communicate with each other and even manipulate us into choosing the goods and services we purchase.

While citizens spend more time fretting about being "smart consumers" than paying attention to what's being done to them, most of our income is siphoned off by what Michael Hudson describes as the FIRE sector (Finance, Insurance and Real Estate). That segment has quietly increased to maximum the already unsustainable level of austerity under which overleveraged citizens live. In 2023, total consumer debt passed the $17 trillion mark, an amount that literally cannot be repaid without catastrophic repercussions: A determined, all-in effort on the part of consumers to pay a big chunk of it back would require such a massive reduction in consumer spending that it would crash the economy. Regardless, consumers are in no position to do such a thing, owing to greed-driven inflation's ("greedflation") consistently outpacing any increases in wages, along with untimely spikes in interest rates that were prescribed by the cabalistic U.S. Federal Reserve (which has a "dual mandate" not only to set interest rates at sensible levels but also to maximize employment rates and stabilize prices, neither of which it does very well).

In a normal world, economists would support and promote ideas for changing the system in order to make it more equalitarian. Unfortunately, we won't see that happening. Owing to academic indoctrination and obliviousness to the challenges working people face, American's mainstream economists are militantly supportive of only one economic philosophy: a combination of monstrously slanted Keynesianism, whose original purpose was trying to figure out a way to pay for clobbering Hitler, and deregulation-oriented neoliberalism, whose continuing mission is clobbering people who aren't rich.

From my seat, one thing that's prevented heterodox economists' ideas from gaining wider circulation is that their platforms haven't been aggregated into one place, which is what I'll try to do here. Completely shunned by the Fourth Estate, heterodox economists are limited to dripping their niche, boutique ideas and findings in the general direction of Fifth Estate media figures, who, because they're not economics scholars, are often unsure what questions to ask those experts during interviews. That's not to blame eclectic podcasters for not researching the subjects, however.

VI. The Problem With Economists

Here it is: Most economists shouldn't be allowed to talk to humans under any circumstances. There are a few exceptions, like Hudson and Richard Wolff, along with the well-intentioned but attention-addicted Robert Reich (Bill Clinton's former Labor Secretary, who was once dismissed as a "foolish policy entrepreneur" by his fellow mainstream economics pundit Paul Krugman[14], who's in turn famous for such doomed predictions as "By 2005, it will become clear that the internet's impact on the economy has been no greater than the fax machine's" in 1998). Aside from the work of those well-known populists, much of the writing and speaking done by the economists I'll attempt to translate in this bit were at first so indecipherable to me that I had to micro-analyze each crouton in their jargon-packed word-salads before I could understand one fucking thing they were saying.

And that's just the heretics, the good guys. At the other end, establishment economists are so obeisant to the gospel of their "trust the free market" creed that they reflexively jump at any chance to insert a dreary, unintelligible corporate buzzword or esoteric, graduate-level shibboleth into the mix if they think it might fit the moment. I'm still undergoing daily psychoanalysis after sloshing through Joseph Stiglitz's 2019 book *People, Power, and Profits*, the single worst wonk-written nonfiction book I've ever read (Simon Schama's dementedly meandering journey into the guts of the French Revolution, *Citizens*, runs a not hopelessly distant second).

Let me defend myself for being so rotten. Every time he opens his mouth, Stiglitz has to walk a mile-high tightrope, given that he's a "Nobel Prize-winning economist," a pedigree he must guard with his life. In 2001, he walked away with one-third of the "Nobel Memorial Prize in Economics" (he also shared a Peace Prize for his "climate-wrecking-capitalists-are-people-too" claptrap in 2007), all of which might lead one to believe that the Nobel Foundation is composed of real-life vampires in power ties.

About that. Many would say that the Nobel Memorial Prize in Economics isn't a legitimate Nobel Prize at all. The first one was awarded in 1969, when, out of nowhere, the Sveriges Riksbank, Sweden's central bank, came up with the idea of awarding them "in honor" of Alfred Nobel, who died in 1896 and thus wasn't around to laugh off the idea. Nobel wouldn't have been the only one to react that way. During a casual online chat with fellow heterodox economist Steve Keen, Michael Hudson noted that Nobel earned his fortune by inventing dynamite, which was ironic, Hudson snarked, given that "The Nobel Prize [for economics] is for *intellectual* dynamite: it blows up the understanding of the economy to leave devastation in its wake!" Chuckling, Keen observed that former Fed chairman Ben Bernanke, who helped engineer the Wall Street bailouts of 2008 (which some believe were completely unnecessary[15]) was awarded the 2022 economics

Nobel for supporting "a model of lending which the Bank of England said is garbage in 2014, and [Germany's Bundesbank] said is garbage in 2017."[16] This all points to the fact that in the final analysis, the "economics Nobel" accomplishes nothing more than celebrating the status quo (the Nobel Foundation has made other cockeyed moves throughout the years, like when they awarded the Peace Prize to none other than Henry Kissinger, remembered by many today as one of history's most prolific war criminals).

Stiglitz has it tough, for sure. Although he's expressed measured amounts of support for deficit spending to help ease the economic pain of the citizenry, he remains more a part of the problem than the solution (one Redditor faint-praised him as "a more humanitarian version of Paul Krugman," a gentle way of saying he's a cheap imitation of a progressive/heterodox economist. And let's not forget that Stiglitz and 16 other Nobel-anointed wunderkinds failed to predict 2022's greedflation tsunami[17]).

I'd feel sorry for any economist who draws the short straw at the annual Bullshit Economics Summit and gets stuck defending anything about American capitalism, especially in these times. The subtitle of *People, Power, and Profits*—which could be the title of a dystopian novel, let's admit it—is *Progressive Capitalism for an Age of Discontent.* "Discontent" indeed; what a deafening understatement, and I'd further add that the phrase "progressive capitalism" has reached the oxymoronic stage of its etymology (the unlucky *Jacobin* reviewer who had the book tossed into his in-basket pointed to the fact that the very idea of "progressive capitalism" is ridiculous, being that wage labor is exploitive from the get-go).

When last we heard from Stiglitz on the subject of the inflation that began engulfing the globe in 2022, he assured his "progressive-minded" readers that the Federal Reserve would eventually bring everything back to normal the old-fashioned way, by raising short-term interest rates, which it did, which, right on schedule, resulted in a horrific stretch of "stagflation," a phenomenon that's normally caused by a combination of rising inflation, slow economic growth and a high-but-not-crazy-high unemployment rate. But this stagflation was different, partly *caused* by the Fed's rate increase. It was a robotic response that proved once and for all that the Fed has only one trick up its sleeve: Even when inflation rears its ugly head owing to completely unhinged corporate greed,[18] the Fed will respond by dicking around with interest rates, the raising of which is, by any rational logic, only supposed to be done if there's a goods-and-services-shortage situation going on, with too many dollars available to too many buyers who all want things that are in legitimately short supply. The thinking goes like this: If you want prices on houses, cars and other consumer goods to fall, make them more expensive to buy by charging consumers more interest when they borrow money to pay for them. The (probably intentional) stupidity of what the Fed did in 2022 was deep and wide: Rate hikes are supposed to help cool down an economy that's burning up with enthusiasm, not make matters worse for people and businesses that are already freaking out.

Amazingly, Biden just let the stagflation fester despite having some power to temper it by publicly and forcefully condemning the rate hikes and/or threatening to fire Fed chairman Jerome Powell. If he'd done one of those things and the rate went back down, there would have been more jobs and cheaper credit available for American worker-consumers and a resulting uptick in the overall economy as businesses were finally driven to compete rather than simply continue to jack prices to Neptune. But Biden declined to preach from his bully pulpit and instead softly "predicted" a rate cut, which told cynics all they needed to know: he was going to allow the stagflation to continue until the 2024 election season rolled around, in order to stir voter enthusiasm over a "strong, rebounding" economy (it'll probably be 2024's "October surprise" but is expected to launch in the summer, which would be the most sensible timing).

That wasn't very neighborly of the Democrats. Indeed, as fundamentally evil as the Republican Party is, its politicians have been known to use the right (more or less) plumbing tools when the system is so clogged that even the capitalists are panicking. When stagflation gripped America in the 1970s, President Richard Nixon—hardly a progressive—ordered a 90-day freeze on all prices and wages in the U.S., a move that worked on contact to end the stagflation, done and done. Unfortunately, stagflation resurfaced just a few years later: Nixon's freezing wages along with prices was a completely unnecessary step that of course did nothing to address core problems like income inequality. Either way, the price-freeze kill switch hasn't been flipped since. During the corporate-driven greedflation of the 2020s, the Biden White House never mentioned the tactic despite its proven success rate. In the same disillusioning vein, we have to note that it was none other than Adderall-snorting lunatic Donald J. Trump who showered barge-loads of capitalism-saving COVID-19 relief money onto the heads of not just the capitalists (thereby giving workers the "opportunity" to stay at jobs they might not have liked rather than march in the streets to demand relief, some critics would be quick to add) but regular citizens as well, to which the Biden administration would later respond by quietly reneging on a sworn-on-a-set-of-bibles presidential campaign promise to provide citizens with a total of $2,000 in economic stimulus money, eventually forking over just $1,400 per person.

While we're here, another thing I want to read into this record is the fact that of all the books that were scattered around my office to inform this one, *People, Power, and Profits* is, appearance-, writing- and even title-wise, much like libertarian arch-villain Charles Koch's 2015 book *Good Profit*, in which the power-deranged billionaire encourages regular people to pull themselves up by their bootstraps in the same superheroic manner as the handful of real-life rags-to-riches stories he presents throughout the book to perpetuate the myth that capitalism will work miracles if one just simply *lets* it. In other words, according to Koch, wealth isn't always inherited (not that he'd know about that, considering that he inherited a fortune from his father, who'd built oil refineries for both Stalin and Hitler).

It sure looked to me that Koch's prime motivation for releasing the book was to encourage his son, Chase, to go full Koch and "fix education," which in this case would mean mindlessly expanding the family's mega-fortune by grooming Chase to become some sort of private education mogul, the sworn enemy of America's public school system. Chase, who may have learned some valuable life lessons after a 1993 incident in which he was found guilty of committing misdemeanor vehicular homicide, was standoffish about it; he appears to be a salvageable human being but time will tell. In 2020, he divorced his wife, Annie, who'd helped launch a private Montessori-type preschool and grade school at Wichita State University. He professes to be politically neutral, for all you want to read out of that; God only knows what people in that income bracket are really thinking from moment to moment.

Anyhow, putting aside the subject of Charles Koch's bad writing to continue indulging in my own, it's exasperatingly common to find economists under-simplifying simple concepts. That habit hobbles the careers of many academics who dedicate their lives to obsessing over obscure elements of their chosen fortes. Their own encyclopedic level of knowledge becomes an albatross, sooner or later rendering them incapable of explaining their ideas to laypeople, a fact that even an expert on experts complained about. In his 2017 book *The Death of Expertise*, international affairs academic specialist Tom Nichols wrote, "[M]any experts, and particularly those in the academy, have abandoned their duty to engage with the public. They have retreated into jargon and irrelevance, preferring to interact with each other only."[19] Nichols points out that experts' impenetrably geeky communication styles (not to mention their countless screw-ups, such as the failure of economics experts to predict the 2001 dot-com crash and the 2008 financial crisis) have convinced laypeople to ignore or actively distrust them, which has given conspiracy theorists all the ammunition they could ever want.

It's not that academics don't *want* to be understood by Joe and Flo Cheeseburger; it's that they're afflicted with a cognitive bias called the "curse of knowledge," or "curse of expertise," which causes people mistakenly to believe that their audiences are familiar with the same terms and concepts they know inside and out. They assume that anyone in the audience can get the gist of what they're saying without defining any of the obscure words and phrases they use.

What's my solution to that messy little communication-gap problem? How about this: Any time an expert speaks to the public through any media platform, their microphone gets muted immediately so that all the audience hears is someone on voiceover, translating the expert's ideas into language that interested newcomers can immediately understand.

Yes, that was a joke. Sort of.

In economically turbulent times like these, when rallying the citizenry behind equalitarian causes is of paramount importance, experts must craft their messaging so that it's accessible to anyone with an eighth-grade education. As we've seen, not all economics wonks are qualified to do that, but the heretics need to learn how, so that their ideas can spread. At present, for the most part, their mousy, indecipherable fringe voices bleat gibberish at captive academic audiences who just want to nap.

Luckily for the heretics, mainstream economics experts suffer from the same problem, and their chosen path doesn't require them to learn any history or foundational truths about the economy, like the basics of what money is and how it works. That gives the heterodox nerds a tremendous advantage. For the most part, orthodox economics students in the West don't investigate the history of economics by getting to know Adam Smith, let alone Marx. They simply view the study of economics, as *Angrynomics* co-author Mark Blyth noted, as "a series of applied models" and after that, armed with no natural curiosity, common sense or historical insight, "jump straight into 'math class'."[20]

That detached, mechanistic approach to economics, especially as practiced by its professional expert class—the members of which blindly adopt a cult-like mindset that views free market capitalism as the only logical path to economic salvation without ever looking beyond it—is discouraging to Hudson as well. He's given up trying to help Western economists understand that America's trusting their "expert thinking" has accomplished nothing more than shortening the timetable for the country's collapse. "What's the point of talking to economists?" Hudson asked aloud at a People's Forum NYC gathering in 2019. "Their minds are gonna go 'clankety clank.' There's nothing that's going to come out of it that they're going to do."[21]

Steve Keen, Hudson's Australian counterpart, doesn't hold up on his swing either. "What an education in economics does is make you into a zealot," he told a *New Economic Thinking* interviewer in 2018. Keen, comparing today's economists to early astronomers who based their theories on the idea that the universe revolved around the Earth, denounced the model studied by today's "neoclassical" economists as having been devised by wishful thinkers working under the assumption that no unforeseen, chaotic event(s) would ever disrupt its progress. They believe the system will simply work without governmental help, intervention, or bailouts; it will function just fine (it never has). Keen argues that the only way the formula could ever work in the real world "is if each last one of us had the intelligence of God," meaning that the system won't crash (as it always does) as long as individuals and businesses constantly work to keep it in harmonious balance and refrain from ever exploiting its weaknesses for their own gain.

Believing that the entire population will always do the right thing to keep the economy in perfect equilibrium is like living in the world depicted in the 2009 film *The Invention of Lying*, where everyone on Earth tells the truth and never fibs about anything. Someone finally does, and, surprise, reaps myriad benefits from it. The economic model upon which the orthodox wonks base all their plans doesn't take into account unexpected "glitches" like natural disasters and wars, so when they do occur, what always results is the wealthy get wealthier. It's what Naomi Klein termed "disaster capitalism" in her 2007 book *The Shock Doctrine*. Pointing to just one example, in the aftermath of Hurricane Maria in 2017, efforts to privatize the beaches of Puerto Rico for the benefit of wealthy mainland investors got an unexpected rocket boost.[22]

Anyhow. If there's anything one can learn from studying economics independently, especially its history, it's the fact that one way or another, America's thuggish system will end or undergo drastic changes in the foreseeable future, probably quite abruptly. In the interest of better informing activists, movement organizers and onlookers as to where to direct their energies, in the following pages we'll look at the most viable fixatives that could serve to preserve the country in these times, when the U.S. empire, facing an array of economic and perhaps even physical threats from an outside world that's grown impatient with its constant bullying, begins stumbling toward a final collapse (a scenario that, Keen assures, would result in an America that resembles the dystopian hellscape depicted in the film *Mad Max*).

It doesn't have to end that way. Let's look at some options heterodox economists have offered as solutions for changing direction. There are other possibilities, but the Fifth Estate has zeroed in on these three in particular, all of which might inspire the public to withdraw from the system en masse—through such actions as widespread participation in debt strikes and other peaceful protests by citizens and wildcat (non-union-approved) strikes by labor—before it's too late. Okay, I mean way too late. You know what I mean.

VII: Option #1: Debt Jubilees, The Great Capitalist Band-Aid

In his 2022 journalistic novella *The Case For A Debt Jubilee*, white-hat venture capitalist Richard Vague endorses comprehensive debt forgiveness for American consumers. Put simply, a "debt jubilee" would act to reset the economy and "clean the slate" by resetting debt balances to zero, not only on student loans but also on credit cards, medical debt and so forth.[23]

Vague begins the book by rattling off a list of establishment-approved alternatives for solving the debt crisis, offering them more as afterthoughts than as workable solutions. For instance, some suggest that individuals and businesses "could always simply pay down" their debts, a notion we've already dismissed.

Or maybe we could somehow magically speed past China and turn America into the manufacturing capital of the world. Unfortunately, that would require rolling back the clock a few decades and focusing on true industrial capitalism—making stuff that people actually need and want—as opposed to the toxic stew of rentier (passive income derived from ownership or control of assets such as real estate), finance and military-industrial capitalism that's hard-wired into nearly every component of the U.S. economy.

In fairness, before we poke too much fun at the idea of suddenly "re-industrializing" America and all the jobs that'd come from it, we should note that there are gears in motion to increase America's "green jobs" count. In 2022, the Democrats passed the Inflation Reduction Act, offering tax breaks to fossil fuel companies to expand their green energy efforts. As always, however, there was a catch: the bill included a set of tax credits for expanding the use of carbon capture technology. That move was condemned by over 100 environmental justice groups, which immediately identified it as a giveaway to the fossil fuel industry, enabling it to continue doing business as usual. One critic noted, "The overwhelming majority of captured carbon to date has been used to *increase* oil production via enhanced oil recovery." In short, trusting the oil companies to do the right thing and work to end oil production, it turned out, was like expecting Colonel Sanders to free all his chickens.

That wouldn't be the only cringe-inducing act in the "let's reboot the American manufacturing sector" follies. In 2023, the establishment had a mild (and quite sensible) panic attack over the rise of the BRICS consortium (a geopolitical bloc comprising Brazil, Russia, India, China and South Africa, a force Goldman Sachs economist Jim O'Neill predicted will collectively dominate the global economy by 2050). In the end, all that really came of it was a hilariously suspicious eruption of propagandist headlines from the Fourth Estate. Suddenly, "The Return of American Manufacturing!" was a top mainstream news story. Wildly overblown reports of "new U.S. government initiatives in manufacturing investment" were ridiculed by Fifth Estate journalists as being long on corporate giveaways and short on middle-class job opportunities.[24]

Anyway, since we assuredly won't be seeing a rebirth of U.S. manufacturing nor a mass movement to pay off all consumer debt, jubilee stands out as a feasible option. Michael Hudson agrees with Vague on debt erasure, suggesting that the fastest way for the capitalist establishment to regain the working classes' favor—and, in fact, save the country from abject economic ruin—is by instituting periodic debt jubilees. Hudson's output, which includes the authorship of more than a dozen books fusing economics with ancient history, is the gold standard on the subject of debt, influencing such luminaries as the late David Graeber, who wrote the 2011 bestseller *Debt: The First 5,000 Years*.

Hudson argues that the American economy has left the era of industrial capitalism behind and become hopelessly mired in rentier and finance capitalism, led by the previously mentioned FIRE sector, which now helps itself to around two-thirds of workers' earnings every month, making it basically impossible for the majority of wage-earners to buy all the things they want and need. But that's not the scariest part, he notes. "Even if workers did not have to buy any of the goods and services they produce—food, clothes and other basic consumer needs—they still could not compete with labor in less financialized and debt-ridden economies."[25] Indeed, given that most of the interest from consumer debt payments is vacuumed up by "savvy investors" who purchase the loans with inherited wealth, Hudson views our current context as "economic apartheid."

The crazily unbalanced but seemingly unalterable nature of America's economic system can be chalked up largely to hubris on the part of the super-rich. Their degree of overconfidence has far surpassed the level that periodically compelled the ancient world's leaders to forgive citizens' debts. It was the fastest way, thought the oligarchs of antiquity, to dissuade the citizenry from banding together and summarily overthrowing the whole lot of them. Rulers instituted "jubilee years" in which all debts were forgiven and all lands held by creditors redistributed to citizens who'd had their property seized to repay loans.

Like the ancient Babylonians and Sumerians of the second and third millennia BCE respectively, the archaic Athenians, under their ruler, Solon, moved to cancel citizens' debts. It was the fastest way to get citizens back to the work of contributing to the whole of society. Without debt jubilees, commoners were too busy working off what they owed to moneylenders to have any time to work on "corvée labor" projects (such as highway construction and repair, not to mention royal vanity projects like statues and walls and such). The only thing Solon didn't do was seize any land from the wealthy classes and distribute it to everyday people who needed it to survive in the city's agrarian society. He would have done so, but the oligarchy refused to cooperate. They supported the feel-goodness of Athenian democracy, yes, but refused to surrender their economic dominance.[26]

In contrast, Rome's leaders, aside from forgiving (mostly rich people's) interest payments and debts to the state's treasury, didn't follow suit and eventually paid the price. Insidiously, along the way, they tried to erase the tradition of jubilee years from public memory As Rome's increasingly corrupt empire began crumbling under the financial weight of maintaining mercenary armies for the purpose of imperial expansion, their need to suppress the Old Testament teachings on debt forgiveness (as mentioned in Deuteronomy 15:1-2 etc.) grew more pressing. Cyril, the Patriarch of Alexandria, Egypt, between 412 and 444 A.D., instituted murderous pogroms, eliminating not only the city's Jewish population—whose members were intimately familiar with the debt jubilees mentioned in the first known versions of the Bible—but also anyone who could read and thus educate themselves about the tradition.

If you'll indulge a slightly *Da Vinci Code*-like detour, the above brings up an interesting side note. Hudson's research has concluded that in the 1300s, St. Augustine took the drastic step of reverse-bowdlerizing the Bible, or at least its popular interpretation, replacing "debt" with "sin" as the offense God would punish. Specifically, the passage "forgive us our debts" in the Lord's Prayer was changed to "forgive us our sins." In my travels, much confusion arose over that. For one thing, in many if not most modern versions of the Bible, the New Testament (which comes from ancient Greek translations of letters originally written in Jesus' own Aramaic language) includes two versions of the prayer. The Matthew 6:12 version is indeed "forgive us our debts," (a direct quote from Jesus' first sermon at Nazareth, according to Matthew). However, Luke 11:4 is translated as "forgive us our sins" (which, it's maintained, Luke said during a conversation with one of his disciples, purportedly quoting Jesus in second-hand fashion). Adding to the confusion is William Tyndale's 1526 Bible translation; in both cases Tyndale switched the wording to "forgive us our *trespasses*" (Tyndale was burned at the stake by order of King Henry VIII for translating the Bible into everyday parlance). Hudson assured me that "The Greek word [specifically referenced] monetary debts, not sins. That is what confirms the Aramaic [original version]. There's no confusion at all among linguists and scholars."

Now, the Aramaic word *ḥōb* (or *khoba*, depending on who's offering their expertise) is the same for both "debt" and "sin," whereas the Greek translation of the Aramaic referred to *opheilema*, which does indeed specifically mean monetary debt. Clear as mud to us non-linguists and non-scholars, I know, but any murkiness dissipates when we accept the all-but-universal popular and academic consensus that during his first sermon, Jesus unrolled the Scroll of Isaiah and announced he'd come to proclaim the jubilee year, when debt slaves would be freed from bondage and lands that had been sold to pay off debts reverted back to the families who were originally going to inherit them. And so, any editing or "reinterpretation" of the Bible to point to "sin" rather than "debt" as the subject of the passage probably was indeed a rather devious, manipulative (and patently obvious) attempt by an oligarch to imply that God tolerates slavery and usury. Hudson contends that Jesus' pro-jubilee activism is what got him killed.

Jesus wasn't the only historical figure who was murdered

for his pro-equalitarian activist efforts. Before Rome's downfall, its political divide was similar to the one we see today in the U.S., with conservative elites using every trick in the book to keep the public focused on matters of empire-building and tolerant of wealth inequality. In contrast, progressive politicians pushed for egalitarian measures, including land redistribution. Naturally, all that friction often led to the violent elimination of the "good guys," for lack of a more appropriate term. Centuries before John and Robert Kennedy were assassinated, Rome was home to the agrarian-reform-minded Gracchi brothers: Tiberius Gracchus, whose political efforts led to the provision of free land to an estimated 75,000 poor Roman families and got him murdered in 133 BCE; and his younger brother, Gaius Gracchus, who continued his work[27] (as we'll see, the similarities between the Roman and American empires never end with all this stuff. Gaius died 10 years after his brother, at the hands of a mob of poor but proud citizens who, in a storyline remindful of the immigrant-hating Trump-worshippers of today, angrily disagreed with his efforts to extend Roman citizenship beyond the city's borders[28]).

Hubris on the part of the rich and powerful—most recently exemplified by the rushed, systematic ethnic cleansing of Palestinians in Gaza allegedly at the behest of wealthy land and fossil fuel speculators—is a sure sign of societal rot. Among other hazards, it signals an intolerable level of wealth inequality, which is dangerous for many reasons, not just the simple fact that obscene levels of hoarded, idle wealth stifle economic growth worldwide.[29] During the fifth century A.D., the collapse of Rome's empire was accelerated when its citizens, fed up with being economically abused for the sole purpose of imperial expansion that benefited only the elites, actively *supported* the Visigoth, Vandal and Ostrogoth invaders who snatched the empire out of the hands of the rich.

Hubris pervades America's oligarchy today. A longtime observer and critic of America's military overreach, Chalmers Johnson saw hubris—a Greek word defined as excessive pride or dangerous levels of overconfidence on the part of a dominant group, leading them to engage in the reckless humiliation of their victims in defiance of the gods—as the defining characteristic of American foreign policy. The enemy of hubris, Johnson noted, is Nemesis, the goddess of retribution. As we speak, she impatiently awaits her meeting with our self-serving billionaires, who view themselves as godlike in their wisdom.

And why wouldn't they? Any voices that question the motives of "philanthro-capitalists" like Bill Gates and Mark Zuckerberg are roundly ignored in establishment circles, where the Fourth Estate fawns over them constantly. In his 2018 book *Winners Take All*, journalist Anand Giridharadas observed that, despite their outwardly "socially conscious" efforts, the super-wealthy are often the creators of the problems they seek to "solve," refusing, like the ancient Greek elites, to make any real sacrifices and instead seeking more and bigger tax breaks.[30]

Instituting debt forgiveness for the masses is a tricky proposition, Vague acknowledges. Aside from questions of fairness (if the government were to wipe out some people's debt, shouldn't others be rewarded for having no debt?), it poses the moral hazard of encouraging spendthrifts to get themselves in hot water all over again. As for paying for debt jubilees, that's the least of its dangers, a point with which Vague agrees nowadays and which we'll discuss in just a few paragraphs. Originally, Vague offered some complicated sliding-scale solutions regarding the forgiveness of only certain kinds of debt, including mortgage debt. Because the U.S. government kind of sucks at "means testing," that scenario would never happen to begin with, so, according to Vague, the most sensible plan would be to issue one-time checks of the five-figure variety to all citizens, say $10,000 to $20,000, which would address the unfairness question while jacking the economy into the stratosphere (such an approach could also possibly lead to a Universal Basic Income [UBI] program being put into place, guaranteeing each citizen enough money to sustain themselves on a regular basis. I won't be covering that in this book, as the question of "how much income would be proper" is the subject of ongoing debate).

Hudson doesn't believe we'll ever see debt jubilees in America, considering that all our establishment "economics gurus" worship the greed-is-good philosophies favored by Margaret Thatcher and Ayn Rand. But it's a fun academic exercise, you have to admit.

"Sounds nice," you mumble. "And this would all get paid for ... how? What, the government has a million-acre orchard of money trees growing somewhere?"

Well, yes. It does. It's been around for decades. Politicians and orthodox economics experts pretend not to know about it. Grab your Pringles and let's chat about it.

VIII: Option #2: Modern Monetary Theory: Preserving Capitalism with a Few Computer Keystrokes

"Modern Monetary Theory," or MMT, is the worst-named simple-stupid concept in human history, and now for a (hopefully illustrative) tangent involving a true story.

It's a beautiful autumn day in suburban Westford, Massachusetts, where all our spooky old trees are ablaze with color, and the air is crispier than a fresh box of saltines. I'm a third-grader, thinking grumpily that we kids should be outside, getting in one last game of pickup baseball before the snows come, but instead we're sitting in a school classroom, and Mrs. Trivers wants to teach us boring math stuff.

She tosses out a few easy questions so the kids in the front row can practice their hand-raising moves. Some blah blah blah, some doofus-level equations, and then it comes, a lightning bolt from Zeus. The Moment Everything Changed.

"I have five sticks," she tells us, instantly losing a kid in the back row who can plainly see she has no sticks whatsoever, why is she even saying that. "Steven here gives me another three sticks. Okay, so *now* I give Margaret seven sticks. How many sticks do I have left?"

Duh, I think, wishing I were crouched at third base, waiting for an easy grounder to come bumbling toward me. *One. You have* one *stupid stick.*

But I don't raise my hand, fearing that I screwed up the count somehow. After all, folks, she said *sticks*, a plural noun. Plural means more than one. No way am I raising my hand and looking like a moron when she reveals that I missed something that only adults or the good kids know about. Nope. Let one of the good kids die on that fucking hill.

Again, I'm not making this up. No one goes for it and raises their hand, not even the A students in the front row. It's a goddamn trap! Maybe this is the part where the truly dumb kids are separated from the rest of us and turned into dog food!

A glacial epoch passes. Finally, Mrs. Trivers, probably thinking we should *all* be turned into dog food, eyeballs us sideways and says, "One. I have one stick."

Ah.

The moral? When you're trying to teach people something, always assume that your audience is smart enough to tie their shoes and nothing past that. Always be sure to fill in any knowledge gaps that might be open, or the concept you're trying to drill into the heads of the masses may suffer the fate of MMT.

When I set out to write this book, the last thing I ever expected to take up most of my research time was the subject of heterodox economics. But I don't regret it. And of all the truths heterodox economists have uncovered, MMT is the most vital for understanding exactly how unfair America's economic system is toward most citizens.

The rich and delicious 50-gigaton truth bomb I'm about to drop on the uninitiated deserves a little more prologue. In the October 1957 issue of *The American Mercury*, Russell Maguire wrote:

> "It was Henry Ford, Sr., who said in substance, 'It is perhaps well enough that the people of the nation do not understand our banking and monetary system, for if they did, I believe there would be a revolution before tomorrow morning'."

That quote, which meme creators always offer without the part that identifies it as a composite paraphrasing of Ford as opposed to anything he ever actually uttered, made the rounds on Twitter and such during the early 2020s after the Fifth Estate and the entire online left began investigating MMT en masse. There's a learning curve to it that really takes only a minute to negotiate, but concerning how MMT hasn't become common knowledge yet, recall that we're dealing with economics academics who are attempting to *Explain Things*, and economists couldn't explain how to change a light bulb without prefacing it with so many unrelated sidebars about electricity, photons and human hand dexterity that the listener would eventually decide to give up and live in merciful darkness forever.

So let's begin.

You know how every time some bank needs a massive bailout, or when the "deficit-hawk" Republicans pass a trillion-dollar tax cut for wealthy people, or some foreign country or military contracting company needs a bazillion dollars to buy or manufacture Air Force jets and other American-made military stuff, they always get it, and politicians from both sides of the duopoly never squawk about it? That's what Modern Monetary Theory brings to America's "budget-management" table.

Basically, it goes like this. The U.S. government can print as many dollars as it wants (it doesn't even do that, really; the only effort required to transfer house-sized piles of money around is having someone log into a Federal Reserve computer and increase or decrease bottom lines in bank accounts) and the recipient can then use those dollars to pay for anything they want, as long as the seller of the good or service accepts American dollars as payment.

Okay, there you go. The end.

Look at you there, wondering, "Wait, where do all those dollars come from, though? China?" (That's what establishment blockheads like Sarah Palin always tell their followers, by the way.)

No. Granted, China invests heavily in U.S. Treasury bonds to keep its export prices lower, but it never *creates* American dollars. It can't. The U.S. dollar is a *sovereign currency*, so the government can "print" as many dollars as it wants. It's basically Monopoly money (often referred to as "fiat currency"), and the government owns the printing press.

Okay, yes, there are mitigating factors affecting whether or not more dollars can be created, but in essence—and MMT proponents will sometimes admit this when they think everyone's distracted—there's no other necessary step. First off, 70% of U.S. debt is owned by U.S. banks and pension funds, but regardless, we'll never have to sell South Dakota to China to pay off a bunch of debt denominated in US dollars, because the U.S. government can conjure up those dollars at will. China can buy as many U.S. Treasury bonds as it wants, but if it suddenly tried to cash them all in for dollars, we'd say "Okay, tough guy," and that'd be the end of it. Everything would be square after someone at the Fed made a few computer keystrokes.

(While we're at this, the growth of the BRICS alliance may eventually isolate America's oligarchs and force the country to behave like a more rational and cooperative business partner if it wants to keep importing raw materials, but we won't be seeing CNN footage of starving citizens in Arizona begging for cheeseburgers or whatnot, not with all the food we have around) (that is until all the environmental misconduct perpetrated by the Big Agriculture guys leads to the Colorado River drying up completely, at which point the American West will become an arid, uninhabitable desert. Just saying.)

One reason Modern Monetary Theory never went completely viral (which might have resulted in the working classes' going apeshit and fulfilling Henry Ford's prophesy) is that it's badly named, consisting of three puzzling word choices. To wit: It's not a "theory"; it's a set of nuts-and-bolts facts. It's not exactly "modern"; it's a logical extension of the ideas laid out by John Maynard Keynes in the 96-page book he published in 1940 that advised ways to fund America's World

War II effort, cryptically titled *How to Pay for the War*. And lastly, it's not speaking to *monetary* policy nerds (i.e., economists who trust that the Federal Reserve's only tactic—adjusting interest rates—is the only way to fix things) but to *fiscal* policy nerds (i.e., economists who'd prefer to see Congress vote on any significant economic decisions, like whether or not the country can "afford" to fix its infrastructure, forgive student debt and so forth).

Other than all that, I love the phrase "Modern Monetary Theory." Truly. If anyone in charge of the National Foundation for Confusey Economics Terminology is reading this, please, don't go changing "Modern Monetary Theory" to "Supersize Me Keynesianism" or "Last Century's Fiscal Policy Approach" or anything similarly obfuscatory. Think of the children. They don't need to know that a "government deficit" is really just a taxpayer windfall.

People often get lost when MMT supporters start describing the details of the paradigm, but common sense handles most of the heavy lifting. The fact is that our fiat-currency-powered system (dollars aren't backed by gold anymore; we've been off the gold standard since 1971, which was done mostly so there'd be no danger of foreign nations suddenly turning in their dollars for gold) only requires citizens to pay taxes to keep them *dependent* on earning or otherwise accumulating U.S. dollars, so they can pay government taxes in the correct currency. In other words, if we're going to pay taxes, we *have* to have those Monopoly dollars. But as I mentioned earlier, some argue (quite correctly) that it's not necessary to tax citizens at all. Any taxes paid to the government are deducted electronically from the taxpayer's bank account, or if the taxes are paid in cash, the physical notes are shredded and sent to landfills or offered as souvenirs to the public on Federal Reserve Bank tours.

So, you can think of taxes as an *optional* step in the government's symbiotic financial relationship with individuals and businesses. Unfortunately, MMT's most well-known spokesperson, Stephanie Kelton, has made MMT hilariously confusing to curious onlookers by consistently including the tax component in the introductions to her talks. It befuddles people right out of the gate. It's like trying to teach a Martian the basics of baseball by opening the discussion with a clarification on what happens to the runners on first and second base when someone hits a ground-rule double at the exact moment a streaker runs onto the field (as we speak, the establishment is taking advantage of all the unintended obfuscation, working to falsely debunk the concept. They've been quite successful at it, nudging dissenting articles to the top of Google searches and so forth). Other MMT proponents are somewhat better at explaining how it works, notably Warren Mosler, who wrote the original paper introducing MMT to the world (shocker: Mosler's not an economist, just a Wall Street executive with an odd fetish for fair play).

My aim here isn't to heap scorn on Kelton. I imagine she's received a mountain of crap for supporting MMT; it's a given that she's tried to explain herself to many roomfuls of blank-faced bureaucrats and establishment economists who laughed in her face. As well, as a senior economic adviser to Bernie Sanders during his 2016 and 2020 presidential campaigns, she must have punched a lot of walls in frustration, listening to him promise to pay for public programs by "taxing rich people" rather than stop to explain MMT to his breathless throngs.

But you can't blame people for refusing to accept the validity of MMT. Anyone who denies its reality simply hasn't had the light bulb go off in their head yet. Its apolitical nature

It's Really, Truly, Madly The Class War, Folks ▪ 187

can be tricky to grasp, since the establishment has thoroughly hypnotized the public into believing there are only so many dollars available for circulation before they're all gone, which of course isn't the case.

When the epiphany does hit you, it's like seeing a real Bigfoot, but some experts aren't wired to accept it. Marxist economist Richard Wolff has dismissed MMT out of hand, dealing the concept a serious blow from, of all places, the Fifth Estate (not for nothing, but considering that MMT could quickly work to make life in a *capitalist* system infinitely more pleasant without instituting any socialist measures, it's not hard to imagine why Wolff would reject it).

MMT deniers who don't try to think it through are intellectually lazy, but that doesn't mean they aren't smart. Guardrails are required for it to work correctly, an "inflation constraint" being the main mitigating factor. The government can't just fill up every citizen's checking account and expect everything to run smoothly. That part, also, is Economics 101: If there are barrels of hundred-dollar bills on every street corner, the currency becomes deflated because there's so much of it around, in too many hands, all chasing the same goods and services, ergo inflation results. But if that were addressed through sensible fiscal policy the way MMT wonks suggest, we sort of *could* print our way out of our troubles and simultaneously avoid inflation.

We're certainly not doing that now. Just the opposite: Money is madly being "printed," but only to rescue corporations and other entities that don't need any rescuing. Or it's hoarded by the rich, which doesn't help the economy and actually hobbles it. As Mark Blyth pointed out to the Senate Budget Committee in 2015—mind you, this was before he bought into the MMT concept, if he even actually has; it's hard to keep up—the U.S. government doesn't have a spending problem; it has a *revenue* problem, obviously brought about by so-called "regressive tax policies" wherein corporate and wealth taxes are routinely lowered while people in the economic majority get their taxes raised.³¹

One quibble I had with Kelton's 2020 book about MMT, *The Deficit Myth*, is that she waits 50-count-'em pages before dropping her most radioactive truth bomb, the fact that under our current "MMT-but-only-for-the-rich" system, a five percent unemployment rate is considered *healthy* by establishment economists, who recommend it even though the musical chairs-style unemployment that comes with it shatters the livelihoods of six million workers every month (according to The Center for Economic and Policy Research) by leaving them with no income stream whatsoever. I think if I'd written that book, I might have titled it *Why There Is No Freaking Reason Whatsoever For People To Suffer From Unemployment* or somesuch. That's not to say she was obfuscating on purpose; she's obviously afflicted with the "curse of knowledge" herself, and regardless, she's certainly made a heroic effort to get the word out, to her credit.

MMT supporters have a ready answer to the unemployment problem. Some, if not most, believe that the way to counter free market capitalism's cruelest blow to the working precariat would be to implement a "government jobs program" (GJP). It's exactly what it sounds like: When private-sector employers experience a slowdown (and even when they don't), government-supplied jobs would be available for any citizen who wanted one.

Australian economist Bill Mitchell, one of MMT's founders, suggested that literally any paying job—even digging holes in the ground and filling them back in again—would keep unemployed workers from suffering financial hardship or falling into bad work habits. If you're laughing over such a suggestion, Mitchell would rebut that there is indeed some small measure of value to society in such a task: At the very least, we'd know how long it takes X number of workers to dig an X-sized hole in the ground and how long it would take them to fill it back in with X amount of dirt. Such information would be valuable to planners and project managers to some degree. They'd write papers!

Okay, if you still aren't sold on the digging-holes thing, maybe America could—and I know how crazy this sounds—work to repair our hopelessly decrepit roads, bridges and railways. That'd be timely. L. Randall Wray, one of the founders of MMT, says the U.S. would need to spend $6 trillion to catch up to China in infrastructure-building. At the moment, the Chinese are basically living like the Jetsons while an American citizen can spend an entire lunch hour watching videos of domestic freight trains going off the tracks and crashing in spectacular heaps. An all-in, long-overdue infrastructure program would be the same sort of win-win as the National Parks program of the Great Depression era. That initiative literally *was* a government jobs program that resulted in the creation of several tourist spots, including Isle Royale, Joshua Tree, and California's Channel Islands.

Mitchell cites a precedent for GJP-style "busy work." In November 1970, the Australian government established a floor price for wool that kept the price reasonable regardless of how much was being produced in any given period, all while keeping workers consistently employed producing it. Here's the deal: If too much wool was produced to meet current demand, the excess was kept in storage facilities while workers kept producing it as usual. In the event of a shortage, the previously stored wool was added to the supply chain. That strategy kept workers consistently occupied (but not overstretched) and prices stable.[32] (Naturally, the system collapsed in the mid-1980s, owing to some still-argued points involving greed, overproduction, etc., but such is the history of ideas that aim to make capitalist systems workable.[33])

Anyhow, there you have it, Modern Monetary Theory, a simple truth that gives the oligarchy night sweats.

In the end, more socialism would solve pretty much all of the precariat's problems, of course, but you know how that goes: the same way as the likelihood of our capitalist reptile-people ever allowing the government to adopt MMT measures or institute debt jubilees or give everyone a free pony. Regardless, let's look at it, for duty and humanity, as the Three Stooges used to say.

IX: Option #3: Socialism, The Final Frontier

> "Whatever is scarce in a market ends up in the hands of the richest people. [That] doesn't square with any morality I'm familiar with, but we celebrate the market in this country. It is in fact the closest we have to a genuine - as opposed to 'pretend' - religion."
>
> -Richard Wolff

It's hard to say how well socialism would work in America or anyplace else for that matter. There's no country in the world whose economy adheres to socialist principles without much deviation. Some countries do include the word "socialist" in the names of their republics, such as the Socialist Republic of Vietnam, which *The Economist* characterized as "ardently capitalist communist," an oxymoron for the ages.

Richard Wolff has stated that Portugal, which operates as a "unitary multi-party semi-presidential representative democratic republic," is the closest to a socialist government of any country in the West. Still, it's not socialist in any real sense; its population is divided into an "owner class" and a "worker class."

I've argued about this with people on Twitter, but in the interest of getting this book off my plate sometime this decade, let's leave it that every nation on Earth is capitalist in some form. That said, barter exchange systems—where businesses simply trade goods and services for other goods and services rather than pay for them with currency—are in wide use throughout the world. The International Reciprocal Trade Association, a non-profit organization that promotes high standards of practice among barter exchange systems, estimated the total worldwide value of barter transactions at more than $12 billion to $14 billion in 2023.

Most American socialists—who generally view our current neoliberal form of capitalism as an economic philosophy that, in line with its "liberal" root, favors individual rights and free enterprise and whose prime motivator is self-serving greed—believe capitalism is unsustainable, so we should talk about that. This section will cover various and sundry realities and precedents facing the online socialist movement today, not any specific "how we can get to socialism" guidance nor a partial (and excruciatingly obvious) list of the socioeconomic benefits everyday citizens would enjoy if the country were guided by a far more humanitarian economic system than our present one.

There are socialist political candidates in the U.S. today, but they receive no mainstream media coverage whatsoever. Indeed, they get even less attention than our sideshow oddballs, for instance the activist/performance artist Vermin Supreme, a recurring presidential candidate who, in interviews, has promised to provide citizens with free ponies and somehow go back in time to "kill baby Hitler."

Unfortunately, Supreme's promises are only slightly less likely to come to fruition than our ever seeing a formidable bloc of socialists elected to the U.S. Congress, not after so many decades of highly coordinated anticommunist agitprop.

Plenty of people and groups are working diligently to make socialism spread in America. Established in 1973, the Socialist Party of the United States of America (now Socialist Party USA) supported "eco-socialist" Green Party co-founder Howie Hawkins for president in 2020 (Hawkins garnered 0.2 percent of the national vote). As of this writing, Socialist Party USA hasn't thrown their support behind any Marxist-adjacent independent presidential candidates like Cornel West for 2024, but it's a safe bet that they'll back either him or the Green Party candidate (most likely Jill Stein). That would put the group in sync with similar organizations, like the Party for Socialism and Liberation, the Peace and Freedom Party, and a dozen or so others.

We won't cannonball into the Olympic-size pool of hopelessness and political establishment trickery that's torpedoed such past leftist presidential candidates as Ralph Nader, Bernie Sanders and Eugene V. Debs. However, a word does need to be said about the difficulties third-party candidates face when they try to get their names listed on voting ballots. There's of course good-old-boy Republican skullduggery afoot in red states when Green Party candidates—the biggest threat to duopoly dominance—are denied ballot access, but the Democrats have likewise been accused of keeping the "Greens" off the ballots under questionable circumstances. In 2022, North Carolina Senate candidate Matthew Hoh, a Green, looked on helplessly as his petition to be added to the state's ballots expired, rendering his candidacy essentially moot. What happened was the state's Board of Elections, under the leadership of a Democrat, found nitpicking fault with a subset of signatures that was too small to have affected the petition's certifiability but which the board's Democratic majority nevertheless deemed significant enough of a voter fraud risk that it needed to be investigated further. The delay in certifying the petition pushed the whole business past the deadline for granting Hoh ballot access, and that's where his fight ended.[34]

If you'll allow me to make a planet-sized understatement, ballot access is crucial to democracy, hence even the slightest effort on the part of the Democrats to deny it to Green Party candidates is a bit, well, fascistic. The fact that no Green Party nominee has ever been elected to office in the federal government doesn't mean that it's a wacky fringe organization. In fact, several Green candidates have received more than 20 percent of the vote in the congressional races in which they've been able to participate.

That said, it's all but certain that the Green Party's presidential candidate won't be on the ballot in every state in 2024 or in the foreseeable future. Because of that, Green Party volunteers—at least the ones I've met—focus mainly on fighting for ballot access for down-ballot races, such as state legislature contests. One would assume that write-in votes could widen the party's reach, but at this early 2024 writing, according to Ballotpedia.org, only 33 states accept write-in votes for candidates, and only if they've officially registered with the state, which can be a hassle. Meanwhile, nine states don't count write-in votes at all.

And so, millions of voters can't even lodge a protest vote. The 2024 election will once again consist of duopoly candidates or bust (in her tireless crusade for solidarity among non-Republicans, Hillary Clinton advised disgruntled voters to "get over yourselves" in an April 2024 soundbite), which will likely result in a new low in voter turnout: A full third of eligible voters didn't bother voting in the 2020 presidential election, and only 52% voted in 2022's general (non-presidential) election.

It's shameful, really. The Democratic Party, which, for decades, was the closest thing America had to an equalitarian party, has fully embraced Reagan-style neoliberalism, straying far from its traditionally socialist-adjacent messaging. In a 1952 speech given in Syracuse, N.Y., then-President Harry Truman, a Democrat, said:

> "Socialism is a scare word they have hurled at every advance the people have made in the last 20 years. Socialism is what they called public power. Socialism is what they called social security. Socialism is what they called farm price supports. Socialism is what they called bank deposit insurance. Socialism is what they called the growth of free and independent labor organizations. Socialism is their name for almost anything that helps all the people."

Contrast that fiery egalitarian rhetoric with the shapeless anodyne hedging of today's New Democrat politicians, who discourage any of their number from so much as uttering the word "socialism." To his credit, in a 2020 Snapchat interview, former Democratic President Obama ripped the party for limiting Progressive Caucus member Alexandria Ocasio-Cortez to a 90-second speaking slot at that year's Democratic National Convention. Obama didn't push the matter very far, however, and, remaining faithful to his party (and personal brand), shifted to the lowest gear possible, spouting toothless rhetoric that included such puffballs as "Instead of talking labels and ideology, we should focus on talking about getting certain things done."[35]

This is all academic of course, but the Democrats, should

they even survive as a coherent party after the 2024 election, can't avoid the subject of socialism forever. It's a hot topic online and off. By my best guesstimate, there are at this writing approximately 32,855,964 YouTubers, Substack writers, Discord group leaders and other thoughtfluencers in the online left who'd love to tell you all about socialism, communism, social anarchism and all that stuff (there are lots of flavors to choose from; the only things their supporters all seem to have in common are that they angrily disagree with at least one relatively minor plank of their "competitors'" platforms and have never met a sesquipedalian word they didn't like).

I'm kidding, I hope you know. Socialism has rarely been as widely accepted as it is today. Many recent polls have indicated that 70% or more of Millennial and Generation Z voters wouldn't hesitate to vote for a socialist candidate. Gallup tells us that 40 percent of all Americans have a favorable view of socialism, as opposed to 60 percent who have a positive view of capitalism.[36]

There are lots of reasons why Americans aren't fully sold on socialism. To begin with, it seems confusing to them. Many study Marx's philosophy as an endless endeavor, like trying to interpret the Buddha. Meanwhile, as Fifth Estate journalist Ryan Chapman stated in a 2022 YouTube "explainer"-style video[37], it's almost impossible for someone to describe a "specific conception of socialism" without being well-versed in its history, which begins much earlier than Marx's teachings.

Some contend that socialism's deepest roots are in Plato and Aristotle's concept of "essence," which German philosopher Georg Hegel used as the basis for his theory of natural sociopolitical evolution, which revolves around humans' inborn tendency to want to work together to build better societies. Chapman does take an admirable stab at defining socialism for the benefit of the uninitiated, describing it as "a socioeconomic philosophy primarily concerned with shaping wealth, institutions or economic activity according to various interpretations of equalitarianism."

The French revolutionary François-Noël Babeuf has been cited as the father of modern communism (the ultimate expression of socialism, i.e. a system that features a fully emancipated workforce) for uttering such quotes as "Since men are absolutely equal, they must not have any private possessions, but must enjoy everything in common." Either way, whether socialism was born in Germany or Russia or emerged naturally from ancient genetic memory pools passed down from early hominids that shared their resources in groups, we won't get into the nuts and bolts of it here. Trillions of words have been written about all the minutiae. Go read them all. I only ask that someone text me when the elites are overthrown and we're hammering out the new order's specifics; I have legislation I'd like to introduce regarding babies being allowed in crowded areas.

Don't get me wrong; a socialist America would be fine by me. Any system that ensures all citizens feel economically secure and content with their work lives is, of course, an admirable, appropriately futuristic vision. But like anything that would greatly benefit the general population and take power away from the oligarchs, any formidable, deeply coordinated movement to replace America's neoliberal system with one that's purely socialistic would be met at every step by negative propaganda from all the tentacles of our ubiquitous capitalist cult. If a socialist movement presented a legitimate threat to the establishment, defensive mechanisms would kick into gear immediately. Wave upon wave of anti-socialist "news and information" would crash upon our cultural shores, funded by hilariously wealthy capitalists and certified by such entities as the intelligence agencies and, of course, the Fourth Estate (which would, without any doubt, continue refusing to report the slightest bit of positive news on any socialist efforts or gains, as has been the case with recent activist actions centered on climate change and the Gaza genocide).

It'd be tough, yes. I don't say this to dissuade anyone, but even an unbreakably united, meticulously organized socialist movement would face such obstacles as, for starters, misinformation-bearing trolls and bot swarms as well as "deep thoughts on the realities of socialism" offered by establishment pundits, venal influencers with footholds in gamer-youth culture, celebrities, and a plethora of other popular fixtures, many of whom would push pro-neoliberal talking points in the media (the latter scenario wouldn't be without precedent. In 2022, American comedian Bobby Lee described a bizarre offer he and a group of other celebrities received from the Israeli government. They would be flown to Israel to tour the country with all expenses paid. The only catch was that they had to tweet Israeli-government-approved messages every day they were there[38]).

There would be movies, too. Right-wing propagandists like Steve Bannon, Donald Trump's former chief strategist, love making movies. After producing the (ironically) Sean Penn-directed *The Indian Runner* in 1991 (Penn would later slam Bannon as "a conniving, hateful, bloated punk who despises mankind"), Bannon went on to direct or produce several kooky, anti-communist films like *Reagan: In the Face of Evil* and *Occupy Unmasked*, which joined such other anti-populist films in the wingnut pantheon as 2016's *Wolf In Sheep's Clothing*, an unintentionally funny hit piece packed with cautionary, Bible-slapping ravings targeting Saul Alinsky.

A big-budget, pull-all-stops movie production of *Atlas Shrugged*, Ayn Rand's zillion-word ode to vulgar greed, would be guaranteed to surface, not that anyone would have ever forgotten laying their eyes on the godawful 2011 TV miniseries treatment of the book. That one starred Taylor Schilling in a career misstep that probably caused Netflix's showrunners to think twice before hiring her to fill the lead role in the popular TV series *Orange Is The New Black* a few years later.

All-in pushback against a strong socialist movement wouldn't stop there by any means. Smear campaigns and shocking "deep fake" videos targeting the movement's principals would surface on a regular basis. Think tanks would disperse to academia laughably weak "realistic, expert-recommended alternatives to socialism" that would, if implemented, leave the core problems of wealth inequality and worker precarity unsolved, after which renowned Fourth Estate hack journalists would write interminably stuffy opinion pieces and books in support of them. Such non-starter "solutions" would of course be artificially viralized on social media by bot swarms.

And as always, the most demoralizing reality checks would come from within the left itself, when well-meaning Fifth Estate figures posed questions steeped in awkward truths, freezing novice radicals in their tracks. A month before the 2020 presidential election, comedian/philosopher Natalie Wynn, a transgender YouTuber famous for her "Contrapoints" videos, released a segment urging her fans to vote for Joe Biden rather than not vote at all. Aware that she'd catch a lot of flak for it from her fellow "BreadTube" personalities, she nevertheless wisely argued that the Republicans and Democrats aren't quite the same, given that, unlike Trump, the Democrats would not have "[filled] the Supreme Court with anti-abortion fanatics, [appointed] climate change deniers to head climate research, [trivialized] a deadly pandemic in the name of delusional macho posturing," etc. She addressed the notion of an armed communist takeover with surgical derision, noting that radical right-wing groups like the Proud Boys et al. have been assembling and organizing armed militias for many years; oh, and by the way, remember kids, the Russian Revolution didn't spontaneously happen overnight; it brought about a six-year civil war.

In the end, though, even if the online socialist left were left undisturbed to go about their business and merrily set about recruiting others to their cause without having their ranks deeply infiltrated and ransacked by trolls and bots and all that stuff, the fact is that they tend to be very tribal in nature, primarily congregating in niche, deeply siloed micro-bubbles with relatively small numbers of mutual followers. It sure looks to me that the average socialism-or-bust Twitter user who posts things on a daily or hourly basis is content with having somewhere around 50 to 300 followers, whereas less politically radical users—predominantly skewing more or less Democratic, of course, and by that I'm allowing that many of those accounts are actually bots—often have upwards of 2,000 to 10,000 mutual followers, not that that means they ever actually communicate with each other. For most center-left Twitter users, the only requirement for mutual "followship" is that they never tweet support for Republicans or criticize Democrats. Once those black-and-white qualifiers are met, most Twitter users simply follow back and that's it. In fact, pro-Democratic Twitter users can be a bit obsessive when it comes to working to increase their follower counts. They gleefully fall into the video-game-like trap of working to amass shit-tons of followers, never minding that the actual engagement they receive in response to their tweets is largely quite shallow at best and completely nonexistent at worst.

During the first two-plus years of growing my sad, undramatic excuse for a Twitter platform, I would occasionally follow hardcore socialists, the really angry sounding ones who'll settle for nothing less than replacing Old Glory's 50 stars with a hammer and sickle. After a quick study of my content, they rarely followed me back, even out of simple courtesy, which, as I said, most people do, regardless of there being a sticking point or two. At first, I felt a little disappointed, even insulted that they didn't follow me back. It wasn't like I was tweeting all kinds of breathless support for the Democrats, not that I could have ever stomached doing that in the first place. I eventually figured it out: In line with their being absolutely convinced that a socialist America is coming sooner than anyone thinks, my potential far-left comrades apparently didn't want anything to do with someone who didn't post a lot of Karl Marx memes or angry mini-rants about how corrupt the Democratic Party is. I stopped taking offense to all the snobbery after absorbing the fact that, in the end, Twitter's aggregate socialist left is a tremendous but infinitely splintered collection of ideologically incestuous echo chambers where most of its users really only want to read tweets from people who think and post the same things they do.

As I see it, the problem with too many "very online" socialists is twofold. For one thing, their litmus tests for accepting potential comrades are almost impossible to pass. It drives them to treat curious outsiders with what can feel like disdainful indifference, as though they have little interest in expanding their base. And second, they seem content with being basically leaderless (at this writing, even the Democratic Socialists of America organization—@DemSocialists—has only managed to attract 350,000 Twitter followers, while Jeffery

Dean Morgan [@JDMorgan], who played the villain Negan on TV's *The Walking Dead*, has a million).

Online socialists can be a bit insular, is what I'm saying, and it works against their own interests. As the German political philosopher Hannah Arendt once said, "While strength is the natural quality of an individual seen in isolation, power springs up between men when they act together and vanishes the moment they disperse." Unfortunately, passionate socialists appear to be oblivious to that simple truth. But to their credit, after the Musk takeover, although "socialist Twitter" was a bit shaken, it, like Twitter's liberal contingent, didn't disappear. Many stayed on the platform, while some shards regrouped on Bluesky and other social media sites, resuming their discussions of Lenin and Trotsky and such.

Hilariously, that "and such" can include, in rare cases, genocidal maniacs like Joseph Stalin (ultimately responsible for at least 20 million deaths by some estimates, as right-wing trolls love pointing out) and Mao Zedong (somewhere between 40 to 80 million). The U.S./Russia conflict in Ukraine in the early 2020s really brought the hardcore communists out in force on social media (for the record, that proxy war was and is outside my scope and, frankly, interest. I view it as a profoundly tangled clash of empires with such a long history of covert and overt transgressions, broken promises and such that all the unvarnished truths will probably never be adequately documented until some academic writes a very fat book about it. I'd direct you to the first half of Serhii Plokhy's 2023 book *The Russo-Ukrainian War: The Return of History* if you're curious about the conflict's background). Suffice to say that the pro-communist "tankies" I mentioned earlier believed Russian President Vladimir Putin should simply level Ukraine and be done with it (when the conflict first broke out, journalist Matt Taibbi predicted exactly that: Putin would reduce the country to a charred jumble of wreckage that would serve just fine as a buffer zone between Russia and current/potential NATO countries like Poland, Hungary et al.). In online spaces, tankies sometimes participate in pro-Russian "campism," a neologism that describes collective support for either the American or Russian empire in conflicts like the one in Ukraine. There's a "western camp" that backs American capitalism and an eastern one that roots for a Russian victory.

There's a disconnect there. Like most Americans, many tankies—the ones who aren't actually bots or trolls, that is—back Putin because they've been led to believe that modern Russia is a legitimately communist country, a Xanadu of equalitarian goodness where workers own the factories and offices where they work, where all citizens have their basic needs met and all that. But that's wrong at a fundamental level, as we've discussed. "Communist Russia" is lorded over by an overclass of self-serving, greed-crazed oligarchs who, like their American counterparts, let politicians, ideologues and elite professionals do all their dirty work (such as making rules that tilt the scales in their favor, crafting their propaganda, etc.). It's actually been an overtly capitalist-imperialist country since Boris Yeltsin became president of the then-newly formed Russian Federation in 1991. Under Yeltsin's leadership, the country pivoted toward modern capitalism. It developed a market economy by implanting market-determined prices and private ownership of its essential functions, such as telecommunications. Today, the only industries the Russian government owns and controls are the oil and gas industries and pretty much nothing else.

Tankies might get more respect if they could point to Russia and declare without any hesitation that it genuinely is a communist country in every sense, run by an army of civic-minded paper-pushers whose every thought revolves around ensuring that citizens feel a sense of socioeconomic security knowing they're guaranteed living wages. Only problem is that it's not.

If there's any statistic that reveals how hardscrabble everyday life can be in a country, it's its rate of homelessness. Moscow analysts say that the official number of homeless people in Russia—64,000 according to Rosstat, Russia's Federal Service for State Statistics—is far too low and that the real number may be as high as 5 million (most analysts believe the actual number is somewhere in between).[39] If we assume Russia's officially reported number of homeless is off by a factor of 10 or so, and also trust the U.S. numbers released by the Department of Housing and Urban Development in 2020—which indicated that over 580,000 Americans experienced homelessness that year[40]—we find that both countries have a disturbingly high number of homeless citizens. That's something the average American might not expect to be the case in Russia, a "communist" country with "zero unemployment," where, many Westerners assume, any worker can obtain a place where they can hang their hat and watch their TV shows.

(While we're at this, last we knew in 2011, "Communist China" had 2,579,000 homeless citizens, which, percentage-wise, was only a little higher than America's homeless rate in 2022. That number could be attributed to China's economic growth spurt during that period, which led to a mass exodus of workers from rural areas to job-filled cities. Many of China's homeless are or were newly transplanted workers who didn't obtain government approval before moving to the cities, resulting in their getting stuck sleeping in railway stations, vacant buildings and so forth until they could become better settled.[41])

As far as employment misery, Russia does have unemployed workers, at least 2.9 million of them (3.9% of the workforce) as of July 2022.[42] Mostly, that can be chalked up to factors that regularly affect all capitalist economies (periodic ups and downs in markets, lack/excess of skilled labor, etc.). But regardless, gone are the days when the Soviets boasted that they'd eradicated unemployment, when Russian workers could be sentenced to six months of corrective labor if they didn't show up for work.[43]

So, if Russia is just a capitalist country wearing a fake Lenin goatee, why are tankies such big fans of Russian military aggression? The first thing I'd say is that, as I alluded to above, I don't believe for a second that every cyber-tankie is an actual tankie. Some unverifiable number of them, I believe, comprises trolls in the employ of right-wing, dark-money-funded think tanks that want to keep leftists distracted by internecine warfare. That's not an "everyone I disagree with is a Russian bot" defense, nor is it an attempt to dismiss all Stalinists out of hand. Quite the contrary; it's an Occam's razor thing, really. It makes the most sense. I can give you my solemn word as a gentleman that if I were hired by some mysterious organization to slap together a disinformation campaign to keep online socialists fighting with liberals and each other instead of working together to accomplish anything, one of the first things I'd do is unleash a brigade of trolls and bots to dump a bunch of extreme pro-Russia bullshit into the mix. It's not rocket science.

Who would hire someone to do something like that? The usual prime suspects, like politically conservative, anti-communist organizers who want the left to keep destroying itself from within. Maybe some are U.S. armed forces recruiters who want to bolster their ranks with people who are itching to "fight the commies" wherever they are. Or cohort number three, our intelligence agencies, which are always interested to know about anyone who's thinking of committing domestic terrorism in the name of, I don't know, borscht?

But all is not completely hopeless on the socialist front. The demise of capitalism has been predicted for generations by thinkers like Rosa Luxemburg, Joseph Schumpeter (who believed capitalism could become stable in the long run) and, of course, Karl Marx. Many 20th-century economists expected capitalism to collapse from such pressures as production capacity reaching its limit, widespread citizens' withdrawal from the system owing to cultural changes, gradual "convergence" (in which capitalism evolves into some form of socialism organically), and/or internal contradictions (ex: as capitalism's desire for limitless growth comes closer to realization, wealth becomes concentrated in fewer and fewer hands, leading to less aggregate demand for goods. British Marxist writer David Harvey's 2014 book *Seventeen Contradictions and the End of Capitalism* offers a thorough study of the subject[44]).

Yet, capitalism persists. It is a chameleon, changing its color to fit the zeitgeist. It rebrands. When times are tough, it becomes a "New Deal" economic philosophy. When the capitalist class thinks it's a good time to put a hurt on the workforce owing to its distracted, comfortable situation, it becomes "neoliberalism." What's worrisome in these times of economic apartheid is the fact that the "owner class" has dropped any pretense of caring about working citizens. Capitalism runs amok.

But happy fluff aside, let's now turn to thoughts offered by other Fifth Estate notables. Michael Hudson's work aside, if a political-economic class is going to hoodwink an entire country, some periodic updating and retrofitting is necessary in order to keep capitalism "progressing." Let's look at some of that.

X: Why the Constitution Sucks

Between October 1787 and May 1788, the *Federalist Papers*, a series of 85 political essays, were published in serial form in various New York State-based newspapers that included the *Independent Journal*, the *New York Packet*, and *The Daily Advertiser*. The *Papers* were written anonymously by Alexander Hamilton, James Madison and, to a minimal extent, John Jay, three of the United States Constitution's framers (point of order, it's rightly considered bad form nowadays to refer to them as the "Founding Fathers" in even the most casual discussion, owing to its paternalistic flavor).

The goal of the *Papers* was convincing the citizens of New York State to vote to ratify (legally approve) the Constitution, which would replace the 1781-ratified Articles of Confederation as the document that would set forth the guidelines by which the states' "league of friendship," or "Perpetual Union," would be organized. The new charter's laws would determine how the states of the fledgling nation would conduct business with each other, direct the war effort, handle diplomacy with foreign governments (including the Native American tribes) and such.

The *Federalist Papers* were central to the country's first major political propaganda campaign. Bent on "manufacturing consent," as Noam Chomsky likes to put it, the articles promoted the idea that constitutional rule by a powerful few was in the best interest of all citizens.

Madison, Hamilton and Jay wrote under the pseudonym Publius, referring to Publius Valerius Publicola, a tidbit that's piqued the interest of many a Fifth Estate thinker. "Well, who was Publius?" Chalmers Johnson once rhetorically quizzed a camera crew. "He was the first consul of the Roman Republic," he replied to himself, without further clarification for viewers who don't know Publius from Alice Cooper (Roman consuls held the highest political office one could achieve, essentially the head of state. Their duties included commanding the Roman army, presiding over the Senate and representing the state in foreign affairs).

We're getting to it. Neither Publius' deeds nor history were essential to Johnson's ensuing talk; his intention was to drive home the point that the 18th-century architects of the American republic took a lot of their cues from the ancient Romans (thus, as one Michael Hudson interviewer "succinctly" observed, the American political system was modeled after one that had been an abject failure).

The loss of Johnson in 2010 at age 79 was a grievous blow to the Fifth Estate, coming in the same five-year period during which it lost three other firebrands: journalist Molly Ivins, comedian George Carlin and author Christopher Hitchens (many would include former Texas governor Ann Richards in that list owing to her talent for anti-Republican one-liners). A semi-reformed cold warrior who was sickened by the constant criminal mistreatment of Japanese citizens by "boneheaded" U.S. soldiers stationed at the 85-odd military bases scattered throughout the archipelago, Johnson spent a lot of leisure time uncovering similarities between the ancient Roman and modern American sociopolitical spheres. There are indeed a lot of parallels. He once wryly noted that at their most decadent point, the Romans had the same sort of adoration for their "celebrity chefs" we see today being heaped upon folks like Guy Fieri and Gordon Ramsay.

Johnson also dabbled with comparing U.S. presidents to

Roman emperors. I'm 99 percent sure that if he were alive today, he'd compare Donald Trump to Caligula and Joe Biden to the last Roman emperor, Romulus. Like Biden, Romulus was an empty figurehead, a cheap imitation of his far more capable progenitor (respectively, Barack Obama and Romulus's father, Orestes, a Roman general who once joined the court of Attila the Hun). After all, both men were hastily chosen by their desperate handlers, mainly to stir nostalgic memories of "the good old days" in the heads of politically naïve citizens.

Anyway. The more intriguing point about the *Papers'* authors' choice of a nom de plume centers on Publius' traditional (and, it's argued today, somewhat inflated) image, that of a wealthy, "egalitarian" military leader who helped to overthrow the Roman monarchy but who was later accused by the citizenry of aspiring to become a king himself, given that he lived in a stately house on a hill; after that, he vacated the mansion for a more modest home, obviously for appearances. Thus we glimpse the devious strategy behind Madison, Hamilton and Jay's writing as "Publius": They wanted to conjure in the minds of their readers visions of a kindly, civic-minded band of aristocrats who "didn't want their intentions misinterpreted." It insinuated that the fact that they lived lives of luxury didn't detract from their wanting the best for all citizens, even if helping the public improve their collective lot might put a dent in their own bank accounts.

Was it all a deception? In his 2022 book *We The Elites*, Robert Ovetz, a mellow-tempered, ponytailed political science lecturer at San Jose State University, decries the Constitution's framers as a group of wealthy, paranoid land- and slave-owners who lived in constant fear of losing their economic dominance over the less-fortunate majority. Ovetz portrays them as a hyper-privileged clique for whom the original

Articles of Confederation and its decentralized, states'-rights-supportive tenor offered scant protection from a triad of threats. There was pushback from Native Americans who'd had their land violently stolen and from rebellious slaves fighting for their fundamental freedoms. And there were rumblings from some of the new country's own citizens, primarily independent subsistence farmers living hand-to-mouth. Although many of those farmers had served on the front lines in the war for independence, scores of them lost their land when the fledgling government rejected their attempts to pay taxes with anything other than gold or silver.

Ovetz spent years poring over reams of papers, notes, diaries, personal letters, and such written by the framers or recorded by various stenographers in the days leading up to the finalization of the Constitution. He couldn't help noticing that the elites had a lot of disdain for common folk and democracy itself. He uncovered a plethora of incriminating remarks directly attributed to such legendary figures as George Washington (writing of his disgust for the Shay's Rebellion and similar revolts that had been perpetrated by the aggrieved subsistence farmers, Washington grumbled, "Mankind, left to themselves, are unfit for their own government").

He's got a million of 'em, our Ovetz. Building his case that the Constitution's authors abhorred real democracy and preferred the ancient Roman system, in which landowning elites always had the final political say, Ovetz points his finger at other legendary figures, for instance John Adams, who once wrote that elections are "productive of Horrors [...] there is great Reason to dread them."[45] On and on it goes: In *The Federalist #10*, James Madison wrote that "Such democracies [like the one practiced in ancient Athens that occasionally held debt jubilees] have ever been spectacles of turbulence and contention ... have ever been found incompatible with personal security or [and here's the money shot] the *rights of property* [emphasis mine]."

Please put down the Cheetos and think about that for a second. Only in a country partly built on the four-on-the-floor-crazy delusion that *inanimate property has rights* could we ever see something come to pass like the 2010 *Citizens United* Supreme Court decision, which threw open the floodgates for corporations to spend as much money on elections as they please, as long as the money isn't given directly to candidates.

Really, if property has rights, why shouldn't a corporation—a legal construct that exists only on paper—be considered an actual private citizen and spend as much money as it takes to tilt the democratic process?

Anyone with a single humanitarian bone in their body saw how bad *Citizens United* was. Shortly after its 2010 passage, former U.S. president Jimmy Carter said the decision was "one of the stupidest rulings ever consummated or perpetrated on the American people."

It's helpful to view *Citizens United* as resulting from an unbreakable *blockchain* of anti-democratic Supreme Court rulings: *Citizens United* wouldn't have come to pass without the 1976 *Buckley vs. Valeo* decision serving as a precedent. In turn, *Buckley*, which removed limits on election expenditures, wouldn't have had a legal leg to stand on if the First Amendment's "protections for free expression" wording had included a clause forbidding any attempt to override the democratic process by members of a filthy rich super-minority.

Let me clarify that property—which nowadays means not just land but also intellectual and artistic works, private debt and so on—doesn't have "rights" in the most literal sense (although right-wingers vehemently disagree[46]), but it does have legal *attributes* that make it a piece of property. In her 2019 book *The Code of Capital*, Columbia University law professor Katharina Pistor lists four main characteristics that make something a legal piece of property: "Priority," which ranks competing claims to the same asset by more than one party to determine actual ownership; "durability," which extends that guarantee of ownership over time; "universality," which guarantees that priority and durability rights are "actually enforced against the world" by the state; and "convertibility," which gives asset owners the right to transfer or sell an asset at will. Pistor reveals that over the last several centuries, laws have been written—"coded"—to favor the rights of property owners over the needs and desires of citizens for hundreds of years, largely through back-room dealings between lawyers. In the 1500s and 1600s, illiterate citizens had basically no idea what the highly skilled legal teams representing wealthy property owners were talking about when they argued points before judges; they were no match for them in court and thus doomed to suffer loss after loss, further tipping the wealth imbalance. The same situation continues today; if an obscure precedent exists, the better-staffed legal team is more apt to find it.

But wait, we're not done with the framers. Their fear of democracy led them to insert several nauseating bits of business into the Constitution. For example, their implementation of voting districts was, Ovetz claims, part of a plot to institute a "divide and conquer" approach to keep citizens separated into factions. Ovetz catches them red-handed, noting that Madison once wrote that although "*divide et impera*" was "the reprobated axiom of tyranny" it is, nevertheless, "under certain (some) qualifications, the only policy by which a republic can be administered on just principles."[47] Translation: Deliberately keeping citizens fighting against each other is the easiest way to keep them governable.

Ovetz's insightful contributions to Fifth Estate journalism are indispensable to truth-seekers. Where establishment-entrenched history teachers and professors describe the Constitution as a holy map to democracy, "democratic government" and the like, Ovetz posits that the "system of checks and balances" was purposely meant to ensure that political privilege always remained in the hands of America's wealthiest citizens.

Those checks and balances still work to prevent progress. Every time a piece of equalitarian or environmentally sensible legislation is submitted, it's guaranteed to fail if it would inconvenience the elites. Somewhere along the "checks and balances" line—which nowadays consists of not just Congress and the Executive Branch but unelected bodies like the Supreme Court and the Federal Reserve—the right judge, politician or bureaucrat will eventually enter the fray to ensure that the wealthy get the result they want.

This is pure heresy, of course, but no more fantastic than other interpretations of the framers' real motives. All we need to do is follow the money. Madison and his cohorts were aristocrats who claimed to want a strong central government and a unified nation that wasn't ruled by a monarchy, but it sure looks like a monarchy now, with a single person—the president, who is awarded their position by the Electoral College rather than through the popular vote—having the final say. Under the president sits a group of 100 wealthy aristocrats (or, as Chris Hedges identifies them, "mandarins")—senators—who, until 1913, were selected not by "the people" but by state legislatures, and who, even now, require a gigantic pile of money to "buy" their seats (in 2022, on average, U.S. Senate candidates spent $13.5 million on their campaigns whether they won or lost[48]).

Keeping in mind that this stuff isn't proper fodder for polite conversation if you're at a kegger hosted by your average Constitutional scholar, I'm inclined to agree with Ovetz's assessment, that the framers often acted as an antidemocratic cabal that sought to expand the dominance and privilege they enjoyed as rich property owners, and in the end, they successfully made it official.

Either way, gaining an understanding of these things is a valuable tool for activists who want to communicate their ideas and aims to others in the 99 percent, whose will is consistently denied by an elite one percent of creditors, landowners and the like in the same manner as the votes of one percent of Rome's propertied elite, by legal decree, overrode the will of the majority of Rome's citizens.

Ovetz is by no means the only Fifth Estate wonk to have concluded that America's democracy problems started in 1787. Rohan Grey, a Modern Monetary Theory proponent and professor at the Willamette University College of Law, likewise believes that the Constitution was intended to formalize the concentration of power at the top. According to Grey, one of the document's objectives was shifting monetary (legal dollar printing) powers from the state level to the federal level so that the federal government would be in total control of the money supply. Given that, Grey maintains that in contrast to the American Revolution, the creation of the U.S. Constitution was an essential element to a *counter*-revolution.

That counter-revolution was completely successful. To this day, U.S. citizens remain reluctant to protest socioeconomic inequality, gravitating instead to culture wars. Many of today's center-left Democratic voters share the same debunked economic beliefs as those of their "Don't Tread On Me"-flag-hugging "opponents" in the Republican voting bloc. The two sides have a lot more in common than they think, is what I mean.

Ovetz is aware of that, but wisely chooses not to pound its truth to stir further division. In fact, he glimpses an opportunity to get both the left and the right to understand that they share common economic cause. That's a tall order, involving more than a little re-education of the majority of liberals who blindly trust the Fourth Estate, not to mention the often paranoid mindset present in the heads of the Fox News crowd, but he does make an admirable effort.

Thinkers like Ovetz get no support from the establishment, of course. Aside from being consistently, dangerously wrong when constructing their economic models, establishment economists often labor under other false impressions. For instance, if you ask any orthodox economist to name the "father of modern capitalism," 99 times out of 100 they'll say it was Adam Smith, the 18th- century economist and philosopher credited with the invention of such concepts as division of labor, gross domestic product and the "invisible hand of the market." If that were the whole story, anyone calling themselves a socialist would curse Smith's name. But the truth, according to University of Southern California professor Jacob Soll, is that Smith was, to a fault, a big believer in the good nature of people, that wealth itself would compel capitalists to give back to their communities and the world.[49]

Soll bases this on years of study, during which he came to interpret Smith as being grounded in the thinking of the ancient Stoics, Cicero in particular, whose pre-Christian faith in the egalitarian nature of humankind led him to believe that wealth was merely "material for virtue to act upon," that the rich would feel compelled to help the less fortunate and contribute to their communities (this was obviously long before Amazon.com billionaire Jeff Bezos decided that a healthy chunk of his Smaug-sized cavern-load of wealth would be better spent founding his own recreational NASA than creating a work environment at Amazon that wasn't so ridiculously awful and pressure-packed that his delivery drivers found it necessary to keep empty milk jugs handy in their trucks in case they needed to urinate[50]).

Soll paints Smith as a bet-hedger, beholden to wealthy patrons but possessed of common sense. For example, Smith was against slavery on ethical and humanitarian grounds but nevertheless stated that it was "perpetuall" [sic], meaning that it would never go away. Toward that, then, I'd say that if anything, he was the prototype of Fourth Estate economics pundits like Joseph Stiglitz, concealing his true feelings and carefully weighing his messaging so that it wasn't too threatening to the elites.

Soll noticed that Smith's convictions weren't shared by Alexander Hamilton, who wrote two-thirds of the *Federalist Papers* and was thus a significant influence over much of the Constitution's content. A self-taught economist, Hamilton believed that the theory of mercantilism favored by 17th-century French Finance Minister Jean-Baptiste Colbert was more "sensible." Philosophical agreement with Colbert inspired Hamilton (and this is a point of contention among economics historians) to urge the new country's leadership to engage in protectionism, violent colonization and forcible extraction of the natural resources of foreign countries. That, Hamilton believed, was the direction the government should take, as opposed to Smith's God-fearing, agriculture-based methods of generating national wealth, which centered on the idea that the infinite wisdom of the market and the guidance of its "invisible hand" would bring balance and rationality to the economy.

And so, if we trust Soll's research, it's safe to say that if Thomas Jefferson—who was, like Smith, a devout believer in agriculture as the means to national prosperity—had helped guide the drafting of the Constitution instead of Hamilton, America might have been much different today. Sure, at some point in more modern times, an archaic but gentler agricultural-based Constitution would have been discarded in favor of a set of rules geared more toward an industrialized but egalitarian society (probably with a lot fewer legal loopholes for the elites to exploit). But would it have evolved into a set of laws that bends over backward to protect a tiny minority of people who own all the stuff that makes stuff? This is all hypothetical, of course, but it's possible that a more Jeffersonian Constitution would have bloviated ad infinitum on the need to protect the land and its farmers.

The fact that one major debate on the proposed future of America was one pitting Smith's naïve agrarianism against Colbert's predatory mercantilism is just one more thing that tells us that the Constitution is laughably obsolete in the Information Age.

XI: Weaving the Austerity Matrix

Now, Hamilton wouldn't be the last self-serving "expert" to spread bullshit in an effort to maintain the elites' dominance. Equally bad people came later, as Clara Mattei lays out in her 2022 book *The Capital Order*.

Things were going swimmingly for the elites during America's first 130-odd years, with little pushback from plebeian interest groups, aside from the odd equalitarian movement. In modern times, the most notable progressive force was the Populist Party, headed by William Jennings

Bryan, who ran for president in 1892. Bryan eventually lost to the Republican, William McKinley, but the elites would be forced to take drastic anti-populist measures only a couple of decades after Bryan's failed run, the necessity of which can be attributed to flaws in the capitalists' anti-humanitarian leanings: Instead of spreading peace throughout the world, the elites, playing a constant game of imperial one-upmanship, gave the world the demented horrors of World Wars I and II. In other words, they overdid it.

In the post-World War I period, there was peace, prosperity and, as a result of all the spectacular warfare, a lot fewer workers around to produce profits for the top of the economic hierarchy. That labor shortage led to an emboldened workforce, whose members wanted to "consume more and produce less." In other words, workers wanted better working conditions and more money. The elites didn't want that, and so workers began to express their disgust with the status quo. They unionized, held strikes and participated in workplace sit-ins. In 1919, one fifth of America's workforce, over four million people, participated in strikes, a number that wouldn't be rivaled until the Great Depression year of 1937. Capitalists, fearing that Bolshevism and widespread worker revolt would challenge the meticulously crafted socioeconomic order atop which they sat, decided they needed to take a drastic step: They needed to bullshit *everyone*.

Mattei claims that in the post-World War I era, when the capital order was threatened by that empowered, increasingly socialist-minded workforce, the elites recruited popular "experts" to help ensure that their gravy train kept running on schedule without interruption. Anointed as omniscient beings and sent to economic conferences in Brussels, Belgium, and Genoa, Italy, during the early 1920s, establishment figures— including a platoon of Italians that included economist Maffeo

Pantaleoni, economist/academic Umberto Ricci and politicians Luigi Einaudi and Alberto De Stefani—birthed a renaissance of popular economic thought based on "common sense" about "truths" such as the "need" for cuts in social spending programs. They advised that such sacrifices would benefit *all* the economic classes if workers voluntarily "consumed less and produced more" through their labor. And so, in the 1920s, austerity spread throughout the land, taking hold in every western country that had (A) survived the war intact, and (B) wasn't communist. "Austerity," writes Mattei, "emerged as an economic, moral, and technocratic message, as economic experts sought to *educate* [my emphasis] restless post-war civil society."

Those experts also recommended establishing omnipotent central banks in order to control money supplies, but the U.S. was already ahead of the game. In 1913, despite pushback from the Republican senate minority, the Federal Reserve was created, ostensibly for the purpose of avoiding future financial crises like the panic of 1907. Central bank control of interest rates is, orthodox economists maintain, essential for "keeping economies running at the right temperature." That means that sometimes an economy needs to be "cooled down" through interest rate hikes, which invariably hurt workers: They lead to higher unemployment rates, owing to the simple-stupid fact that businesses have less capital with which to hire more people or keep all the workers they have.

One notable item that snuck its way into the malevolent mix of "expert" wisdom was the "fact" that central banks should be independent from any governmental or democratic constraints. Naturally, that bit of advice was followed to the letter, and the Federal Reserve was imitated around the world. In America, it is a rogue, unelected body, answerable to no one, and, as some heterodox economists contend, isn't even necessary, owing to the existence of the U.S. Treasury. It's been suggested in some Modern Monetary Theory circles that the Fed could, more or less, be replaced by an Excel spreadsheet.[51] That's been dismissed as being a bit extreme, but as we've seen, the Fed does have an odd habit of raising interest rates at inadvisable times, such as the aforementioned hike it implemented in 2022, when, by suspicious coincidence, the U.S. labor force was participating in the "Great Resignation," in which a record 50.5 million people quit their jobs (albeit mostly to move to better ones owing to COVID-19's taking people out of the workforce for various reasons). Not to put too fine a point on it, but like the worker rebellions of the World War I-era, the burst of worker confidence in 2020 was obviously worrying to the oligarchy, and of course their crack corps of orthodox economics experts. The 2020 interest rate hike, coming after more than a decade of low-to-zero interest rates that served to benefit only Wall Street and other wealthy interests, was quite clearly a shot across the bow to the labor force, which, in the rate hike's aftermath, suddenly found that fewer jobs were available, the fact of which muzzled any real worker rebellion that might have arisen.

6

Putting It All Together: Rules For Online Radicals

I: Piddling and Twiddling

In the Broadway musical *1776*, John Adams curses his fellow members of the Second Continental Congress. They can't seem to agree on anything, least of all the big question of whether America should declare independence from England. The group of legendary figures, Adams complains to the air, "piddle, twiddle and resolve" nothing but inconsequential matters, spending their time bloviating at great length over such items as whether the Congress should reimburse such-and-so state representative 20 dollars for the upkeep of their mule. It's dangerously stuffy in their Philadelphia enclave, and the sweat-soaked assembly can't even agree to open a window to get a break from their own stench. They seem more interested in hearing their own voices than discussing workable strategies that might address the issues that had brought them there: unfair taxes imposed by their mother country, the ever-present threat of Redcoats randomly detaining colonists or conducting unannounced searches of their homes, etc.

Piddling and twiddling with others over major, minor and

microscopic points of ideological contention is the online left's favorite pastime. It provides an inexhaustible supply of debate fodder for Fifth Estate personalities who need to fill hours of content on their talk shows. It's hard to picture a scenario in which all the separate left-leaning bubbles on corporate social media would ever settle on a comprehensive plan of coordinated action, from a hashtag campaign to a national workers' strike. But it's not completely impossible. It only appears so because we focus more on promoting our individualism than collaborating to advance the needs of the greater collective, which is an infinitely more interesting puzzle.

No matter how unbreakable they may feel to us in our minds, the ties that bind leftists to each other on social media are astonishingly fragile, ready to snap at the first sign of disagreement. When one of our (officially designated) "Friends" or "mutual followers" writes something we disagree with, we don't ask them to explain their thinking; we reach for the Block button, instantly severing our link forever. Any camaraderie we may have shared is forgotten in a flash, and future opportunities to exercise our critical thinking with that person disappear. Worst of all, it tells the blocked person that they're disposable, that they're somehow "not properly leftist."

Out of the hundreds of personal connections I've made on Twitter, one stands out, not for its degree of camaraderie but for the discouraging way it ended. During the first year of my Supersize Me experiment, a 60something woman, whom I'll call "Shelly," began engaging with my tweets on a daily basis and we became friends. A retiree subsisting on disability payments, she was a Democratic voter with a good sense of humor. Politically, all she really knew about me was that I disapproved of Donald Trump, which was how I wanted it in those days. We chatted nearly every day, usually in a kidding-around manner, sometimes "offline" in private Twitter messages. Neither of us had a lot of friends, she because she wasn't very active on the platform, and me because my tweets weren't very emotional and thus kind of sucked by Twitter standards. But we had fun. She was open about being romantically interested in me but wasn't expecting anything to happen; being married, I parried a few of her more risqué comments with distractive jokes and such.

One day, she announced she'd been diagnosed with cancer. Naturally, I was very supportive of her. In an instant, I made it one of my responsibilities to keep her spirits up. I scoured the web and collected dozens of animated GIF files (short film clips) of stupid animal tricks—chickens chasing farm kids, baby pigs eating stuff, a guy riding an emu—and every day, I'd post one on her timeline.

A few months passed, and both of us were becoming mildly "popular"; more people were interacting with the things we posted. I began to let my guard down, tweeting fewer digs against the Republicans and taking a few relatively tame potshots at the Democrats. Then, at some point, I tweeted something about Biden not being the best 2020 Democratic candidate, and within minutes, Shelly "unfollowed" and blocked me. In an instant, I'd been "ghosted," banished from her circle.

I won't lie; it hurt a bit. I mean, I'm not completely stupid; maybe Shelly's interest in me was deeper than I suspected, and she'd been looking for an excuse to take me down a notch. But the blocking seemed completely irrational to me. We'd shared a lot of very personal information with each other, and it was disappointing that she'd resorted to *that* over a harmless comment about Joe Fucking Biden.

But such is life online. With all the internecine fighting

that rages on the internet between online leftist groups, it's no wonder organizers dismiss the idea that social media could ever be of any use to them. By and large, they're convinced that the only way to get people to agree on strategy is when they're physically gathered together in one place, where seasoned pros can address questions and concerns in real time, face-to-face. Even then, it's not easy to persuade a sizable group of workers to agree on a set of union demands or convince the majority of the activists in one's group to agree on which physical route for a protest march would yield the best visibility.

Along with knowing that a Niagara Falls of disinformation will greet anything they post on corporate social media that supports their causes, organizers don't take internet spaces seriously because they're always thrumming with distractions: fresh news stories, memes, and a million other things. It's hopeless to get anything organized online, they think.

And at present, they're not wrong. Social media users have normalized a lot of bad habits over the years. They've completely forgotten a few rules of thumb that would make our virtual gathering places much less chaotic and divisive if the vast majority put them into practice. As things are, we'll probably never see an online renaissance of solidarity between movements take hold unless centralized, for-profit social media is abandoned by pretty much everyone on the planet.

As you've seen, I believe that the right sort of decentralized, independent social media platform—namely the fediverse—could help activist movements to connect with each other. "Federated" spaces like Mastodon, most of whose servers are built and maintained by techie tinkerers as labors of love, offer fertile ground for Fifth Estate figures to grow their platforms and for political junkies to share uncensored information with each other. It is the "gray web," if you will, a purely organic segment of the social media sphere, where users aren't manipulated and psychologically abused in the name of corporate profits. And unlike darkweb users, visitors to the fediverse aren't in constant danger of having their devices hacked or subjected to humanity's darkest impulses. In 2024, I talked with a Brazilian who was quitting Twitter for Bluesky; she said that Brazilian activist communities are already moving to the fediverse. American movements should definitely follow suit in order to collaborate in peace.

That said, corporate social media will not go quietly into the night, despite its inevitable demise. It will distract, it will obfuscate, and it will continue to benefit from its close relationships to the Fourth Estate, the imperial-industrial complex and various other well-funded misinformation dispensers. It will remain stubbornly, immovably "politically correct" on a selective basis, which it will use as an excuse to silence Fifth Estate critics at will. Even the Mastodon constellation of the fediverse has some censorship going on, with some administrators enforcing policies of zero tolerance for critics of the establishment. An acquaintance of mine had a few posts removed from a Mastodon instance because they were critical of IDF actions in Gaza. What all that means, however, is that the fediverse isn't perfect. If you're going to participate in it, make sure you research the instance and know what's okay to post there.

It's a given that longtime corporate social media users would resist switching to the fediverse. Millions of people have spent years building friendships and soapboxes on their corporate platforms of choice. Some have tapped into revenue streams they've grown to count on to pay the bills. In the process, they've come to accept, or at least ignore, that corporate social media companies constantly work to keep them siloed within bubbles while rudely invading their privacy and manipulating their thoughts and emotions through cynical algorithms.

Realistically, online activist actions should be much less difficult to organize than actions that require people to be physically present. On paper, if an activist wants to accomplish something online, all they really need to do is grow widespread support for the ends they seek, such as launching a boycott or a labor strike. Once a goal is set and popular support for it grows, whether through viral hashtags, "tweet storms" (rapid-fire bursts of tweets posted by multiple users simultaneously over a set period of time) or some other method, large groups of netizens will simply take it from there. In that, online protest campaigns can spread the word and attract more people to movements, which can in turn lead to things like increased participation in movements, locating volunteers who'd be willing to commit their spare time to causes, and even free mainstream publicity (on the rare occasions when major media outlets—all of which are by now well aware that people have very active online lives and that they therefore cannot ignore things that trend on the internet—deign to cover an organization's online doings).

And yet the piddling and twiddling continues, and will until the online left consciously takes up the habit of finding common cause instead of picking at ideological nits, and finally moves out of its squalid, oppressive corporate social media digs. It's steadily happening but at the same glacial pace as the implementation of Jane McAlevey's "whole person-oriented" approach to activist organizing, a deeply nuanced method we see in pro-labor spaces. It's a paradigm McAlevey recommends as an alternative to Saul Alinsky's "mobilization method," which is now over 50 years old.

But while we're at it, was Alinsky really so bad?

II: The Mob Rules

Saul Alinsky was a labor organizer whose best-known book, *Rules For Radicals*, was published in 1971, the year before his passing. The book's lessons have inspired countless activist organizations, including Fred Ross's Community Service Organization, the National People's Action network and Chicago's United Neighborhood Organization.

Alinsky's methods are still in wide use today. His organizing work was informed by his college years at the University of Chicago, where he studied gangs and mobs as a "nonparticipant observer," including a stint during which he claimed to have hung out with Al Capone. "*That's* the model," McAlevey once spat in disgust to an assembly of Canadian labor activists.

McAlevey, who largely took over Alinsky's role as the front-person of labor organizing, argued that Alinsky's overarching goal—mobilizing, i.e., getting as many warm bodies as possible to protest events, regardless of how dedicated to the causes those bodies actually are—is outdated. That's largely true, but along the way, critics have taken issue with her often brusque dismissal of Alinsky, given that he did get things accomplished now and then. For example, there was his 1964 threat against Chicago Mayor Richard Daley for refusing to follow through on some political promises he'd made, measures that would benefit poor Blacks on the city's South Side. Alinsky proposed a prank in which teams of activists would invade all the public bathrooms at O'Hare Airport. Participants planned to line themselves up four or five deep at the stalls and urinals, either standing or sitting there for five minutes before leaving and being replaced by a co-conspirator, after which they'd head to another restroom and do the same thing. "What's some poor sap at the end of the line going to say," Alinsky told *Playboy* magazine in 1972, "'Hey, pal, you're taking too long to piss'?"

The proposed "shit-in" never took place, luckily for everyone involved. Two days after word of the action leaked (so to speak), City Hall, not wanting to deal with hundreds of angry flight returnees running around looking for places to relieve themselves, broke down and kept its word.[1]

Obviously, Alinsky did have his troll side. Also in 1964, he took umbrage with Eastman Kodak's exploitation of Black workers at the company's Rochester, N.Y. facility, which had resulted in race riots. He proposed a "fart-in" at a performance of the Rochester Philharmonic Orchestra: The organization would purchase 100 seats for the show and give them to Black workers, who would be treated to a preshow banquet of baked beans. That one never got off the ground, but Alinsky's idea to disrupt a classical music performance did become reality in 2014, when 50 protesters, inspired by a Facebook campaign launched by a 42-year-old white woman, Sarah Griesbach, interrupted the St. Louis Symphony by singing "justice for Michael Brown"—beautifully, according to the crowd—to protest the recent murder of the Ferguson, Missouri, African American man by police officers.

(Regarding the Black Lives Matter movement, there's no shortage of wisdom available for the Fifth Estate to diffuse in the area of police misconduct. Police officers, rarely if ever vetted for intolerant beliefs through psychological testing processes, continue to use deadly force on non-whites as if they have a legal imperative to do so. Not only is there no national testing standard in use for keeping intrinsically violent, trigger-happy cops off the streets;[2] police officers likewise aren't evaluated for high levels of racist and/or other bigoted beliefs that might make them unfit for the job, which can actually be diagnosed through tests like the one offered by the non-profit organization Project Implicit.[3])

Some of Alinsky's Rules haven't stood the test of time, especially when people are doing any activism online. Two Rules I feel have passed their expiration dates have become fused together in center-leftist meme-culture, namely, "Ridicule is man's most powerful weapon" and "Pick the target, freeze it, personalize it, and polarize it." They constitute an invitation to beat transgressively divisive jokes to death. Not everyone has a knack for comedy, let's face it, and when you have too many unfunny people crafting their own memes in the hope of racking up Likes and shares and such, the whole point sort of deflates. For example, poking fun at U.S. Representative Matt Gaetz for the (admittedly large) size of his forehead was funny for the first day or so, but it also served to distract from the Florida representative's denying the 2020 presidential election results and claiming Trump had every right to contest them. What's even less funny is watching "targets of online abuse" completely ignore all the noise and continue doing business as usual. Republicans have become experts at pretending their trolls aren't there.

In online left circles, widespread adherence to the Alinsky model has inspired such unconstructive nonsense as cancel culture, dogpiling, shunning and other tactics that cater to a mob mentality. Such behavior is the opposite of a "whole person" activist recruitment approach, a phrase derived from McAlevey's "whole worker" model of labor organizing, a technique focused less on gathering mobs of faceless people than on taking the time to identify "the most respected worker on each shift, in each department," i.e., the individuals who can only be found by questioning and getting to know *all* the workers in the organization. Once activists identify potential leaders or potential comrades, they can focus on enlisting them to their cause.

Applying that recruiting/organizing strategy to the online left, the "just Google it" snobbery needs to stop. Just because you've explained your thinking to one person on one occasion, it doesn't mean you can't repeat yourself to any other curious minds, calmly and clearly, over and over. There may be "no such thing as a stupid question," but it's as though seasoned social media users believe the opposite, that all questions are stupid. I saw it constantly on Twitter and took the opposite tack, repeating myself ad infinitum to people who asked why I thought such and so about a particular thing. No one ever complained. In fact, for what it's worth, I think people who'd seen me post the same things before kind of appreciated being reminded about them.

It could be said that Alinsky's greatest strength—his transgressive nature—was also a liability. Some people don't enjoy insulting others or engaging in pranks. But on the other hand, Alinsky's seventh Rule—"a tactic that drags on too long becomes a drag"—is helpful because it encourages activists to stay sharp, flexible and enthusiastic about their actions.

In fact, that Rule directly relates to the concept of "conjunctural analysis," an awkward but useful little term that's become a hot topic of late within activist circles. It urges activist groups to "mobilize in the moment," to look at a recent event or development and change, adjust or altogether abandon their current strategy and take advantage of it. For example, if an activist group has been focusing all their energies on organizing protests against Starbucks' management for their alleged union-busting efforts,[4] and it suddenly comes to light that XYZ Coffee Company has been doing something even worse, the activist group's focus may need to shift, and very quickly.

While we're here, like any other Fifth Estate-centric

concept that sounds a lot more complicated than it is, conjunctural analysis has been so obfuscated by well-meaning academics that they shouldn't be allowed to speak its name. In 2024, Christina Heatherton of the Trinity Social Justice Institute interviewed scholar Jordan Camp on his favorite subject, the work and life of Italian Marxist theorist Antonio Gramsci. In the 1920s, Gramsci developed a method of conjunctural analysis to collate and understand the swirl of factors that allowed Mussolini to come to power. Knowing that Camp was so familiar with Gramsci's thinking that he thought it was possible to "talk" to the long-dead philosopher as if he were still around, Heatherton asked Camp what he thought Gramsci would say about today's cockeyed political environment. Camp begins addressing the question but never answers it, instead launching into a six-minute-long soliloquy about Gramsci's life and upbringing. It was like watching a shy 10-year-old boy talk about his favorite Imagine Dragons songs.

Good organizers are rare. The best ones want to know when something is working and when it isn't. They have the confidence to ask their people for feedback, be prepared to hear criticism, and, if criticism does come, be possessed of enough maturity that they don't take it personally. That seems obvious enough, but by the same token, a good activist should always endeavor to temper their criticism of an organization's strategies. As activists, it's okay for us to find fault with a tactic, and it's okay not to pretend to be mindlessly upbeat about every plan an organizer suggests. But the best way to express our disagreement with someone else's thinking is to come to them with an alternative solution rather than a blank-faced complaint.

Yes, that's basic *One-Minute Manager* stuff. But we need to think about those things and work to improve our communication so that we can cohere at a fundamentally human level. The only way for individual activists and groups to challenge the powerful is by building real solidarity. In that effort, everyone needs to communicate mindfully.

Toward that, Chris Dixon cautions that activists need to be aware that there are two approaches constantly at work in movements that can sometimes cause friction between teams of activists. Activists who are involved in strategizing protests against bad things—activists who are in "tear-down mode"—may see activists who are promoting positive things like relationship-building—working in "build-up mode"—as being "in a dream world," whereas activists whose efforts focus on building power in positive ways can tend to question why activists from the "tear-down" side are "being so negative." Both teams have the same end goals, and that needs to be kept in mind. It makes me think of when my friends and I are playing street hockey and a bunch of guys are battling for the ball without looking at whom they're tussling with: Sometimes we have to yell "same team" so that our teammates know that they're working against their own players.

Is there such a thing as a one-size-fits-all organizational strategy? I asked Stephanie Luce, co-author of *Practical Radicals*. "[Organizations need] to understand that they are just part of a larger eco-system," she said, "and that there are different strategies needed to make transformative change. An electoral organizer may believe their strategy is the best, but when they look at a larger eco-system they will see that other units—such as organizations that do base-building and disruption—play crucial roles."

What about the fact that early on, Jane McAlevey became so disillusioned with climate activists' "disregard for 'just transition'" (ensuring that workers have jobs to go to if their fossil fuel jobs disappeared) that she switched to labor organizing? Luce believes the climate movement's tune has changed over the years. "I find it hard to generalize about climate activists since I've worked with a huge range of people who would consider themselves climate activists. Some are fully focused on just transition. Some climate activists see unions as a key force in the climate movement and see labor and climate work as intertwined."

Either way, the sidelining of McAlevey is a devastating setback to all activist movements, but it isn't insurmountable. In a February 2024 conversation with activist/author Cynthia Kaufman on the subject of McAlevey's battle with cancer, I asked her whom she thought might one day take McAlevey's place as the front-person of organizing. "McAlevey trained a lot of people and leaves behind an important body of work on organizing," Kaufman told me, then added, "We don't need a messiah. Our movements need to be leaderful."

That may be true of individual movements, but the United States is running far behind its international counterparts in building alliances among movements in order to remain politically relevant. That includes the Democratic Socialists of America, which, even with a relatively meager 90,000 members, still "lacks a united political program even on such basic matters as whom to endorse for president," as Arash Azizi wrote in *The Atlantic* (in a March 2024 piece that looked to me like a preview of the Fourth Estate's inevitable cattle call for the left to cohere behind Biden in the upcoming presidential election, point of order).[5] Azizi is correct when he writes that, in contrast to the American left, "the international left seems largely to recognize that it is too small to survive on its own and must therefore build coalitions," and that after the 1970s, the left "[placed] itself outside the political system, condemning itself to marginality," which is where we stand now.

Aside from the internet-centric advice I've given here, the precise steps required for building leftist convergence are outside the scope of this book. I recommend Luce and Bhargava's *Practical Radicals* to those seeking deeper answers.

III: Being The Change (Before It's Too Late)

It's plain that the oligarchs who own and operate our current system aren't going to address the issues of climate change or worker misery without pushback from a united left. Not to be overly dramatic, but time is running out. Solidarity must take hold, one way or another, so that the left can begin to coordinate strategy and demand change, if not for more livable work lives, then for drastically reducing humankind's use of fossil fuels for the benefit of future generations.

Some believe that the oligarchs and corporate elites who control America have survival strategies of their own regarding any upheaval that may be coming, whether from disease, societal collapse, or the fast-spreading climate crisis. Toward the latter, it's safe to assume that the wealthy—in particular fossil fuel super-barons like Charles Koch and Harold Hamm—know that their reckless, greed-driven refusal to end the use of fossil fuels threatens a huge swath of humanity, which could at some point affect them as well.

In some areas of the world, climate collapse has already arrived. Americans are familiar with the heat waves, droughts and flood-inducing downpours that have been brought on by climate change, but it is much worse elsewhere. In the Jacobabad district of Pakistan, the streets empty in midsummer, when temperatures reach 52°C (126°F) and wet bulb temperatures rise to 160°F. Under those conditions, even if someone were outdoors, lying unclothed in the shade and drinking water constantly, they'd die in a few hours.[6] Only a drastic reduction in greenhouse gases will prevent further devastation occurring during this century.[7]

There's a bumper sticker that reads "Nature Bats Last." That's true. She alone will determine how many, if any, humans will survive any tumult that may be ahead. If the super-rich do have plans for surviving the catastrophes they've invited, they've kept them secret. The idea that they'll take off in a giant spaceship for years or decades until they reach a habitable planet is a non-starter: If exposure to radiation didn't bring on gastrointestinal cancer, our hyper-privileged astronauts would face myriad other threats: anemia, loss of midrange vision (they'd either be looking at their immediate surroundings or out a window into the void of space), bone deterioration,[8] etc.

That leaves conspiracy buffs with the "secret mountain enclave" theory, in which the elites would purportedly ensconce themselves and their families in some sort of hideout, waiting in luxury until it's safe to come out again. Some of the elites are said to be busily preparing for the apocalypse, such as Mark Zuckerberg, who's reported to be building a $270 million underground fortress on Hawaii's Kauai island, and Paypal founder Peter Thiel, who, last anyone knew, was trying to obtain permission to build a bunker-style mega-lodge in New Zealand.[9]

Turning to preventive, non-insane plans, Chris Hedges believes that the only strategy that will work to prevent societal breakdown at this point is one that involves widespread civil disobedience. Luce concurs. "It's hard to predict what will work," she told me, "but right now, it's hard to see a path for climate justice that won't involve major disruption. The status quo is not working; mainstream strategies to address climate chaos are moving far too slow - and in some cases, moving backwards."

Kaufman addresses the matter diplomatically. "Saying that there is only one strategy doesn't help us build synergy between the many strategies we need. Different people are attracted to different tactics, and different problems require different strategies. Civil disobedience is one important tactic among many."

There's no doubt that disruptive events are in our future, Shawn Fain's proposed 2028 national strike for one. While we prepare for whatever lies ahead, the broad left needs to start coming to agreement on what it wants exactly.

Unfortunately, corporate social media doesn't reward efforts to build solidarity. It hampers prefigurative movements simply because "netiquette" is a long-lost art. People have come to expect the worst from others when they communicate online. Basic politeness, much less the practice of behaving as though one desires to educate others, has gone out of fashion. It's as though people prefer getting into arguments with patently obvious trolls and bots over helping others understand their points of view. The old saying "Please don't feed the trolls" is widely ignored, to progress' peril. When you encounter a garden-variety rabble-rouser attacking your thoughts in a public forum, there's no need to worry that observers might think less of you. If you know you're right, don't retaliate or defend yourself. There's no need for it. Savvy observers will ignore the nonsense and respect you for your restraint.

In the meantime, we should seriously consider committing to an all-in rejection of corporate social media, which, along with the inevitable demise of Fourth Estate media owing to the high cost of cable television subscriptions and the corresponding rise of the Fifth Estate, would reduce confusion, starve attention-seeking troublemakers and put the online left on track to build the solidarity—and thus the power—required to challenge the elites. If all citizens understood the need for worker and activist solidarity, universal socioeconomic equality and climate preservation as informed by history and our Fifth Estate, we wouldn't have had any need for this discussion.

Acknowledgments

Unlike my first book, which was basically a labor of love for my wife, Jen, I have many people to thank for their input and assistance, whether sought or unsought, with this one. Jen does get top billing of course. For the second time in our marriage, she gave me the time and space I needed to research all this horrible business. My gratitude to her is bottomless.

During the writing process, I barely saw the rest of my family at all. To my sister and her husband, Valerie and Dan Compagna; my nephews Chase and Rane Markgren; my niece Brandie Markgren; James Brown Sr. and Jr.; Beth Brown and Evan and Anna Brown, here's to a fun summer ahead.

My "spirit animal" for this project was Kiss guitarist Ace Frehley. During writing breaks, I relaxed by watching his press interviews, which are comedy gold. Seeing him constantly crack up laughing over "serious rock 'n' roll business" always helped me tamp the emotions that came up while delving into these awful, depressing subjects. I feel a special kinship with the guy, not just because I'm also something of a jackass who literally cannot take American politics seriously for one second, but also because neither of us were ever professionally trained in our chosen passion. Where Ace never took a single guitar lesson but nevertheless perfected his own "double-picking" lead guitar technique, only ever picking up the odd trick here and there from his friends, I never attended a college English course (please at least pretend to look surprised). I took any bit of advice or criticism that came to me from the group of editors who've had to make sense out of my rushed attempts at music journalism over these many years: Amy Diaz, Meghan Siegler, Jenn Stevens, Steve Almond, Arielle Castillo and resident taskmistress Lisa Parsons, who exceeded my wildest expectations in editing this book.

I ran a test copy of this book by three readers, all of whom I met on Twitter and are truly dear to me: Mary Smith, the pseudonymed Jack Fortunati (see what he did there?) and presidential candidate Michael Dean. They and many other "tweeps" upped my mood when things felt hopeless: Adirondack Fella, Delilah Rose, Patricia Obiezierska, Shannon Day, Laurie Yoder, Angelo Angelli, Linda Mason, Scott and Brenda, Amy LeFave, Christlike Atheist, Caroline O'Driscoll, Mike "Mitch" Mitchell, Amy Harmon, and countless others.

I'm indebted to four authors who contributed invaluable thoughts to this book: Catherine Liu, Cynthia Kaufman, Michael Hudson and Stephanie Luce. Green Party/animal rights activist Stephanie Voltolin was also amazingly generous with her time.

A special thanks to Dan Szczesny, a local author whose friendship has made me feel part of the New Hampshire writing community.

A few veteran trolls from my Usenet days helped keep my spirits up in various social media spaces: Jeroen van Kessell, Mark "Menjy" Bullock and Bill Cleere.

Gary Poirier's support for my work has been appreciated more than he'll ever know.

The fonts I chose for this book are all shareware and were used free of charge. The main body of the book is printed in a variation of Philipp H. Poll's "Libertinus Math" typeface. The title is set in Aaron Amar's "Dozer." Chapter titles were rendered in Themnific's "Fava." I'm unusually happy with them and can't praise their creators enough.

Notes

Meet The Online Left

1 : John G. Matsusaka, "Popular Control of Public Policy: A Quantitative Approach," USC Gould School of Law, revised April 2010, https://gould.usc.edu/assets/docs/Matsusaka_Popular_Control.pdf

2: Alex Kotch, "Koch Brothers Bankroll Move to Rewrite the Constitution," Billmoyers.com, March 27, 2017, https://billmoyers.com/story/kochs-to-rewrite-constitution/

3: "Study: US is an oligarchy, not a democracy," BBC News, April 17, 2014, https://www.bbc.com/news/blogs-echochambers-27074746

4: Ryan Grim, "Cable News Viewers Have a Skewed Attitude Toward Gaza War, Survey Finds," The Intercept, April 30 2024, https://theintercept.com/2024/04/30/gaza-israel-palestine-cable-news-poll/

5: Malcolm Gladwell, "Small Change: Why the revolution will not be tweeted," *The New Yorker*, September 27, 2010, https://www.newyorker.com/magazine/2010/10/04/small-change-malcolm-gladwell

6: Dave Pell, "The Revolution Will Not Be Tweeted (Unless It Is)," *NPR*, September 29, 2010, https://www.npr.org/sections/alltechconsidered/2010/09/29/130215057/the-revolution-will-not-be-tweeted-unless-it-is

7: Aisha Majid, "Top 50 news websites in the US: AP and Axios among fastest-growing in September," Press Gazette, October 13, 2023, https://pressgazette.co.uk/media-audience-and-business-data/media_metrics/most-popular-websites-news-us-monthly-3

8: David Winner, "How the left enabled fascism," The New Statesman, October 3, 2018, https://www.newstatesman.com/world/europe/2018/10/how-left-enabled-fascism

9: School History, "Operation Mockingbird Facts & Worksheets," https://schoolhistory.co.uk/modern/operation-mockingbird/

The Decline of Corporate Social Media

1: Jamie Waters, "Constant craving: how digital media turned us all into dopamine addicts," The Guardian, August 22, 2021, https://www.theguardian.com/global/2021/aug/22/how-digital-media-turned-us-all-into-dopamine-addicts-and-what-we-can-do-to-break-the-cycle

2: Bruce Y. Lee, "'Vaccine Police' Founder Claims Drinking Urine Is COVID-19 Antidote," *Forbes*, January 10, 2022 https://www.forbes.com/sites/brucelee/2022/01/10/vaccine-police-founder-claims-drinking-your-own-urine-is-COVID-19-antidote/?sh=6e674da93735

3: Stefan Wojcik and Adam Hughes, "Sizing Up Twitter Users," Pew Research Center, April 24, 2019, https://www.pewresearch.org/internet/2019/04/24/sizing-up-twitter-users/

4: Aja Romano, "Twitter users can't stop tweeting about how much they don't want tweets to get longer," *Vox*, Sep 28, 2017, https://www.vox.com/culture/2017/9/28/16373268/twitter-users-hate-new-280-character-limit

5: P.W. Singer and Emerson T. Brooking, *Like War* (Mariner, 2018)

6: Influencer Marketing Hub, June 2022:
https://influencermarketinghub.com/how-much-do-youtubers-make/

7: Amal Moursi, "The 2022 Instagram Rich List—Who Earns The Most From Sponsored Instagram Posts?" *Hopper HQ*, https://www.hopperhq.com/blog/2022-instagram-rich-list/

8: 'The Great Reset Conspiracy Flourishes Amid Continued Pandemic," Anti-Defamation League, December 29, 2020, https://www.adl.org/resources/blog/great-reset-conspiracy-flourishes-amid-continued-pandemic

9: Brady, et al, "Emotion shapes the diffusion of moralized content in social networks," June 26, 2017
https://www.pnas.org/doi/10.1073/pnas.1618923114

10: *The Majority Report*, "How To Spot A Grifter On YouTube," June 3,2022, https://www.youtube.com/watch?v=_uZmi4QsN1U

11: The Jimmy Dore Show, "Is Rachel Maddow Dangerous To Journalism?" November 13, 2017,
https://www.youtube.com/watch?v=SDo0AUtW_Bo

12: Majid Padellan, *The Liddle'est President*.
https://www.amazon.com/gp/product/1734666439

13: Stephanie Lai, "Campaigns Pay Influencers to Carry Their Messages, Skirting Political Ad Rules," *The New York Times*, November 2,2022, https://www.nytimes.com/2022/11/02/us/elections/influencers-political-ads-tiktok-instagram.html

14: Sophia Cai, "Biden's digital strategy: an army of influencers," *Axios*, April 29,2023,
https://www.axios.com/2023/04/09/bidens-digital-strategy-an-army-of-influencers

15: Oliver Darcy, "Trump invites right-wing extremists to White House 'social media summit'," CNN Business, July 11, 2019, https://www.cnn.com/2019/07/10/tech/white-house-social-media-summit/index.html

16: Edward-Isaac Dovere, "Bernie Sanders Just Hired His Twitter Attack Dog," *The Atlantic*, March 19, 2019, https://www.theatlantic.com/politics/archive/2019/03/sanders-promised-civility-hired-twitter-attack-dog/585259/

17: Keith A. Spencer, "There is hard data that shows "Bernie Bros" are a myth," *Salon*, March 9, 2020, https://www.salon.com/2020/03/09/there-is-hard-data-that-shows-bernie-bros-are-a-myth/

18: A.J. Katz, "These Are the Top-Rated Cable News Shows for August 2022," *Adweek*, August 30, 2022, https://www.adweek.com/tvnewser/these-are-the-top-rated-cable-news-shows-for-august-2022/513419/

19: "Abby Martin Deplatformed By Youtube," Against The Current, March 15, 2022, https://nzagainstthecurrent.blogspot.com/2022/03/abby-martin-deplatformed-by-youtube.html

20: Jane McAlevy, *Unions, Organizing, and the Fight for Democracy* (Ecco, 2020, excerpted in https://janemcalevey.com/writing/why-unions-matter-excerpt-from-a-collective-bargain-unions-organizing-and-the-fight-for-democracy/)

Twitter is Dead, Long Live the Fediverse

1: Mark Maurer, "How Elon Musk's Twitter Faces Mountain of Debt, Falling Revenue and Surging Costs," Wall Street Journal, Nov. 21, 2022, https://www.wsj.com/articles/how-elon-musks-twitter-faces-mountain-of-debt-falling-revenue-and-surging-costs-11669042132

2. Kevin McGill, "Elon Musk Loses Appeals Court Ruling On 2018 Union-Busting Tweet," *Associated Press*, March 31, 2023,

https://www.huffpost.com/entry/nlrb-elon-musk-uaw-unionization_n_64286850e4b01284198da44d

3: Caleb Naysmith, "'I Refuse to Be the First Fatality': Elon Musk's The Boring Company's Safety Record Reportedly Left Employees Fearing For Their Lives," Benzinga, April 1, 2024, https://www.benzinga.com/startups/24/04/38023883/i-refuse-to-be-the-first-fatality-elon-musks-the-boring-companys-safety-record-reportedly-left-emplo

4: Kayla Gogarty, "Anti-LGBTQ hate has increased on Twitter since Elon Musk officially acquired the company," *Media Matters*, December 13, 2022, https://www.mediamatters.org/twitter/anti-lgbtq-hate-has-increased-twitter-elon-musk-officially-acquired-company

5: Yuvraj Malik, "Twitter rolls back COVID misinformation policy," Reuters, November 29, 2022, https://www.reuters.com/technology/twitter-rolls-back-COVID-misinformation-policy-2022-11-29/

6: Sharon Kann, "In less than a month, Elon Musk has driven away half of Twitter's top 100 advertisers," *Media Matters*, November 22, 2022, https://www.mediamatters.org/elon-musk/less-month-elon-musk-has-driven-away-half-twitters-top-100-advertisers

7: Joanna Slater, "Connecticut jury orders Alex Jones to pay nearly $1 billion to Sandy Hook families," *The Washington Post*, October 12, 2022, https://www.washingtonpost.com/nation/2022/10/12/alex-jones-sandy-hook-verdict/

8: I assume that was partly the case, although shortly before Musk reinstated Alex Jones in December of 2023, he claimed that Jones' ban would remain in force out of respect for the memory of his first-born son, who died of Sudden Infant Death Syndrome in 2002. "I have no mercy," Musk commented at the time, "for anyone who would use the deaths of children for gain, politics or fame."

9: Mia Sato, "Twitter is running ads next to tweets from Holocaust deniers," The Verge, Feb 10, 2023, https://www.theverge.com/2023/2/10/23594756/twitter-ads-toxic-content-holocaust-deniers-media-matters-report-study

10: "'The Dawn of Everything and the Fediverse: How the Fediverse could help humanity to embrace its full potential of different forms of society" *Fungiverse Tales*, January 14, 2024, https://fungiverse.wordpress.com/2024/01/14/the-dawn-of-everything-and-the-fediverse-how-the-fediverse-could-help-humanity-to-embrace-its-full-potential-of-different-forms-of-society/

11: Adi Robertson, "Twitter wants to decentralize, but decentralized social network creators don't trust it," *The Verge*, December 12, 2019, https://www.theverge.com/2019/12/12/21012553/twitter--decentralized-social-network-developers-reaction-mastodon-activitypub

12: Dave Lee, "Bluesky Repeats Most of Twitter's Mistakes," *Bloomberg*, May 3, 2023, https://www.bloomberg.com/opinion/articles/2023-05-03/many-will-use-jack-dorsey-s-bluesky-like-they-use-elon-musk-s-twitter-badly

13. "Can Cryptocurrency Be Hacked?" *Worldcoin*, https://worldcoin.org/articles/can-cryptocurrency-be-hacked Crypto is outside our scope. I talked about blockchain and such in my previous book, and until there are reliable, fully functioning quantum computers around—built with next-generation technologies that make today's mainframes look like abacuses—to bring blockchain into everyday use, I've little interest in the subject at the moment.

14. Mike Masnick, "Lazy Reporters Claiming Fediverse Is 'Slumping,' Despite Massive Increase In Usage," *Techdirt*, February 8, 2023 https://www.techdirt.com/2023/02/08/lazy-reporters-claiming-fediverse-is-slumping-despite-massive-increase-in-usage/

15: Jay Peters, "Twitter is back after struggling on a random Wednesday," The Verge, February 15, 2023, https://www.theverge.com/2023/2/15/23601449/twitter-down-outage-ios-for-you-page

16: Green Bay Packers stock doesn't pay dividends and cannot be traded, but you can purchase stock at packersstock.com if you don't mind that all the money, profit or not, goes to team operations and local community projects and programs. A 45-member board of directors is elected by the Packers' stockholders, who in turn elect a seven-member executive committee. The executive committee runs the football team, a $4 billion-and-growing franchise, and is ultimately responsible for the direction of the team and its organization.

17: Tamara Cohen, "Are we hard-wired to be rebellious? How part of our brain controls whether we fit in with the crowd," *Daily Mail*, February 20, 2012, https://www.dailymail.co.uk/sciencetech/article-2103859/Are-hard-wired-rebellious-How-brain-controls-fit-crowd.html

Digital Divides

1: Ogi Djuraskovic, "Big Data Statistics 2022: How Much Data is in The World," *First Site Guide*, updated January 10th, 2022, https://firstsiteguide.com/big-data-stats/

2: Fraser Cain, "Are There More Grains of Sand Than Stars?" *Universe Today*, November 25, 2013, https://www.universetoday.com/106725/are-there-more-grains-of-sand-than-stars/

3: Rory Carroll, "Welcome to Utah, the NSA's desert home for eavesdropping on America," The Guardian, June 13, 2013, https://www.theguardian.com/world/2013/jun/14/nsa-utah-data-facility

4: Jon Hamilton, "Without Language, Large Numbers Don't Add Up," *NPR*, February 9, 2011, https://www.npr.org/2011/02/09/133601966/language-essential-for-understanding-large-numbers

5: Richard Henderson and Owen Walker, "BlackRock's black box: the technology hub of modern finance," *Financial Times*, February 24, 2020, https://www.ft.com/content/5ba6f40e-4e4d-11ea-95a0-43d18ec715f5

6: Saad Qureshi, "From tech-savvy to digitally literate: the era of the T-shaped graduate," Navitas, December 17, 2018, https://learningandteaching-navitas.com/tech-savy-digitally-literate-t-shaped-graduate/

7: Anna Merod, "Report: More high schools offer computer science courses, but enrollment disparities persist," *K-12 Dive*, November 11, 2021, https://www.k12dive.com/news/report-more-high-schools-offer-computer-science-courses-but-enrollment-di/609890/

8: Peter Beaumont, "The truth about Twitter, Facebook and the uprisings in the Arab world," *The Guardian*, February 25, 2011, https://www.theguardian.com/world/2011/feb/25/twitter-facebook-uprisings-arab-libya

9: Felix Richter, "Have we passed the peak of the smartphone era?" World Economic Forum, Aug 18, 2021, https://www.weforum.org/agenda/2021/08/smartphone-growth-peak-5g-apple-samsung-iphone-tech/

10: Jean Twenge et al, "Increases in Depressive Symptoms, Suicide-Related Outcomes, and Suicide Rates Among U.S. Adolescents After 2010 and Links to Increased New Media Screen Time," *Sage Journals*, November 14, 2017, https://journals.sagepub.com/doi/abs/10.1177/2167702617723376

11. Annie Lennon, "Is depression linked with social media use in adults," *Medical News Today*, November 27, 2021, https://www.medicalnewstoday.com/articles/flimsy-evidence-for-social-media-worsening-adult-mental-health

12: Eliza Mackintosh, "Facebook knew it was being used to incite violence in Ethiopia. It did little to stop the spread, documents show,"

CNN, October 25, 2021,
https://www.cnn.com/2021/10/25/business/ethiopia-violence-facebook-papers-cmd-intl/index.html

13: Euan McKirdy, "Facebook: We didn't do enough to prevent Myanmar violence," *CNN*, November 6, 2018, https://www.cnn.com/2018/11/06/tech/facebook-myanmar-report/index.html

14: Catherine Herridge and Graham Kates, "Copy of what's believed to be Hunter Biden's laptop data turned over by repair shop to FBI showed no tampering, analysis says," CBS News, November 21, 2022, https://www.cbsnews.com/news/hunter-biden-laptop-data-analysis/

15: Bart Jansen, "Special counsel John Durham criticizes FBI Trump-Russia probe but recommends no wholesale changes," USA Today, May 15, 2023, https://www.usatoday.com/story/news/politics/2023/05/15/john-durham-report-fbi-russia-donald-trump/70179728007/

16: Zachary B. Wolf, "COVID 'lab leak theory': What we've learned," *CNN*, February 27, 2023, https://www.cnn.com/2023/02/27/politics/covid-lab-leak-what-matters/index.html

17. Dan Falcone, "Creating the Horror Chambers: An Interview with Noam Chomsky," *Jacobin*, July 28, 2015, https://jacobin.com/2015/07/chomsky-interview-citizens-united-democracy-higher-education/

18: *Real News Network*, "Inflation, Europe's energy crisis, and the Fed with Richard Wolff," at 31:40 of the YouTube video https://www.youtube.com/watch?v=I43uC1mfHKc

19: Josh Salman, Matt Wynn and Dinah Voyles Pulver, "Tens of thousands left the president option blank, though 'undervotes' were down from 2016," *USA Today*, November 11, 2020, https://www.usatoday.com/story/news/investigations/2020/11/11/t

housands-who-voted-didnt-choose-president-competitive-states/6244098002/

20: Ian Spiegelman, "After CPAC Taunts, Caitlyn Jenner Gets Little Support from Prominent Conservatives," *Los Angeles Magazine*, July 12, 2021, https://www.lamag.com/citythinkblog/caitlyn-jenner-cpac/

21: Sybil Davis, "'Oppenheimer' Shows the Betrayals of Stalinism and the Dangers of Lesser Evilism," Left Voice, March 10, 2024, https://www.leftvoice.org/oppenheimer-shows-the-betrayals-of-stalinism-and-the-dangers-of-lesser-evilism/

22: Human Action Podcast, "The Managerial Revolution," December 23, 2020, https://www.youtube.com/watch?v=LwHkXGNEBQ0

23: Barbara and John Ehrenreich, "The Professional Managerial Class," *Radical America*, March-April 1977, https://library.brown.edu/pdfs/1125403552886481.pdf

24: Amber A'Lee Frost, "The Characterless Opportunism of the Managerial Class," *American Affairs Volume III, Number 4* (Winter 2019), https://americanaffairsjournal.org/2019/11/the-characterless-opportunism-of-the-managerial-class/

25: "Debating Piketty's theories on 'Capital' and inequality," May 13, 2014, *PBS Newshour*,
https://www.youtube.com/watch?v=kBl5V-pQOAw
As long as we're picking on Piketty, we may as well take a minute to marvel at the agitated manner in which conservative pundits took to attacking *Capital in the Twenty-First Century*'s conclusions; they went at it like ducks to a Dumpster full of doughnuts. For example, there was the time in May of 2014, when Kevin Hassett, a glad-handing American Enterprise Institute cacodemon who'd later go on to serve as Donald Trump's Chairman of Economic Advisers, appeared on an episode of *PBS Newshour*. He served as the debate opponent of Heather Boushey from the Washington Center for Equitable Growth, a "left-leaning" economics-education-grant-dispenser that's been dismissed by more than one critic as a self-serving group of Washington insiders who

"helped lay the foundations for the repulsive and dehumanizing economic order under which we currently live" (it's a given that when two duopoly-attached mouthpieces start throwing important-sounding sentences at each other while Fourth Estate cameras are trained on them, neither of them is gravely concerned about whether or not our neo-Gilded Age ever actually ends).

Hassett, wearing the Ronald McDonald grin of a televangelist who's about to give away free Bibles to the first 10,000 viewers who call in, pronounced Piketty's analysis "an historic blunder." He reached that ridiculously pedantic conclusion owing to the fact that Piketty had identified "capital" (as opposed to—I guess—"systemic wealth-cronyism" or some other dummy-proof term) as the enemy of economic equality. That, along with a few other quibbles, such as Piketty's "ignoring pre-tax rates," conveniently convinced Hassett that Piketty had based all his research on nothing more than the cost of *buying houses* (as Hassett babbled his nonsense, Boushey turned to *Newshour* host Gwen Ifill, begging with her eyes for help, which Ifill dutifully provided in the form of a few easily swattable Nerf-ball questions).

26: Barbara and John Ehrenreich, "Death of a Yuppie Dream: The Rise and Fall of the Professional-Managerial Class," Rosa Luxemburg Foundation, February 2013,
https://www.rosalux.de/fileadmin/rls_uploads/pdfs/sonst_publikationen/ehrenreich_death_of_a_yuppie_dream90.pdf

27: Matt Krupnick, "Restrictions on tenure and academic freedom have college professors eyeing the exits," *USA Today*, December 19, 2023,
https://www.usatoday.com/story/news/education/2023/12/19/cuts-tenure-academic-freedom-send-college-professors-exits/71925104007/

28: Cynthia Kaufman, "Belonging and Social Change: A Critique of the Politics of Wokeness," January 21, 2019,
https://cynthiakaufman.net/2019/01/21/belonging-and-social-change-a-critique-of-the-politics-of-wokeness/

29: Clara Mattei, "When Liberals Fell in Love With Benito Mussolini," *Jacobin*, October 8, 2022,
https://jacobin.com/2022/10/mussolini-fascism-liberalism-austerity

30: Daisy Grewal, "How Wealth Reduces Compassion," *Scientific American*, April 10, 2012, https://www.scientificamerican.com/article/how-wealth-reduces-compassion/

31: Claudia M. Elsig, The Psychology of Wealth and How It Affects Mental Health, Calda Clinic, September 13, 2022, https://caldaclinic.com/the-psychology-of-wealth-and-how-it-affects-mental-health/

32: River Page, "The CIA and the New Dialect of Power," *American Affairs Journal*, Winter 2021, Vol V, Number 4, https://americanaffairsjournal.org/2021/11/the-cia-and-the-new-dialect-of-power/

33: Chalmers Johnson, "Improve the CIA? Better to abolish it," *SF Gate*, February 22, 2004, https://www.sfgate.com/opinion/openforum/article/Improve-the-CIA-Better-to-abolish-it-2792378.php

34: James Petras, "The CIA and the Cultural Cold War Revisited," *Monthly Review*, November 1, 1999

35: Politics and Prose, book discussion on *A Collective Bargain*, at 15:20 of the YouTube video https://www.youtube.com/watch?v=rR8QmFpJgfU

It's Really, Truly, Madly The Class War, Folks

1: Lydia Saad, "At Year Three, Americans Split on Whether Pandemic Is Over," *Gallup*, March 9, 2023, https://news.gallup.com/poll/471734/year-three-americans-split-whether-pandemic.aspx

2: Lydia Saad, "Americans Still Glum About State of the Union in Most Areas," *Gallup*, February 2, 2023, https://news.gallup.com/poll/469241/americans-glum-state-union-areas.aspx

3: Jeff Jones and Lydia Saad, "Americans' Views on Economic Mobility and Economic Inequality in the U.S. (Trends)," *Gallup*, January 2-7, 2018, https://news.gallup.com/poll/228980/americans-views-economic-mobility-economic-inequality-trends.aspx

4: "Environment [poll]," *Gallup*, 2023, https://news.gallup.com/poll/1615/environment.aspx

5: "Real and nominal value of the federal minimum wage in the United States from 1938 to 2022," Statista.com, January 30, 2023, https://www.statista.com/statistics/1065466/real-nominal-value-minimum-wage-us

6: J Geiman, "The Psychological Toll of Student Debt," Center for Law and Social Policy, October 8, 2021, https://www.clasp.org/blog/psychological-toll-student-debt/

7: Summer Meza, "Biden Doesn't Want to Hear Millennials Complain: 'Give Me a Break'," Newsweek, January 12, 2018, https://www.newsweek.com/joe-biden-says-millennials-dont-have-it-tough-780348

8: Indigo Olivier, "Conservatives claim canceling US student debt will be expensive. They're wrong," *The Guardian*, June 22, 2022, https://www.theguardian.com/commentisfree/2022/jun/22/us-student-loan-debt-cancellation-joe-biden-cost#:~:text=As%20the%20Urban%20Institute%20points,dollars%20to%20the%20national%20debt

9. Robert Farrington, "Supreme Court Rejects Biden's Student Loan Forgiveness Plan," The College Investor, June 30, 2023, https://thecollegeinvestor.com/43140/supreme-court-rejects-down-biden-student-loan-forgiveness-plan/

10: Ayelet Sheffey, "Biden made it harder for student-loan borrowers to get rid of debt when they go bankrupt," *Business Insider*, May 9, 2022, https://www.businessinsider.com/biden-made-it-harder-to-discharge-student-debt-through-bankruptcy-2022-5

11: Alex Pareene and Laura Marsh, "Joe Biden's Debt Cancellation Games," The New Republic, June 15, 2022, https://newrepublic.com/article/166764/joe-biden-student-debt-cancellation-games

12: Michael P. Barry, "Defining the Retirement Crisis, Part 3: It's Going to Get Worse Before it Will Ever Get Better," The American Society Of Pension Professionals & Actuaries, September 19, 2022, https://www.asppa.org/news/defining-retirement-crisis-part-3-it%E2%80%99s-going-get-worse-it-will-ever-get-better

13: Brittany King, "Those Who Married Once More Likely Than Others to Have Retirement Savings," United States Census Bureau, January 13, 2022, https://www.census.gov/library/stories/2022/01/women-more-likely-than-men-to-have-no-retirement-savings.html

14: Paul Krugman, "Incidents From My Career," Princeton University, https://www.princeton.edu/~pkrugman/incidents.html
I occasionally dabble in trolling Reich myself on Twitter—not that he personally sees it, I'm sure—catcalling him with my nickname for him, "Captain Obvious." He earned it for his bottomless supply of virtue-signaling, eyeroll-inducing, pro-Democratic-establishment tweets, one of which got him into hot water with women's rights proponents.

15: Dean Baker, "Op-Ed: The bank bailout of 2008 was unnecessary. Fed Chairman Ben Bernanke scared Congress into it," Los Angeles Times, September 14, 2018, https://www.latimes.com/opinion/op-ed/la-oe-baker-bailout-20180914-story.html
While we're at it, some observers asked why Bernanke's Federal Reserve didn't simply send the bailout money to debt-drowned homeowners for the express purpose of paying off their mortgage loans, thereby killing two birds with one stone and making the economy work more smoothly.

16: Michael Hudson, Steve Keen et al, "How Finance Capitalism Ruined the World - Dr. Michael Hudson & Dr. Steve Keen, DSPod #203," YouTube, https://www.youtube.com/watch?v=1q8wgMQjDFI

17: Carl Schramm, "Nobel economists were dead wrong on inflation: Don't expect an apology," *The Hill*, April 5, 2022, https://thehill.com/opinion/finance/3259197-nobel-economists-were-dead-wrong-on-inflation-dont-expect-an-apology/

18: Julia Mueller, "'Greedflation' is the new inflation as corporate profits balloon," *The Hill*, June 19, 2003, https://thehill.com/business/economy/4057722-greedflation-is-the-new-inflation-as-corporate-profits-balloon-report/

19: Tom Nichols, *The Death of Expertise* (Mariner, 2017)

20: Rhodes Center Podcast, "The 'Free Market' is a Fever Dream and Adam Smith Wasn't in It," YouTube, March 31, 2023, https://www.youtube.com/watch?v=LuJOQks1tmY

21: The People's Forum NYC, "Empire and Economics: The Long History of Debt-Cancelation from Antiquity to Today," YouTube, Apr 15, 2019, https://www.youtube.com/watch?v=M4DkZ3CWFOk

22: Alexander C. Kaufman and Hermes Ayala Guzmán, "The Battle Over The Last Piece Of Puerto Rico That Wasn't For Sale," The Huffington Post, October 14, 2021, https://www.huffpost.com/entry/puerto-rico-beaches-privatization_n_6160a321e4b0cc44c50c93e3

23: Michael Hudson, "A Debt Jubilee is the Only Way to Avoid a Depression," *Counterpunch*, March 23, 2020, https://www.counterpunch.org/2020/03/23/a-debt-jubilee-is-the-only-way-to-avoid-a-depression/

24: Hirsh Chitkara, "The Hollow Return of American Manufacturing," Tablet, March 20, 2023, https://www.tabletmag.com/sections/news/articles/hollow-return-american-manufacturing

25: Michael Hudson, "Reality economics," December 19, 2012, https://michael-hudson.com/2012/12/reality-economics/

26: Isabella Trope, "How Did a Debt Crisis Lead to Athenian Democracy?" *The Collector*, November 22, 2021, https://www.thecollector.com/athenian-democracy-debt-crisis/

27: David Lebedoff, "RFK and the brothers Gracchus: An ancient parallel," Star Tribune, May 31, 2018, https://www.startribune.com/rfk-and-the-brothers-gracchus-an-ancient-parallel/484225511

28: "The Gracchi Brothers," United Nations of Roma Victrix, https://www.unrv.com/empire/gracchi-brothers.php

29: Fatema Z. Sumar, "Hoarding billionaires stunting global growth," Asia Times, November 2, 2022, https://asiatimes.com/2022/11/hoarding-billionaires-stunting-global-growth/

30: Andrew Anthony, "Winners Take All: The Elite Charade of Changing the World—review," *The Guardian*, March 26, 2019, https://www.theguardian.com/books/2019/mar/26/winners-take-all-anand-giridharadas-review

31: "Blyth Devastates Congress' Approach to Budget," Real News Network, March 14, 2015, https://www.youtube.com/watch?v=AQUv1U0r-wM

32: Bill Mitchell, "Modern Monetary Theory—what is new about it?" William Mitchell - Modern Monetary Theory, https://billmitchell.org/blog/?p=34200

33: Bob Richardson, "Expensive Lessons for Government and Rural Industry from the Wool Stockpile," Australasian Agribusiness Journals Online, https://www.agrifood.info/Agrifood/Connections/2001_1/richardson.htm

34: Howie Hawkins, "The Democrats' Third-Party Massacres," Counterpunch, July 15, 2022, https://www.counterpunch.org/2022/07/15/the-democrats-third-party-massacres/

35: Katelyn Caralle, "Socialism still too 'loaded' for Democrats says Barack Obama as he blasts DNC for only giving AOC a 90 second slot at convention saying it should have been much more," Daily Mail, December 2, 2020, https://www.dailymail.co.uk/news/article-9009911/Socialism-loaded-Democrats-says-Obama-blasts-DNC-AOCs-one-minute-slot.html

36: Jeffrey M. Jones, "Socialism, Capitalism Ratings in U.S. Unchanged," December 6, 2021, https://news.gallup.com/poll/357755/socialism-capitalism-ratings-unchanged.aspx

37: Ryan Chapman, "SOCIALISM: An In-Depth Explanation," YouTube, Aug 27, 2022, https://www.youtube.com/watch?v=lrBRV3WK2x4

38: Bad Friends, "Soy Boys, Cuck & High-T," YouTube, June 20, 2022, https://www.youtube.com/watch?v=lmBr5Rw3xlg

39: Paul A. Goble, "Russia has as many as 5 million homeless, not the 64,000 Rosstat reports," Euromaidan Press, July 8, 2017, https://euromaidanpress.com/2017/07/08/russia-has-as-many-as-5-million-homeless-not-the-64000-rosstat-reports-euromaidan-press/

40: National Alliance to End Homelessness, "State of Homelessness: 2022 Edition,"
https://endhomelessness.org/homelessness-in-america/homelessness-statistics/state-of-homelessness/

41: Jenny Hammond, "Homelessness in China," *GB Times*, July 17, 2012,
https://web.archive.org/web/20160829114015/http://gbtimes.com/life/homelessness-china

42: "Russia jobless rate stays at record low of 3.9% in July," Reuters, August 31, 2022,
https://www.reuters.com/markets/europe/russia-jobless-rate-stays-

record-low-39-july-2022-08-31/

43: Andrei Sokolov, "Forced Labor in Soviet Industry: The End of the 1930s to the Mid-1950s," July 2004, https://www.hoover.org/sites/default/files/uploads/documents/0817939423_23.pdf

44: Marx & Philosophy, review of David Harvey's Seventeen Contradictions and the End of Capitalism, June 19, 2014, https://marxandphilosophy.org.uk/reviews/7906_seventeen-contradictions-and-the-end-of-capitalism-review-by-anon/

45: "To Thomas Jefferson from John Adams, 6 December 1787," *Founders Online*, https://founders.archives.gov/documents/Jefferson/01-12-02-0405

46: Brian Balfour,"Property Rights Are Human Rights," John Locke Foundation, June 16, 2022, https://www.johnlocke.org/property-rights-are-human-rights/

47: "James Madison to Thomas Jefferson," University of Chicago Press, https://press-pubs.uchicago.edu/founders/documents/v1ch17s22.html

48: Taylor Giorno, "'Midterm spending spree': Cost of 2022 federal elections tops $8.9 billion, a new midterm record," OpenSecrets, February 7, 2023, https://www.opensecrets.org/news/2023/02/midterms-spending-spree-cost-of-2022-federal-elections-tops-8-9-billion-a-new-midterm-record/

49: Jacob Soll, "Adam Smith: Why it is unfair to label Scottish economist and philosopher a proponent of 'greed is good'," *The Scotsman*, July 9, 2023, https://www.scotsman.com/news/opinion/adam-smith-why-it-is-unfair-to-label-scottish-economist-and-philosopher-a-proponent-of-greed-is-good-4209908

50: Ken Klippenstein, "Documents Show Amazon Is Aware Drivers Pee In Bottles And Even Defecate En Route, Despite Company Denial," *The Intercept*, March 25, 2021, https://theintercept.com/2021/03/25/amazon-drivers-pee-bottles-union/

51: Real Progressives, "Episode 34—The Legal Nature of Money and the History of the Federal Reserve with Rohan Grey," September 21, 2019, https://realprogressives.org/podcast_episode/episode-34-the-legal-nature-of-money-and-the-history-of-the-federal-reserve-with-rohan-grey/

Putting It All Together: Rules For Online Radicals

1: Drew Forbes, "The O'Hare Shit-In: Airports, Occupied Infrastructures, And Excremental Politics," *Society & Space*, October 3, 2017, https://www.societyandspace.org/articles/the-ohare-shit-in-airports-occupied-infrastructures-and-excremental-politics

2: Candice Bernd, "Evaluating Police Psychology: Who Passes the Test?" *Truthout*, February 20, 2015, https://truthout.org/articles/evaluating-police-psychology-who-passes-the-test/

3: Julia Thomas, "Am I racist? Take this scientific quiz and find out," *Brain Fodder*, December 26, 2022, https://brainfodder.org/implicit-association-test/

4: John Logan, "Starbucks's Howard Schultz Isn't a Caring Liberal Boss. He's a Vicious Union Buster," Jacobin, October 2022, https://jacobin.com/2022/10/starbucks-howard-schultz-lawbreaking-union-buster-labor-violation-media-narrative

5: Arash Szizi, "Too Much Purity Is Bad for the Left," *The Atlantic*, March 21, 2024,

https://www.theatlantic.com/international/archive/2024/03/america
n-left-socialist-lessons-from-abroad/677804/

6: Ben Farmer, "Hotter than the human body can handle: Pakistan city broils in world's highest temperatures," *The Telegraph*, June 28, 2021, https://www.telegraph.co.uk/global-health/climate-and-people/hotter-human-body-can-handle-pakistan-city-broils-worlds-highest/

7: Seth Borenstein, "'Code red': UN scientists warn of worsening global warming," Associated Press, August 10, 2021, https://apnews.com/article/asia-pacific-latin-america-middle-east-africa-europe-1d89d5183583718ad4ad311fa2ee7d83

8: Doug Hullander, Patrick L. Barry, "Space Bones," *NASA*, October 1, 2001, https://web.archive.org/web/20011006181643/http://science.nasa.gov/headlines/y2001/ast01oct_1.htm

9: Katherine Fidler, "From pools to bowling alleys and a flaming moat – inside the bunkers where billionaires will ride out the apocalypse," Metro, Mar 31, 2024,
https://metro.co.uk/2024/03/31/inside-doomsday-bunkers-mark-zuckerberg-billionaires-building-2-20556222/

Index

4chan, 83-86, 119
Adams, John, 209, 220
African-American Vernacular
  English, 145
Ahmadinejad, Mahmoud, 16
Aladdin (investment software
  program), 104
algorithms, 46, 75, 80, 85, 89, 92,
  111, 122, 225
Alinsky, Saul, 5, 146, 197, 225-
  229
Amazon Web Services (AWS), 95
America Online (AOL), 91
American Psychiatric
  Association, 40, 111, 113
Anderson Cooper 360, 73
Anglin, Andrew, 82
anocracy, 4, 5
Arab Spring protests, 107
Arendt, Hannah, 201
Aristotle, 2, 195
ARPAnet, 102
Articles of Confederation, 206,
  209
artificial intelligence (AI), 103,
  114, 137
Athar, Sohaib, 52
Atwood, Margaret, 52
Azizi, Arash, 232
Babeuf, François-Noël, 196
Babylonians, 153, 175
Bankruptcy Abuse Prevention
  and Consumer Protection Act,
  157
Bannon, Steve, 197
basket of deplorables, 156
beatniks, 145
Benattia-Vergara, Nabilla, 64
Bernanke, Ben, 164

Bernie bros, 71, 141
Bezos, Jeff, 95, 215
Bhargava, Deepak, 30, 233
Biden, Joe, 20, 27, 43, 60, 62, 63,
  68, 69, 70, 118, 128, 153, 155-
  157, 166, 167, 198, 208, 222,
  232
Black Lives Matter, 32, 227
BlackRock, 104
blockchain, 74, 210
Bluesky, 87-90, 92, 97, 224
Blyth, Mark, 57, 152, 170, 187
Boebert, Lauen, 47
Booker, Cory, 63
bot swarms, 29, 31, 32, 71, 75, 76,
  98, 197-199, 204
Bouazizi, Mohammed, 107
BRICS consortium, 174, 184
Brown, Michael, 227
Buckley Jr., William F., 132
Buckley vs Valeo decision, 210
Bureau of Intelligence and
  Research (INR), 143
Burnham, James, 133, 134, 138
Bush, George W., 3, 36, 62
Buttigieg, Pete, 20, 69
Buzzfeed, 73
Caligula, 208
carbon capture technology, 173
Carlin, George, 207
Carlson, Tucker, 68, 131
Carlyle, Thomas, 152
Central Intelligence Agency
  (CIA), 29, 142-145
Chaplin, Charlie, 110
Chapman, Ryan, 195
Chapo Trap House, 17
Cheney, Elizabeth, 35
Chichester, D.G., 48

chickenpox, 154
Chomsky, Noam, 120, 206
Church of Bob Dobbs, 145
Cirtru (app), 160
Citizens United decision, 210
Clinton, Bill, 26, 157, 163
Clinton, Hillary, 71, 141, 156, 193
CNN, 18, 20, 35, 73, 131, 184
co-housing, 160
Colbert, Jean-Baptiste, 215, 216
Communications Decency Act, 114
Communications Decency Act, Section 230, 114
computer-class enrollment in schools, 106
Congress of Cultural Freedom, 144
conjunctural analysis, 229, 230
conspiracy theories, 31, 56, 57, 63, 169, 234
Constitution of the United States, 3, 4, 206, 208, 209, 211-213, 215, 216
Corporate Proxy Movement, 25
Counter Social, 98
countries with free college, 155
Covid-19, 47, 57, 59, 83, 152- 154, 219
curse of knowledge, 169, 188
Cyril of Alexandria, 176
Dahl, Eivind, 147
Daily Kos, 31
dark money, 31, 70
Davis, Sybil, 134
debt jubilees, 172-179, 180, 190
democratic socialist, 34, 67
Democratic Socialists of America, 200
dengue fever, 154
DeSantis, Ron, 96, 126
dialect of power, 143

Discord, 195
Dixiecrats, 24
Dixon, Chris, 148, 231
DIY, 100
Doleac, Jennifer, 152
dopamine, 39, 40, 122
Dore, Jimmy, 59, 65, 72
Dovere, Edward Isaac, 69
duopoly, 3, 11, 36, 71, 128, 156, 157, 183, 192, 193, 249
Dutton, William, 5, 6, 8, 9, 10
Ehrenreich, Barbara, 135-137, 138
Emperor Romulus, 208
Everett, Dolly, 108
Facebook, 10, 19, 28, 32, 44, 48, 49, 51, 53, 55, 80, 87, 91-93, 95, 97, 98, 107, 112-115, 119, 120, 162, 227
Fail Whale, 95
Fain, Shawn, 235
Federal Reserve, 162, 166, 183-185, 212, 218, 219
Federalist Papers, 206, 208, 209, 215
fediverse, 80, 81, 85, 87, 88, 90-94, 96, 98, 100, 112, 223, 224
Fifth Estate, 1, 5-13, 17-19, 38, 58, 65, 66, 72, 73, 75, 93, 107, 120, 121, 125, 133, 135, 151, 152, 163, 172, 174, 182, 187, 195, 198, 205, 207, 212, 213, 221, 223, 224, 227, 229, 235, 236
finance capitalism, 175
Financial Times, 17
FIRE sector, 162, 175
First Amendment, 115, 210
Fisher, Mark, 12
Fleets (Twitter-app), 95
Floyd, George, 118
Force The Vote, 65
Ford, Henry, 182
Fortnite, 50

Fourth Estate, 5-9, 11, 14, 17, 51, 58, 62, 68, 72, 116, 141, 142, 151, 163, 174, 179, 197, 198, 214, 215, 224, 232, 235
Fox News, 18, 31, 34, 62, 68, 141, 214
Frank, Thomas, 42, 68, 127
free speech, 81-84, 86, 115-117, 138
Friedman, Milton, 127
Friedman, Thomas, 6
Frost, Amber A'Lee, 17, 135, 139
Frum, David, 34
future shock, 102, 105
Gaetz, Matt, 228
Gates, Bill, 179
gerontocracy, 70
Gill, Allison, 61
Giridharadas, Anand, 179
Gladstone, William E., 28
Gladwell, Malcolm, 14-17, 93
Goldberg, Michelle, 17
Google Cloud, 94, 95
Gracchi brothers, 178
Graeber, David, 174
Gramsci, Antonio, 230
Gray, Briahna Joy, 11, 65
Great Reset, 57
greedflation, 162, 165, 167
Green Bay Packers, 96
Green Party, 29, 32, 192, 193
Greenfield, Jeff, 146
Greensboro Sit-In, 15
Greenwald, Glenn, 73, 74, 117
Grey, Rohan, 149, 213
Halligan, Ryan, 108
Halper, Katie, 11
Halpern, Justin, 52
Hamilton, Alexander, 206, 208, 215, 216
Hamm, Harold, 233
Harris, Kamala, 63

Harvey, David, 205
hashtag campaigns, 98, 221
Hedges, Chris, 75, 125-127, 142, 146, 212, 234
heterodox economics, 152, 163-165, 170, 172, 182, 218
Hitchens, Christopher, 207
Hobbes, Thomas, 103
Hoh, Matthew, 192, 193
Holmesian fallacy, 56
homelessness, 154, 159, 160, 203
Hudson, Michael, 153, 162-164, 170, 171, 174-177, 180, 205, 207
Inflation Reduction Act, 173
"informational generation gap", 106
International Reciprocal Trade Association, 191
internet addiction, 109, 111
internet hivemind, 6, 10, 19, 45, 111
Israel Defense Force, 11, 224
Ivins, Molly, 207
Jackson, Michael, 53
Jay, Paul, 11
Jefferson, Thomas, 216
Jenner, Caitlyn, 129, 130, 131
Jennings Bryan, William, 68, 217
Jin-ri, Choi, 108
Johnson, Chalmers, 3, 17, 143, 179, 207
Jones, Alex, 84, 85
Kaufman, Cynthia, 139, 232, 234
Keen, Steve, 164, 171, 172
Keep On Truckin', 144
Kelley, William Melvin, 145
Kelton, Stephanie, 186, 188
Keynes, John Maynard, 184
Keynesianism, 162
Kissinger, Henry, 165
Klein, Naomi, 26, 171

Koch, Charles, 4, 9, 32, 168, 169, 233
Koch, Chase, 168
Koubaa, Khaled, 107
Krugman, Paul, 165
Krystol, Bill, 35, 36, 87
Kulinski, Kyle, 71, 72, 114, 117
lab leak theory, 117, 247
Lahren, Tomi, 130
lateral orbitofrontal cortex, 99
liberal class institutions, 142, 146
libertarians, 9, 32, 129-131, 168
Liu, Catherine, 136, 139
Lord's Prayer, 176
Luce, Stephanie, 30, 231, 233, 234
Luxemburg, Rosa, 22, 161, 205
Machiavelli, Niccolò, 3
macroeconomics, 151
Maddow, Rachel, 73
Madison, James, 206, 208, 209, 211, 212
managerial class, 133, 134, 138
Mann, Thomas, 25
Mao Zedong, 45, 201
Martin, Abby, 11, 59, 75
Marx, Karl, 205
Mastodon, 80, 81, 88, 91-93, 98, 223, 224
Mattei, Clara, 7, 140, 151, 216-218
McAlevey, Jane, 78, 146, 225, 226, 228, 231, 232
McCarthy, Joseph, 29
McDaniel, Ronna, 35, 132
McGann, James, 9
Medicis, 3
Meier, Megan, 108
Melber, Ari, 91
Meza, Summer, 156
Michaelson, Elex, 62
Milano, Alyssa, 91
Mitchell, Bill (Australian economist), 188, 189

Mitchell, Bill (conspiracy theorist), 63
Miura, Haruma, 108
Modern Monetary Theory (MMT), 8, 180, 182-188, 190, 213, 219
Moore, Michael, 12, 13
Mosler, Warren, 186
Mother Jones, 13
Musk, Elon, 53, 82, 84, 85, 96
Mussolini, Benito, 140, 230
mutual aid, 148
Nader, Ralph, 24, 144, 192
National Review, 132
National Rifle Association, 31, 84
National Vehicle Residency Collective, 159
Netanyahu, Benjamin, 11
netiquette, 124, 235
Newfield, Jack, 146
NFTs (Non-Fungible Tokens), 116
Nichols, Tom, 169
Nixon, Richard, 24, 25, 167
Nobel Memorial Prize in Economics, 164, 165
O'Rourke, Beto, 63
Obama, Barack, 69, 73, 194, 208
Ocasio-Cortez, Alexandria, 65, 194
Occupy movement, 126, 148, 197
October surprise, 167
Olivier, Indigo, 156
Omar, Ilhan, 65
Operation Mockingbird, 29
Oppenheimer, Robert, 134
Ornstein, Norm, 25
Orwell, George, 133
Ovetz, Robert, 208, 209, 211-214
Padellan, Majid, 60, 61, 64
Page, River, 142, 143
Pantaleoni, Maffeo, 218

Parscale, Brad, 130
Pell, Dave, 16
Pelosi, Nancy, 28, 65, 141
Peterson, Jordan, 123
Pfeifle, Mark, 16
Piketty, Thomas, 136
Pistor, Katharina, 211
Plokhy, Serhii, 201
Pod Save America, 73
populism, 3, 11, 16, 65, 66, 68, 125, 146, 163, 197
Post.news, 97
Powell memo, 25, 155
Powell, Jerome, 166
Practical Radicals, 30, 231, 233
precariat, 160, 161, 188, 190
prefiguration, prefigurative politics, 43, 147-149, 235
Pressley, Ayanna, 65
Priebus, Reince, 132
Prince, Eric, 4
Professional Managerial Class (PMC), 132, 134-139, 141-143
Progressive Caucus, 66, 194
Project Implicit, 228
protest votes, 128, 193
Pruss, Graham, 159
Publius Valerius Publicola, 206-208
Putin, Vladmir, 201, 202
QAnon, 63
Raekstad, Paul, 147
Raffensperger, Brad, 132
Rand, Ayn, 132, 198
Reagan, Ronald, 26, 157, 160, 194, 197
RealDonnyBot, 87
Reddit, 8, 39, 44, 49, 51
Reed Jr., Adolph, 136
Reich, Robert, 163
relational databases, 105
Ricci, Umberto, 218

Ronaldo, Cristiano, 55
Roosevelt, Franklin, 67
Roy, Deb, 59
Russia Today, 75
Russiagate, 117
Russian Nazi Troll Bots, 30, 42, 102
Sagan, Carl, 103, 104
Sanders, Bernie, 20, 29, 32, 38, 60, 63-72, 141, 174, 186, 192
Sandy Hook shooting, 31, 84
Schama, Simon, 164
Schicklgruber, 22
Schilling, Curt, 62
Schilling, Taylor, 198
Schumpeter, Joseph, 205
Seder, Sam, 11, 58, 59
Seymour, Richard, 110
Sh!t My Dad Says, 52
shadowbanning, 111
Shay's Rebellion, 209
Shock Doctrine, 171
Short Message Service (SMS), 53
Signal (messaging app), 99
Silicon Valley Bank, 57
Sirota, David, 63, 64
skeet, skeeting, 89, 90
Skouras, Spiro, 57
sleep deprivation, 40
Smith, Adam, 170, 214-216
Snapchat, 64, 112, 194
Snowden, Edward, 73, 99, 143
Social Democratic Party of Germany, 22
social democrats, 66, 67
social media influencers, 55, 61-64, 76, 197
Social Security, 149, 159
Socialist Party USA, 192
Sockington, 53
sockpuppets, 98
Soll, Jacob, 214-216

264 ▪ Index

Spareroom (app), 160
Spurlock, Morgan, 41, 42
stagflation, 166, 167
Stalin, 22, 134, 144, 201, 204
Stalin, Josef, 134
Standing, Guy, 160
Stein, Jill, 192
Stiglitz, Joseph, 164, 165, 215
"Stop The Steal" movement, 113
Substack, 52, 55, 195
Sun Tzu, 32, 150
Supreme Court, 140, 157, 198, 210, 212, 251
Supreme, Vermin, 48, 191
Sveriges Riksbank, 164
Taibbi, Matt, 17, 74, 86, 117, 202
tankies, 45, 201, 202, 204
Taylor Greene, Marjorie, 130
Taylor, Astra, 157
Thälmann, Ernst, 21, 22
Thatcher, Margaret, 160, 180
The Demon-Haunted World, 103
The Divine Comedy, 37
The Invention of Lying, 171
The Jester, 98
Thiel, Peter, 234
thoughtfluencers, 10, 11, 74, 122, 195
Threads (Meta app), 87, 88, 90, 91
TikTok, 61, 62, 112
Tlaib, Rashida, 65
Toffler, Alvin, 52, 102, 105
Tribel (social media app), 97
Trump, Donald, 10, 21, 22, 27-29, 34-36, 60, 63, 68, 74, 83, 126, 136-142, 147, 167, 178, 197, 198, 208, 228
Truth Social, 74, 81, 82
T-shaped graduate, 106
tweet storms, 225
Twitch.com, 51
Twitter, 10, 11, 16, 19, 21, 23, 27, 30, 32, 33, 35, 37-39, 41-53, 55, 57, 60-63, 67, 71, 74, 79, 83, 85, 96, 119, 129, 141, 148, 182, 199, 200, 229
Twitter Blue, 53, 97
Twitter Files, 86
Tyndale, William, 177
Ukraine, 59, 75, 201
undervotes, 128
Universal Basic Income (UBI), 180
US Capitol seige of January 2020, 21, 35, 113
Usenet, 49, 91, 119
Utah Data Center, 102
Vague, Richard, 172-174, 179
Varoufakis, Yanis, 161
vehicle dwellers, 159
Vietnam War activism, 156
Wall Street bailout (2008), 164
Wallace, George, 132
Walter, Barbara F., 4, 5
Washington, George, 209
Watergate, 8
wealth inequality, 30, 67, 107, 152, 167, 178, 198, 213
Weimar Republic, 21
Weinstein, Harvey, 108
West, Cornel, 192
WhatsApp, 99
Winner, David, 22
wokeness, 20, 57, 139, 143-147, 149
Wolff, Richard, 125, 126, 127, 152, 163, 187, 190
Wray, L. Randall, 189
Wyden, Ron, 118
Wynn, Natalie, 198
Yeltsin, Boris, 202
Young Republicans, 31
Young, Kimberly, 109, 111

YouTube, 5, 19, 51, 54, 55, 57, 58, 72, 74, 75, 146, 195

Zuckerberg, Mark, 88, 90, 179, 234

About The Author

The leader of the cult punk-metal band Druid in a previous life, Eric Saeger has written for New Times Media, Hippo Press and many other publications. He lives in Manchester, New Hampshire with his wife, Jennifer, and their three rescue cats, Patchy, Roobs and Babypuss.

www.ingramcontent.com/pod-product-compliance
Lightning Source LLC
Chambersburg PA
CBHW011521070526
44585CB00022B/2492